Ray Browne on the Culture Studies Revolution

Ray Browne on the Culture Studies Revolution

An Anthology of His Key Writings

RAY BROWNE

Edited by BEN URISH

Foreword by John Cawelti

McFarland & Company, Inc., Publishers
Jefferson, North Carolina, and London

LIBRARY OF CONGRESS CATALOGUING-IN-PUBLICATION DATA

Browne, Ray B. (Ray Broadus), 1922–2009.
Ray Browne on the culture studies revolution :
an anthology of his key writings / Ray Browne ;
edited by Ben Urish ; foreword by John Cawelti.
p.   cm.
Includes bibliographical references and index.

ISBN 978-0-7864-4162-4
softcover : 50# alkaline paper ∞

1. Popular culture — United States — History.
2. United States — Social life and customs.
3. Social history — United States — History.
4. Browne, Ray B. (Ray Broadus), 1922–2009.
5. Popular Culture Association — History.
I. Urish, Ben.   II. Cawelti, John G.   III. Title.

E161.B787   2011   306.0973 — dc22   2010037560

British Library cataloguing data are available

Front cover © 2011 Shutterstock

Manufactured in the United States of America

*McFarland & Company, Inc., Publishers
Box 611, Jefferson, North Carolina 28640
www.mcfarlandpub.com*

Editor's Acknowledgments
(Ben Urish)

I wish to thank the library staff of Central Michigan University for easing the workload considerably. Additional thanks go to Ray Browne's former students (if the term "former" is applicable) Jack Nachbar and Gary Hoppenstand for sharing their insights so willingly; and to Browne's colleague John Cawelti for his sterling foreword to this book.

Special thanks to Emma Hennesey at Wiley-Blackwell, Tim Lloyd of the American Folklore Society, and Rosa Griffin of the Johns Hopkins University Press. Thanks also to Adam Hirschberg of Cambridge University Press and Rebecca Soares of the University of Wisconsin Press.

On a more personal level I am grateful to Sharon Barbour for providing a "safe work zone," John Dowell for technical assistance, and Colleen Vallo for editorial insights.

I first contacted Ray Browne about an anthology of his writing in 2005; he told me that he had been "vain enough" to consider such a collection himself and jokingly applauded my being "in the vanguard of timely ideas." He gave me the materials he had begun pulling together for the project, and for the next four years answered all of my questions regarding this project, while never trying to influence my choices or considerations.

As this project neared completion, Ray Browne passed away. It would be impossible to truly thank Ray Browne for all he has done for me (and so many others), directly and indirectly, over the years. This collection then, will have to suffice as a token of my deepest appreciation and gratitude, and is dedicated to him, for helping us to follow our hearts as we follow our minds.

"On Redefining Cultural Studies" composed August 2005, previously unpublished. Used by permission of Ray Browne.

"Popular Culture: Notes Towards a Definition" originally printed in pamphlet form by the Popular Culture Association in 1970. Reprinted by permission of Ray Browne. Published in *Popular Culture and Curricula*. Edited by Ray B. Browne and Ronald J. Ambrosetti. Bowling Green, OH: BGSU Popular Press, 1972, p. 3–11; and in Ray B. Browne, *Popular Culture Explosion* (Dubuque, Iowa: Wm. C. Brown, 1972), p. 205–207. *Popular Culture and Curricula* © 1972 by the Board of Regents of the University of Wisconsin System. Reprinted by permission of the University of Wisconsin Press.

"Popular Culture: New Notes Toward a Definition" originally published in Nachbar, Jack, and Christopher Geist, eds. *The Popular Culture Reader*, 3rd ed. Bowling Green, OH: BGSU Popular Press, 1983, p. 13–20 © 1983 by the Board of Regents of the University of Wisconsin System. Reprinted by permission of the University of Wisconsin Press.

"The Many Faces of American Culture: The Long Push to Democracy" originally printed as part of the University Professor Lecture Series. Lecture given on 11–7–77. Copies were printed in pamphlet form, but the speech was not officially published. Reprinted by permission of Ray Browne.

"The Humanities as Redefined Through Popular Culture" originally published in and edited from "Popular Culture as the New Humanities." *Journal of Popular Culture*, Spring 1984, 17:4, p. 1–8. Reprinted with the permission of Wiley-Blackwell; and from "Redefining the Humanities." *Pennsylvania English* 13 (Spring/Summer 1989) p. 16–28. Reprinted with permission of *Pennsylvania English*.

"Popular Culture: Medicine for Illiteracy and Associated Educational Ills" originally published in *Journal of Popular Culture* (Winter 1987) 21:3, p. 1–15. Reprinted with the permission of Wiley-Blackwell.

"Up from Elitism: The Aesthetics of Popular Fiction" originally published in *Studies in American Fiction*, Vol. 9 (1981), p. 217–231. Reprinted with permission of Northeastern University English Department and *Studies in American Fiction*.

"The Repressive Nature of TV Esthetics Criticism" originally published in *Journal of American Culture*, (Fall 1983), 6:3, p. 117–122. Reprinted with the permission of Wiley-Blackwell.

"The Face of the Hero in Democracy" edited from "The Concept of the Hero Against Democracy." *Profiles of Popular Culture: A Reader.* Edited by Ray B. Browne. Madison: University of Wisconsin Popular Press, 2005, p. 47–53. © 2005 by the Board of Regents of the University of Wisconsin System. Reprinted by permission of the University of Wisconsin Press; and from "Hero with 2000 Faces." *The Hero in Transition.* Edited by Ray B. Browne and Marshall W. Fishwick. Bowling Green, OH: BGSU Popular Press, 1983. p. 91–106. © 1983 by the Board of Regents of the University of Wisconsin System. Reprinted by permission of the University of Wisconsin Press.

"The Theory-Methodology Complex: The Critics' Jabberwock" originally published in *Journal of Popular Culture* (Fall 1995) 29:2, p. 143–156. Reprinted with the permission of Wiley-Blackwell

"Internationalizing Popular Culture Studies" originally published in *Journal of Popular Culture* (Summer 1996), 30:1, p. 21–37. Reprinted with the permission of Wiley-Blackwell.

"The Vanishing Global Village" originally published in *The Global Village: Dead or Alive?* Ray Browne and Marshall Fishwick, eds. Bowling Green, OH: BGSU Popular Press, 1999, p. 24–35. © 1999 by the Board of Regents of the University of Wisconsin System. Reprinted by permission of the University of Wisconsin Press.

"Whale Lore and Popular Print in Mid-Nineteenth-Century America: Sketches Toward a Profile" originally published in *Prospects* 1 (1975) p. 29–40. Reprinted with the permission of Cambridge University Press.

"The Seat of Democracy: The Privy Humor of 'Chic' Sale" originally published in *Journal of American Culture* (Fall 1980) 3:3, p. 409–416. Reprinted with the permission of Wiley-Blackwell.

"Sherlock Holmes as Christian Detective: *The Case of the Invisible Thief*" originally published in *Clues: A Journal of Detection* (Spring/Summer 1983) 4:1, p. 79–91. Reprinted with the permission of Ray Browne and *Clues.*

"The Rape of the Vulnerable" originally published in *The God Pumpers: Religion in the Electronic Age.* Ray Browne and Marshall Fishwick, eds. Bowling Green, OH: BGSU Popular Press, 1987, p. 183–190. © 1987 by the Board of Regents of the University of Wisconsin System. Reprinted by permission of the University of Wisconsin Press.

"Class Reunions as a Folk Festival" originally published in *Journal of Popular Culture* (Summer 1985) 19:1 p. 107–113. Reprinted with the permission of Wiley-Blackwell.

"The ASA and its Friends" originally published in *American Quarterly* (1979), 31:3, p. 354–358. © 1979 The Johns Hopkins University Press. Reprinted with the permission of the Johns Hopkins University Press.

"Folklore to Populore" originally published in *Popular Culture Studies Across the Curriculum*, edited by Ray Browne (Jefferson, N.C.: McFarland, 2005), p. 24–27. Reprinted with permission of McFarland & Co., Inc.

"Replying to a Rejoinder" originally published in *Preview 2001+: Popular Culture Studies in the Future.* Ray Browne and Marshall Fishwick, eds. Bowling Green, OH: BGSU Popular Press, 1995, p. 35–37. © 1995 by the Board of Regents of the University of Wisconsin System. Reprinted by permission of the University of Wisconsin Press.

"American Studies and Humanity's Dream" originally published as "Introduction." *Journal of American Culture* (2004) 27:2, p. 130–132. Reprinted with the permission of Wiley-Blackwell.

"Russel B. Nye: The Richness of His Life" originally published in *Journal of American Culture* Vol. 16:1, p. 1. Reprinted with the permission of Wiley-Blackwell.

"Review of *The Unembarrassed Muse*" originally published in *Journal of Popular Culture* (1971), 4:3, p. 737–741. Reprinted with the permission of Wiley-Blackwell.

"Review of *The Study of Folklore*" originally published in *The Journal of American Folklore*, Vol. 80, No. 317 (Jul.-Sep., 1967), p. 301–302. Reprinted with the permission of the American Folklore Society.

"Review of *The Benjamin Lee Whorf Legacy*" originally published in *Journal of American Culture* (June 2009) 32:2, pg. 182. Reprinted with the permission of Wiley-Blackwell.

"Review of *The Devil Gets His Due: The Uncollected Essays of Leslie Fiedler*" originally published in *Journal of American Culture* (June 2009) 32:2, p. 184. Reprinted with the permission of Wiley-Blackwell.

"Review of a Theme Issue of the *Journal of Folklore Research*" originally published in *Journal of American Culture* (June 2009) 32:2, p. 171. Reprinted with the permission of Wiley-Blackwell.

"Review of *Postmodernism and Popular Culture: A Culture History*" originally published in *Journal of Popular Culture* (Winter 1996) 30.3, p. 244–245. Reprinted with the permission of Wiley-Blackwell.

"Review of *Re-Reading Popular Culture*" originally published in *Journal of American Culture* (2006) 29:1, p. 92. Reprinted with the permission of Wiley-Blackwell.

"Review of *Inventing Popular Culture*" originally published in *Journal of American Culture* (2003), 27:1, pg. 115. Reprinted with the permission of Wiley-Blackwell.

"Review of *Society's Impact on Television: How the Viewing Public Shapes Television Programming*" originally published in Journal *of Popular Culture* (Spring 1996), 29:4 p. 252–253. Reprinted with the permission of Wiley-Blackwell.

"Review of *The McDonaldization of Society: Revised Edition*" originally published in *Journal of American Culture* (2003) 27:3, p. 359–360. Reprinted with the permission of Wiley-Blackwell.

"Book Review of *Cowtown Wichita and the Wild, Wicked West*" originally published in *Journal of American Culture* (2007), 30:3 p. 336. Reprinted with the permission of Wiley-Blackwell.

"Education: Forward to Democratic Fluency" originally published as "Preface," p. i-iii, and "Windshield No Rear-View Mirror," p. 194–195, in *The Many Tongues of Literacy*. Bowling Green, OH: BGSU Popular Press, 1992. © 1992 by the Board of Regents of the University of Wisconsin System. Reprinted by permission of the University of Wisconsin Press.

Table of Contents

PART FOUR: MEANDERINGS AND EXCURSIONS

Foreword
(John Cawelti)

Ray Browne was the man who, with the invaluable assistance of his wife, Pat, created popular culture scholarship, with its journals, its associations and its publications. For this alone, he is deservedly a legend. His indefatigable energy and organizational know-how were always amazing to me. In a way it's too bad that Ray was not in charge of General Motors, for with his entrepreneurial skill and openness to new ideas, he might have run that major component of the auto industry a lot better than those in charge actually did. But it is certainly fortunate for those of us who became interested in popular culture that Ray chose the inspiration and organization of a new kind of scholarship as his life's work.

But even more astounding is that this is only half of the Ray Browne story. While he was in the process of organizing the major institutions of popular culture scholarship, Ray was equally busy writing and editing books, articles and reviews about popular culture. His own scholarly books and articles have further helped to inspire and define our understanding of popular culture. His work in this regard is of far-reaching interest, though much of it has been eclipsed by Ray's role as an organizer and facilitator. Fortunately, in this volume, Ben Urish has brought together an excellent representative sampling of Ray's own scholarly projects. The book should become a basic starting point not only for the appreciation of Ray Browne's personal scholarly achievement, but for the understanding of the development and significance of popular culture studies in America.

As an historian and analyst of popular culture Ray had always been extraordinarily broad in his interests and open-minded about the ways we interest ourselves in human creations of all kinds. He was instinctively skeptical about fashionable or academic hierarchies of taste and might rightly have adopted as his own the famous motto of the Roman playwright Terence "*humani nil a me alienum puto*"—nothing human is foreign to me. Curiosity remained his perennial byword and he was always fascinated by what lay on the other side of all sorts of cultural borders, geographic, ethnic, linguistic, artistic, and intellectual. This collection shows the extent to which he was always on the trail of new cultural phenomena.

Characteristically, when Ray encountered some new or hitherto unstudied area of popular culture he would either write about it himself or find some collaborator to join him in the quest. Many of his books are anthologies edited with the involvement of others, for Ray was never unwilling to share his delight in the scholarly enterprise. Though Ray wrote about things from a challenging new point of view, he was, in many ways, like one of those great Victorian men of letters who wrote about everything.

The centerpiece of this collection is rightfully two groupings of essays, "Blazing the Trail" and "Clearing the Horizon," which sample the evolution of Ray's thinking about popular culture. By following these essays one can get a very good idea of the history of popular culture scholarship, from its emergence out of folklore and American studies, to its increasing significance to our understanding of our evolving global culture.

Among the many things that amazed me about Ray was his productivity—almost every time I opened my copy of the *Journal of Popular Culture* or *The Journal of American Culture,* I would turn to the review section and find a large number of insightful reviews by Ray. Many of them were about mystery fiction or about books on the literature of mystery, an interest that Ray and I shared. However, there were many other areas in which Ray read and reviewed, one of the most important being books about the concept of popular culture. I never understood how Ray could read so many books, and his comments were never facile or superficial. I'm very glad that a sampling of these reviews is included in this collection.

Ray Browne was one of the most generous people I ever knew. His generosity of spirit is evident in the range of interests and ideas displayed in this collection of his writings. But Ray was also the kind of person who continually helped others and encouraged them in their own work. I will never forget that, at a key point in my life, he greatly aided me by publishing *The Six-Gun Mystique*. The number of others whose work he both encouraged and also supported through publication and the opportunity to present papers at national and regional conventions is beyond counting. He lived a life that made an enormous difference to scholarship, to culture, and to thousands of individuals. It is to me both a pleasure and a privilege to be able to say a few words at the beginning of this fascinating collection of Ray's own writings.

John Cawelti has been involved with the popular culture studies movement since its beginning and has been instrumental in legitimizing studies in the field. He is the author of the landmark classics The Six-Gun Mystique *(1971) and* Adventure, Mystery and Romance *(1976). He is a professor emeritus of English at the University of Kentucky in Louisville.*

Preface

Ray B. Browne, Freely Engaged
(Ben Urish)

Engaging the Academy[1]

Ray Broadus Browne was a legendary scholar with an international reputation. Browne's early mark was made in the fields of folklore studies and literary criticism. That background, plus a strong interest in the then emerging field of American Studies, led Browne to consider a broader approach to the study (and definition) of the humanities as filtered through the social sciences. With a handful of like-minded colleagues, Browne became one of the prime founders of what became known as "the Popular Culture Studies movement."

And it was indeed a movement. Post–World War II America saw a general shake-up in the academy precipitated by an influx of war-experienced veterans thanks to the G.I. Bill of Rights. The dawn of the atomic age, the rise of the Cold War, and the birth of the modern civil rights movement made the old curricula and bureaucracies inadequate, irrelevant, or both. Changes came, but were sometimes erratic and slow, and their acceptance was frequently sporadic and institutionally or systemically blocked.

An obvious example is the creation of the field of American Studies. At the outset, American Studies was, perhaps, too many things to too few people. But soon its impact was felt, first in the fields that it drew heaviest from, American history and American literature, and later in the academic world at large. Like the later popular culture studies, it meant to supplement, not supplant, the more traditional methodologies. Also like Popular Culture Studies, key among its tenets was an attention paid to things relevant to the lives of the common people, and not just the life-ways and concerns of the elite classes or canonized literatures.

Cultural anthropology, too, began a long process of reinvention. Rather than look to "other" and "exotic" cultures, anthropologists more and more broadened their critical and theoretical approaches to include their own (largely western and industrialized) cultures, whole and in part. Anthropology's holistic approach resonated (to some degree at least) with American Studies and helped to reinvigorate the study of folklore as well.

Ray Browne entered the academic scene in this time of vibrancy and change. Like so many, his education had been interrupted by the war. He resumed his education and then began his academic career after his military service was completed at the war's end. From the start, Browne was attracted to both the study of literature and the study of folklore. He taught and researched while he earned his M.A. in 1947 and his Ph.D. in 1956. Even the growing field of American Studies and the broadening approaches of other relevant disciplines were not enough to contain Browne's interests.

Also after the war, scholars of various backgrounds (with a large number of them from sociology), perhaps influenced by the Frankfurt school and spurred by the wide-reaching impact of television, the paperback book explosion, and the promise of satellite communication, turned their interests toward what was termed "mass culture." The term had a largely (though not exclusively) negative connotation and had been in use in mainstream as well as academic writings since at least the end of the First World War. The default position was that if "the masses" enjoyed something (such as a pop song, a television show, or a crime novel) it must be appealing to the lowest common denominator and therefore be devoid of artistic, aesthetic, and intellectual value. The Frankfurt scholars went even further and often saw such permutations as evidence of the vagaries of capitalistic systems' oppression and deflection of the masses.

The fusion of Browne's academic interests and pursuits led him to consider the same cultural phenomena and materials as the scholars of "mass culture"—but with a decidedly different outlook. The combination of Browne's training in anthropologically informed folkoristics and American Studies' growing attention to the personal and popular literatures of "everyday people" gave him a much more benign appreciation of such cultural phenomena and artifacts. And a growing cadre of social science and humanities scholars were of a similar mind.

In addition, Browne soon came to see these cultural forces, primarily in the United States, as reflections and expressions of the dynamic tensions within a large-scale capitalist system and the historically expanding tangent of democratic egalitarianism. Browne saw those dismissive of "mass culture" as failing to acknowledge the cultural complexities at issue and only judging merit by misapplying entrenched "elite" cultural standards and outmoded scholarly practices. Browne's largest pedagogic motivation was the belief that an educated and aware citizenry is required for a properly functioning democracy. To ignore aspects of popular culture is to remain ignorant, and, as a result, lose the democratic impulse. Likewise, since popular culture was seen as expressing and disseminating democratic ideals, deriding popular culture forms and aspects outright was tantamount to deriding egalitarian principles. For Browne and others, the Popular Culture Studies movement was much more than an academic issue.

Predictably, Browne and his like-minded cohort were accused of overly "celebrating" what they studied, applying only a decidedly unrigorous, "gee-whiz" fan-based approach to cultural expressions of limited, if any, value. In a move to distinguish it from the narrowly defined "folk culture" and the largely derisive positions of most "mass culture" scholars, the approaches of Browne and others, at their own behest, became known as "Popular Culture Studies."

Two decades past the war and a decade past Browne's Ph.D., larger cultural upheavals brought the academic world again into a state of heightened flux. Academic and institutional boundaries seemed more permeable and scholars dealing with such things as, for example, the music of The Beatles, might be taken seriously. Such things as Marshall McLuhan's analyses of mass media forms and their potential cultural effects caught the public's attention as well as that of the academic world.

Browne's career was also in a state of flux. In 1967 he left his position in American Studies at Purdue and came to Bowling Green State University in Ohio as a folklore specialist housed in the English department.

Around that time, disgruntled with what they saw as the increasingly entrenched and narrowing theoretical and methodological aspects of the field of American studies in general and the American Studies Association in particular, Browne and Russel Nye began the serious planning that would eventually lead to the founding of the *Journal of Popular Culture* and, with Marshall Fishwick and Carl Bode, the Popular Culture Association. The men sought a more unified network for scholarly communication and focus, as well as a means of obtaining increased visibility and academic respectability. Such luminous scholars as John Cawelti, David Madden, and a growing host of others quickly joined them. The process continued to be an uphill battle, as colleagues and academic institutions not only failed to see the value in the emergent field but actually saw it as a non- or even anti–intellectual pursuit, with no justifiable reason to be included in the academy.

National and regional conferences followed. A few years later, Browne was the founding chairperson of the Popular Culture Department at BGSU. He remained chairperson and taught there until 1992. In addition, he co-founded (and was active in) the American Culture Association and its respective journal, as well as the Popular Press, the BGSU Popular Culture Library and several additional journals.

Browne edited the movement's flagship journal for over three decades while helping to helm the Popular Press and maintaining positions of prominence in both the PCA and ACA. Furthermore, he traveled around the world, lecturing on a variety of topics and spreading the gospel of Popular Culture Studies. In his career he authored more than eighty articles and book chapters, eight books, and around a thousand reviews. He also edited fifty scholarly volumes. At the time of his death, he was working on at least three books, co-editing a theme issue of the *Journal of American Culture,* and composing several book reviews.

Engaging with Ray Browne[2]

I first heard of Ray Browne when I was a graduate student in cultural anthropology at Wichita State University in the early 1980s, when a national PCA conference was held there. He was presented as a celebrator of popular culture — or perhaps I should say he was largely dismissed as a *celebrator* of popular culture.

Though I knew only a little about Ray Browne, I could not dismiss him so easily. I began to read Browne on my own. I found (and still find) Browne to be a freshly pragmatic thinker and, as such, quite utilitarian in any number of academic arenas.

After a six-year absence, I returned to higher education in pursuit of a doctorate in American culture studies at Bowling Green State University, the institution where Browne had established so much. One of my first classes was a seminar on detective fiction, taught by Ray Browne. I was given a collection of Victorian and Edwardian era crime literature and told to report on it the next week. I prepared an overview of the volume and presented it to the class. Browne's response was not what I had expected. He looked at me and said "Well, from your report we learn that you understand what you read. But I was expecting you to be profound." There was no harshness or irony in the statement, and though a bit taken aback and slightly embarrassed, I was also kind of thrilled: Ray Browne had expected me to be profound! I would soon come to understand that expecting and bringing forth the best in his students was one of Ray Browne's many talents.

One day a year or so later, after a class in which we read current books on cultural theory, I was discussing ideas with a few fellow students and was surprised to learn of their take on Ray Browne. They respected him for all of his pioneering work on organizations, the department of Popular Culture and the journals—but they hadn't read anything he wrote except his landmark article "Popular Culture: Notes Toward a Definition" and knew nothing of his extensive scholarship. Enrolling in some of the last classes taught by Browne at BGSU, and subsequent professional and personal dealings with him, only strengthened my belief that this aspect of Browne's work was unjustly overlooked.

Engaging the Writings

Browne's scholarly work was, and remains, not only "contemporary and relevant" but a vital missing element in modern cultural studies and research, placing Browne beyond his obvious niche as a pioneer in founding academic associations and journals. Browne's far-reaching but malleable underlying ideas, and his deep readings of the social effects and affectations of democratic-capitalistic enterprises, make him an especially insightful and invigorating (if unrecognized and unacknowledged) cultural studies voice.

The ideas (and no less, his applications of them) expressed by Ray Browne in his often-intriguing essays are in need of a broader audience, both in popular culture studies itself and in sister disciplines that attempt to analyze and document cultures and cultural phenomena. Despite the age of some of his essays, Ray Browne's thinking marks him as a revolutionary and radical scholar — still. Browne's writings are crisp and clear and even essays over a half-century old read as if they are freshly composed, a particular rarity for academic articles. It is not surprising that, given the circumstances and his intended readership, Browne wrote for what might now be termed a trans- or cross-disciplinary audience, and so avoided the jargon in vogue in a particular field at the time, allowing the articles to have broader application and relevance today than they might have retained otherwise. More significantly, his concepts and queries have an immediacy and freshness that is genuinely inspiring. The essays themselves range from research in anthropologically based folklore studies, literary criticism, media analysis, and theory and methodology critiques; to commentary on the state of academia, and to the values of various approaches to popular culture studies in particular and cultural studies in general.

Browne's work is clearly of value to a variety of academic fields and his importance to and influence on the development of several of them needs to be acknowledged. Quite a few fields of study and disciplines that made no note of the pieces in their original incarnations will continue to do so at their academic and intellectual peril. There is, however, a more vital reason why this volume is useful.

The endlessly recurrent, dissembling state of any of the many fields involving culture studies means the time is *always* right for Browne's fundamental, inclusive, and eclectic voice to be heard. Browne's pioneering and still relevant work merits close attention by contemporary scholars of all culture studies-based fields. His work clearly dispels the theoretical Maginot Lines that many of those academic endeavors have become. Somewhat sadly, his thinking has lost little of its revolutionary message for several disciplines.

Browne's work, then, is of significant relevance not just to popular culture studies, but also to other fields and disciplines that study culture and cultural phenomena. This includes cultural anthropologists who study state societies past and present, mass media scholars, entertainment scholars, folklorists, sociologists, literary critics, social psychologists, historians, those who pursue the study of the humanities, American studies, and cultural studies scholars. Work after work in these areas unknowingly struggle and flail about, trying to reinvent Browne's groundwork concepts and explanations. Regrettably, few have the eloquence or conviction of Browne.

Browne's work can therefore be used to cover the theoretical and methodological gaps between fields and disciplines that attempt culture-based investigations. It may also draw the attention of scholars towards popular culture studies as a significant, relevant location of contemporary discourse on all matters cultural.

Engaging This Collection

There is then, easy justification for introducing or reintroducing Browne via his key articles and other writings. This is a selection of those writings spanning nearly six decades of academic publishing. The intention of this volume is not to present a mere "collection of classics" but to demonstrate the vigor, viability, and at times revolutionary character of the approaches and underlying ideas within the pieces.

Nor is this a comprehensive overview — or even a representative sampling — of his remarkable output. For example, volumes could (and should) be comprised solely of Browne's essays on literature, or on folklore, or on media studies, or of his reviews. The focus here is on his more overt commentaries on and explanation of the benefits of popular culture studies, and some key exemplars of his application of those ideas. Some then-contemporary references and examples may be dated, but the ideas expressed and points made are not.

These writings can be organized and categorized a number of ways. Chronologically he moves by topic, from folklore, to literature, to media, to arguing the case for Popular Culture Studies both in the academy generally and in certain disciplines specifically. But as in his diverse though disciplined approach, there are no clear-cut boundaries.

Another organizing strategy is evident in that once the *Journal of Popular Culture* and the Popular Press were established, Browne began to limit (but did not curtail) his output through other academic publishing venues. Prior to that, Browne felt that the case in support of Popular Culture Studies must be restated to some degree for each discipline/audience anew. On his home ground, knowing he was addressing the at least partially converted and that the victory for academic legitimacy was in sight, Browne allowed himself to increasingly shift his focus to broader issues. From the late 1970s on, Browne's writings largely either deal with broad issues within the tenuously established field of Popular Culture Studies, or with his then-current personal academic research interests. Several times, he did still adapt his larger pieces into smaller ones for particular audiences outside of Popular Culture Studies proper. This volume is organized by way of several general but not exclusive themes, and combines aspects of topic, subject, and chronology.

As this collection demonstrates, the ideas of Ray Browne have relevance to all sorts of contemporary social sciences and humanities oriented fields. Browne's work should (and must) appeal not just to investigators of popular culture phenomena, but also to any and all that study culture and cultures— in any discipline or from any approach. This includes but is not limited to all of the aforementioned fields potentially and profitably informed and influenced by popular culture studies: anthropology, history, American studies, sociology, cultural studies, etc.

Since this collection represents in both breadth and scope the apex of Browne's most mature thinking on the value of Popular Culture Studies, there is some minor polishing and rehashing in evidence to any who read the volume in its entirety. Collectively, the selections demonstrate the range of Browne's interests and developing thinking from a variety of perspectives. In his quest to demonstrate the viability of Popular Culture Studies, Browne's scope broadened and he became more holistic in attempting to explain the "hows and whys" of certain historical developments and social dynamics to various disciplines and subdisciplines.

Ideally what will be seen here is the raw force and almost overwhelming range of Browne's primary thinking on issues still investigated and debated by scholars of varied backgrounds and interests. To that end, the digressive flow of Browne's approach, in both form and content, is a major strength and is replicated in the organization of the selections chosen.

The book is divided to four main parts; each part has a brief general explanatory introduction, and each piece within has a short introduction of its own. In addition, each inclusion has its original publication credit listed at the beginning and in a briefly annotated bibliography that encapsulates the content of the piece in question. Occasional minor editing has been done, but the articles, including citation styles, are largely as they appeared when first published and at the end of the appropriate pieces and not in toto at the end of the volume. On a handful of the selections, more significant editing has been done and in those few cases it is noted and explained in the pieces themselves or their introductions, as seems most fitting.

Here is Ray Browne, engaging freely with all manners of topics, artifacts, approaches, genres, theories, disciplines and perspectives, while gently prodding and encouraging us to attempt to do the same.

Bibliography

[1]For a more complete overview of Browne's career see

Hoppenstand, Gary. "Ray and Pat Browne: Scholars of Everyday Culture," in *Pioneers in Popular Culture Studies*, Ray Browne and Michael T. Marsden, eds. (Bowling Green, OH: BGSU Popular Press, 1999), pp. 32–65.

For Browne's take on the early years of the PCA in particular and the movement in general, see his

Against Academia: The History of the PCA/ACA and Popular Culture Movement, 1967–1988 (Bowling Green, OH: BGSU Popular Press, 1989). A revised update of the book has the less incendiary title of *Mission Underway* and continues the story through 2001.

[2]For a revealing look at Browne as classroom educator and a commentary on Browne's scholarly motivations, see

Nachbar, Jack. "Casting His Hope with the People: Selected Articles by Ray B. Browne," in *Eye on the Future: Popular Culture Studies in the 21st Century*, Marilyn F. Motz, John G. Nachbar, Michael T. Marsden and Ronald J. Ambrosetti, eds. (Bowling Green, OH: BGSU Popular Press, 1994), pp. 203–206.

Prologue

On Redefining Cultural Studies

In this previously unpublished and very personal essay fragment, Browne presents his overall argument for a more inclusive definition of "cultural studies." He argues that the study of popular culture is essential to the proper approach of American Studies. And, given the importance of the U.S. socially, politically, historically, and economically on the planet, Browne further contends that American Studies, as a discipline, must in fact be global in its ultimate orientation. We end up, therefore, with a reconstructed field of Cultural Studies, fueled by a transnational approach to the study of popular culture. Of special interest is Browne's brief and bittersweet telling of his and Russel Nye's early attempts to define "popular culture" where, with the benefit of hindsight, he expresses some minor regrets.— The Editor.

> Let me not to the marriage of [inquiring] minds
> Admit impediments
>
> Shakespeare, *Sonnet 116*

The world, I have always thought, is such a complex and wide mixture of things that one owed it to himself or herself to try to reach out and grasp them and try to understand all. One need not be as enthusiastic as Robert Louis Stevenson to believe indeed that if we could just understand the "number of things" that make up the world we might be, if not as "happy as kings," at least as curious as detectives.

Other persons have felt that first of all one should understand himself or herself — that the world is a projection of oneself and one needs to understand this projection before the world is taken on. The microcosm is to be understood before the macrocosm is tackled. In other words one should recognize the godship of oneself before searching for the godhead in creation.

Perhaps both points of view are equally valid. To understand the world and oneself one needs to spend much time studying the "masters" of thought to reap the benefit of their experience and wisdom about themselves and any light they might shed upon themselves, the world and their experience in it.

To a certain extent the attitude of trying to understand the world through one's own eyes is self-indulgent. It tries to use oneself as the spot of emanation of the essence of existence and to become god-like in appreciation of oneself and the world through oneself.

But what in fact does the world care whether an individual — one out of ten billion on earth — understands himself or herself? The world rolls on in its own complex course controlling the existence or terminating it. The self-exploring individual is in some ways examining their own navel on a body that is important only to their selves.

Another way an individual can face the world is by looking beyond their own nose and his reflection in a mirror and sees the big, complex reality that constantly enriches the

9

person who tries to understand it. The world is indifferent to the individual but the individual should not be indifferent to it. They cannot be, in fact, if they want to be a part of it rather than trying to make it a part of them. Tennyson's Ulysses was "a part of all that [he] had met," because he realized that the universe is a big, largely indifferent mass of power and opportunities.

The role of education of us all then might well be that of eye-opener and stimulant — eye-opener to the possibilities of the world of outside knowledge, and stimulant to determination to learn of it and understand it.

To those of us interested in the Humanities, our dedication demands that we try to understand *humanity* in all its shapes, colors and cultures. To do so is to understand ourselves in conjunction with the outside world. We need to remember that recent discoveries in DNA have taught us that we are all practically the same, that differences are superficialities and surface things, and that we come to understand ourselves by understanding others.

Seeing and being interested in the wonders of the world as revealed in the human aspects of life and cultures has driven my academic career. I have always wanted to begin with the individual — myself — as a point of departure and work outward — to family, community, county, state, country, and world. The geography is staggering in its immensity but the journey profitable if travelers look out from themselves, grasp the world and bring it to them.

So, my academic career has always been a reaching out from my known to the unknown. I've always wanted to discover the new — to be the pioneer — and leave to somebody else the pleasure of settling and understanding.

This action has always been what people dramatically like to call a "probing of the edges." In fact, however, the more proper descriptive term might be "outreach from the known to the unknown," tracking the trickle of water from the center to the edges and then following the heart of the flow with the hope that I would find there the essence of human existence.

The search has not always been fruitful or pleasant. Some academics have looked upon the inquiry on the outer edges to be fruitless until those edges have been demonstrated to contain the essence of truth. In its simplest statement this logic has dictated that nothing is worth studying until it has filtered through time and been proved to be lasting. This is indeed a strange kind of reasoning that turns in upon itself and has the mouth sucking the tail. In such logic are many basic blind spots. If the pioneer — on earth, in the sky, in science, etc. — does not make the first probes then there is never any general movement toward the new possible discoveries. Poet Frost's *Reluctance* suggests the proper attitude of the academic explorer:

> Ah, when to the heart of man
> Was if ever less than a treason
> To go with the drift of things,
> To yield with a grace to reason,
> And bow and accept the end
> Of a love or a season?
> ["Reluctance" (1913), stanza 4]

Or as he says in *The Road Not Taken*, choosing the path less traveled has "made all the difference." Daniel Boone discovered far more beyond the Appalachians than he dreamed of and opened up a new territory in which the settler could pursue detailed investigation, and Whitman voiced the exhilaration of the search for the new:

> Lighthearted I take to the open road,
> Healthy, free, the world before me,
> The long brown path before me leading wherever I choose.

Perhaps Mark Twain, beloved iconoclast of both elite and popular critics, gives us the most desirable model in the conclusion of *The Adventures of Huckleberry Finn*, with only the slightest paraphrase into literary phraseology. Tom, Jim and Huck decide to take off for the west where new adventures await them. But Huck soon realizes that he can have no lasting new experiences with these two representatives of the old order. So he decides to go alone in order to escape both Tom and Huck and Aunt Sally. Aunt Sally has tried to "sivilize"—that is, canonize—him in the past and he can't stand it. There are too many canonized worshippers already in the congregation. He has to go west and find his new culture and new literature of values. Academics who find in this novel in essence Ernest Hemingway's approval of it as the mother of all American literature need to take to heart its conclusion about the individual and existence.

Although the term "Popular Culture" has been around ever since at least the Romans who constantly talked of *Vox Populi*, in the late sixties and early seventies when it came into use again it seemed bewildering to most scholars. Even anthropologists did not use it with conviction. Because everybody seemed to think he or she knew what the term means since they were living in the everyday world, although they did not have much to do with it except through the media of entertainment, most people simply assumed that they knew what the term means without thinking much about it. Unfortunately the drive was aided and abetted through careless reading of the early main book, Russel B. Nye's *The Unembarrassed Muse* (1970), which became the bible of early popular culture scholars.

Nye had subtitled his book *The Popular Arts in America* and had begun his "Introduction" with the single paragraph stating that, "The term 'the popular arts' cannot be used accurately to describe a cultural situation in Western civilization prior to the late eighteenth century." Though most scholars then and now might have argued with the time restriction, harm from the book came about despite Nye's intentions when nearly all readers of the study mistook "popular arts" for popular culture. In academia, as in the world at large, when a tag line or idea—no matter how foolish and incorrect—gets its head on crooked it is virtually impossible to set it straight.

Such has been the fate of the term "popular culture." Before Nye's book was published several of us tried in different ways, by conference and publication, to establish a working definition. In 1970 I published my "Popular Culture: Notes Towards a Definition."* Nye published a pamphlet called "Notes on a Rationale for Popular Culture." I had read the "Introduction" to Nye's *Unembarrassed Muse* before it was published and concluded that together our statements should help toward a definition, or at least should outline our approach. Unfortunately our directions were concerned with the arts and entertainment as popular culture, or popular culture as the arts and entertainment.

In my publication I tried to outline a working definition of the concept. In addition

---

Browne is referring to the pamphlet version of the article, printed and distributed by the Popular Culture Association in 1970. It was then more widely published in 1972.—The Editor.

to trying to establish that the folk and their culture has always been with us, I tried to point out that folklore, a very fiercely ambitious subject in academia at the time, was and is the unlettered popular culture. Nye's book and my article were matches that set off explosions among both the students of all the humanities and the folklorists. The latter group felt that popular culture students were trying to poach on the older discipline and would corrupt and steal it. Although we in popular culture studies tried to allay such fears, in fact their apprehensions have proved at least partially prophetic. Popular Culture Studies have spilled over into folklore studies, as the more astute folklorists now recognize and admit, and popular culture studies are reaching out to encompass all aspects of the humanities and social sciences as they impinge on cultures that have everyday existences—which means all.

Many statements made in my early publications were uttered by a pioneer in a new land and would have been said much differently if the terrain had been more familiar or if the pieces had been written later when the study of the subject had been more thoroughly worked out and stabilized.

At this point, therefore, before venturing into the world of popular culture studies, it will be useful to define the *present* understanding of the term, largely as I stated it in my article "Internationalizing Popular Culture Studies."

Popular culture, as is increasingly being understood, is the system of attitudes, behavior patterns, beliefs, customs and tastes that define the people of any society. It is the entertainment, diversions, icons, rituals and actions that shape a society's everyday world. Popular culture is the way in which and by which most people in any society live. In a democracy like the United States it is the voice of the people — their practices, likes and dislikes— the lifeblood of their daily existence, a way of life. The popular culture is the voice of democracy, speaking and acting, the seedbed in which democracy is born and grows. Popular culture in all societies—from the most authoritarian to the most democratic — it democratizes them and makes democracy truly democratic. It is a people's way of life they inherit, practice, modify as they please, and then pass on to their descendants. It is what the people do while they are awake; it is the dreams they dream while asleep, as well as where and how they sleep and how long.

Studies of American cultures have generally aspired to follow the dynamics of everyday cultures but have been held back by clinging to the theories and methodologies of conventional attitudes. Now, however, American Studies are rapidly and expanding into Popular Culture Studies. Students of culture increasingly realize that old formulas, myths and symbols, interpretations and readings of facts must be reconsidered and that they must take into consideration all aspects— all drives, all expressions of life and culture if they are to understand the world and the interconnectedness around them. Old approaches must be reconsidered because they are no longer sufficiently comprehensive or appropriate. In a dynamic world, old methods of study are not satisfactory.

Cultural Studies must move into the 21st century.

PART ONE

BLAZING THE TRAIL

The first four years of Browne's earliest publications were in folklore collection and folklore studies. In the decade after that, his folklore publications lessened and studies analyzing literature came to predominate. Even in these early writings, however, Browne's approach was eclectic and wide-ranging. For instance, popular songs are included in the folklore studies as well as in an analysis of Shakespeare. Browne also documented the influence of folktales on the writings of Nathaniel Hawthorne, and so on. All the while Browne was fusing elements of various disciplines and working his way toward an expanded and more inclusive approach to the fields and disciplines in which he worked.

Other scholars, especially in the relatively new domain of American studies, were on a similar course, and in the late 1960s the nascent popular culture studies movement fully arrived. It remained for the movement and the field to be described, defined, defended, and justified.

This section includes the formative articles Browne published over the ensuing decade, plus the key articles published thereafter that elaborated upon and further developed the thrust of those early ideas. A later section contains pieces that introduced newer concerns and approaches that arose as the field, and Browne's thinking, matured.

1

*Popular Culture: Notes Toward a Definition**

By the time of this landmark article's publication Browne had been instrumental (and successful) in solidifying the popular culture studies movement and helping to provide it with a solid foundation. The Journal of Popular Culture, *the Popular Culture Association and its meetings, the BGSU Popular Press, and the (brand new in 1972) Department of Popular Culture were all in operation. Browne's task here was to try to provide functional parameters for the growing discipline, while not closing off any potential research topics or interested scholars.*

Browne had pondered the matter for some time, creating a draft of the piece in response to Russel Nye's Unembarrassed Muse *introduction before Nye's volume had even seen print. This version was printed in pamphlet form by the Culture Association and distributed to members at the early conferences. John Cawelti then had published his early thinking on the term ("Notes Toward an Aesthetic of Popular Culture" among other works), and Nye's "Notes on a Rationale for Popular Culture" had also received the pamphlet treatment by the time Browne let the article see official publication, nearly simultaneously in two volumes, one aimed at career academics, the other at students and the public at large. David Madden, Marshall Fishwick, and others, all chimed in with their considerations, as published in the* Journal of Popular Culture.

The negative scholarly connotations tied to the term "mass culture" (see preface) are not directly addressed in this piece, and Browne claims not to have considered them at the time, but by positing that mass culture is a particular aspect of popular culture, Browne must have been aware that his potential audience was grappling with the term. His explanation, however, that mass culture is popular culture that is mass disseminated eventually seemed insufficient to Browne. It forces Browne to deal with issues of dissemination in his definition, and corrals him into what he would later disavow: an explication of popular cultural phenomena reduced to, and too closely aligned with, the popular arts.

Browne would rarely deal with the "mass culture" term again, properly leaving it to the dustbin of academic history, and the distinction he makes here would be dropped in his later thinking. The notable (and expected) exception is his later similarly titled article "Popular Culture: New Notes Toward a Definition" (seen elsewhere in this collection). There, he corrects and bolsters the mass culture/popular arts/dissemination issues. One of the few other significant (though brief) considerations of "mass culture" came in the book chapter "American Studies and Popular Culture" from the book he edited, Popular Culture Studies Across the Curriculum *where Browne notes that the term "mass" in "mass culture" had largely political ramifications as a result of its theoretical origins.*

---

*Also published as "Popular Culture: The World Around Us."— The Editor.

15

His evaluations of the usefulness of the ideas of Susan Sontag and Marshall McLuhan to popular culture studies would also somewhat diminish. Browne often cherry-picked the concepts of others that he found useful and rejected those he did not.— The Editor

"Popular Culture" is an indistinct term whose edges blur into imprecision. Scarcely any two commentators who try to define it agree in all aspects of what popular culture really is. Most critics, in fact, do not attempt to define it; instead, after distinguishing between it and the mass media, and between it and "high" culture, most assume that everybody knows that whatever is widely disseminated and experienced is "popular culture."

Some observers divide the total culture of a people into "minority" and "majority" categories. Other observers classify culture into High-Cult, Mid-Cult, and Low-Cult, or High-Brow, Mid-Brow, and Low-Brow, leaving out, apparently, the level that would perhaps be called Folk-Cult or Folk-Brow, though Folk culture is now taking on, even among the severest critics of popular culture a high class and achievement unique unto itself. Most of the discriminating observers agree, in fact, that there are perhaps actually four areas of culture: Elite, Popular, Mass, and Folk, with the understanding that none is a discrete unity standing apart and unaffected by the others.

One reason for the lack of a precise definition is that the serious study of "popular culture" has been neglected in American colleges and universities. Elitist critics of our culture — notably such persons as Dwight MacDonald and Edmund Wilson — have always insisted that whatever was widespread was artistically and esthetically deficient, therefore unworthy of study. They have taught that "culture" to be worthwhile must necessarily be limited to the elite, aristocratic, and the minority. They felt that mass or popular culture — especially as it appeared in the mass media — would vitiate real culture. This attitude persists today among some of the younger critics. William Gass, for example, the esthetician and critic, takes the extreme position that "the products of popular culture, by and large, have no more esthetic quality than a brick in the street.... Any esthetic intention is entirely absent, and because it is desired to manipulate consciousness directly, achieve one's effect there, no mind is paid to the intrinsic nature of its objects; they lack finish, complexity, stasis, individuality, coherence, depth, and endurance."

Such an attitude as Gass' is perhaps an extreme statement of the elitist critic's point of view. Luckily the force of numerous critics' arguments is weakening such attitudes. Popular Culture has a dimension, a thrust and — most important — a reality that has nothing to do with its esthetic accomplishment, though that has more merit than is often given to it.

This point of view is demonstrated by the talented young stylist Tom Wolfe, who, perhaps writing more viscerally than intellectually, thumbs his nose at the prejudice and snobbery that has always held at arm's length all claims of validity if not esthetic accomplishment of the "culture" of the masses.

Susan Sontag, a brilliant young critic and esthetician, is more effective in bludgeoning the old point of view. Far from alarmed at the apparent new esthetic, she sees that it is merely a change in attitude, not a death's blow to culture and art:

> What we are getting is not the demise of art, but a transformation of the function of art. Art, which arose in human society as magical-religious operation, and passed over into a technique for depicting and commenting on secular reality, has in our own time arrogated to itself a new function — neither religious, nor serving a secularized religious function, nor merely secular or profane.... Art today is a new kind of instrument, an instrument for modifying consciousness and organizing new modes of sensibility.

To Sontag the unprecedented complexity of the world has made inevitable and very necessary this change in the function of art. This is virtually the same attitude held by Marshall McLuhan:

A technological extension of our bodies designed to alleviate physical stress can bring on psychic stress that may be much worse.... Art is exact information of how to rearrange one's psyche to anticipate the next blow from our own extended psyches ... in experimental art, men are given the exact specifications of coming violence to their own psyche from their own counter-irritants or technology. For those parts of ourselves that we thrust out in the form of new inventions are attempts to counter or neutralize collective pressures and irritations. But the counter-irritant usually proves a greater plague than the initial irritant like a drug habit. And it is here that the artist can show us how to "ride with the punch," instead of "taking it on the chin."

An equally important aspect of popular culture as index and corrector is its role as comic voice. Popular humor provides a healthy element in a nation's life. It pricks the pompous, devaluates the inflated, and snipes at the overly solemn. For example, such organs of popular culture as the magazines spoofed Henry James' pomposity during his lifetime, spoofed his "high" seriousness and in general tended to humanize him.

A more reasonable attitude than Gass' and one that is becoming increasingly acceptable is that held by the philosopher Abraham Kaplan: That popular culture has considerable accomplishment and even more real possibilities and it is developing but has not realized its full potential. All areas draw from one another. The Mass area being largely imitative draws from the others without altering much. Elite art draws heavily from both folk and, perhaps to a slightly lesser degree, popular arts. Popular art draws from Elite and Mass, and Folk, but does not take any without subjecting it to a greater or lesser amount of creative change. That popular culture has "no more esthetic quality than a brick in the street" or at least no more esthetic potential is a contention refuted by America's greatest writers— Hawthorne, Melville, Whitman, Twain, to name only four — as well as the greatest writers of all times and countries— Homer, Shakespeare, Dickens, Dostoevsky, and Tolstoy.

Melville provides an excellent case in point. *Moby Dick* is the greatest creative book written in America and one of the half dozen greatest ever written anywhere. Its greatness derives from the sum total of its many parts. It is a blend of nearly all elements of all cultures of mid–nineteenth century America. Melville took all the culture around him — trivial and profound — Transcendentalism and the plumbing of the depths of the human experience, but also demonism, popular theater, the shanghai gesture, jokes about pills and gas on the stomach, etc., and boiled them in the tryworks of his fiery genius into the highest art.

Many definitions of popular culture turn on methods of dissemination. Those elements which are too sophisticated for the mass media are generally called Elite culture, those distributed through these media that are something less than "mass," that is such things as the smaller magazines and newspapers, the less widely distributed books, museums and less sophisticated galleries, so-called clothes line art exhibits, and the like — are called in the narrow sense of the term "popular," those elements that are distributed through the mass media are "mass" culture, and those which are or were at one time disseminated by oral and non–oral methods— on levels "lower" than the mass media — are called "folk."

All definitions of such a complex matter, though containing a certain amount of validity and usefulness, are bound to be to a certain extent inadequate or incorrect. Perhaps a workable definition can best be arrived at by looking at one of the culture's most salient and quintessential aspects— its artistic creations— because the artist perhaps more than anyone else draws from the totality of experience and best reflects it.

Shakespeare and his works are an excellent example. When he was producing his plays at the Globe Theater, Shakespeare was surely a "popular" author and his works were elements of "popular" culture, though they were at the same time also High or Elite culture, for they were very much part of the lives of both the groundlings and the nobles. Later, in America, especially during the nineteenth century, all of his works were well known, his name was commonplace, and he was at the same time still High art, Popular (even mass) art and Folk art. In the twentieth century, however, his works are more distinguishable as parts of various levels. *Hamlet* is still a play of both High and Popular art. The most sophisticated and scholarly people still praise it. But *Hamlet* is also widely distributed on TV, radio and through the movies. It is a commonplace on all levels of society and is therefore a part of "popular culture" in the broadest sense of the term. Other plays by Shakespeare, however, have not become a part of "popular" culture. *Titus Andronicus*, for example, for any of several reasons, is not widely known by the general public. It remains, thus, Elite culture.

Wideness of distribution and popularity in this sense are one major aspect of popular culture. But there are others. Many writers would be automatically a part of popular culture if their works sold only a few copies— Frank G. Slaughter and Frank Yerby, for example. Louis Auchincloss also, though his works are of a different kind than Slaughter's and Yerby's, because his subject is Wall Street and high finance, and these are subjects of popular culture.

Aside from distribution, another major difference between high and popular culture, and among popular culture, mass culture and folk culture, is the motivation of the persons contributing, the makers and shapers of culture. On the Elite or sophisticated level, the creators value individualism, individual expression, the exploration and discovery of new art forms, of new ways of stating, the exploration and discovery of new depths in life's experiences.

On the other levels of culture there is usually less emphasis placed upon, and less accomplishment reached in, this plumbing of reality. Generally speaking, both popular and mass artists are less interested in the experimental and searching than in the restatement of the old and accepted. But there are actually vast differences in the esthetic achievements attained in the works from these two levels, and different aspirations and goals, even within these somewhat limited objectives. As Hall and Whannel have pointed out:

> In mass art the formula is everything—an escape from, rather than a means to, originality. The popular artist may use the conventions to select, emphasize and stress (or alter the emphasis and stress) so as to delight the audience with a kind of creative surprise, Mass art uses the stereotypes and formulae to simplify the experience, to mobilize stock feelings and to 'get them going.'

The popular artist is superior to the mass artist because for him "stylization is necessary, and the conventions provide an agreed base from 'which true creative invention springs.'" It is a serious error therefore to agree with Dwight MacDonald (in *Against the American Grain*) that all popular art "includes the spectator's reactions in the work itself instead of forcing him to make his own responses." Consider, for example, the reactions of two carriers of non–Elite culture, the first of popular culture, the banjo player Johnny St. Cyr. He always felt that the creative impulses of the average person and his responses in a creative situation were immense:

> You see, the average man is very musical. Playing music for him is just relaxing. He gets as much kick out of playing as other folks get out of dancing. The more enthusiastic his audience

is, why the more spirit the working man's got to play. And with your natural feelings that way you never make the same thing twice. Every time you play a tune new ideas come to mind and you slip that one in.

Compare that true artist's philosophy with that of Liberace, to whom the "whole trick is to keep the tune well out in front," to play "the melodies" and skip the "spiritual struggles." He always knows "just how many notes (his) audience will stand for," and if he has time leftover he fills in "with a lot of runs up and down the keyboard."

Here in condensed form is the difference between popular and mass art and popular and mass artists. Both aim for different goals. St. Cyr is a truly creative artist in both intent and accomplishment. His credentials are not invalidated merely by the fact that he works in essentially a popular idiom. Given the limitations of his medium — if indeed these limitations are real — he can still be just as great a creator as — perhaps greater than — Rubenstein. It is incorrect to pit jazz against classical music, the popular against the elite. They are not in competition. Each has its own purposes, techniques and accomplishments. They complement each other rather than compete.

Another fine example can be found among the youth of today and their rebellion against what they consider the establishment. They are obviously not a part of the static mass, to whom escape is everything. Instead they are vigorously active, and in their action create dynamic and fine works of art, as examination of their songs, their art, their movies, etc., dramatically demonstrates.

It is also unfair to give blanket condemnation to mass art, though obviously the accomplishments of mass art are less than those of "higher" forms. Liberace does not aspire to much, and perhaps reaches even less. His purposes and techniques are inferior, but not all his, or the many other workers in the level, are completely without value.

All levels of culture, it must never be forgotten, are distorted by the lenses of snobbery and prejudice, which the observers wear. There are no hard and fast lines separating one level from another.

Popular culture also includes folk culture. The relationship between folk culture and popular and elite cultures is still debatable. In many ways folk culture borrows from and imitates both.

Historically folk art has come more from the hall than from the novel, has depended more upon the truly creative — though unsophisticated — spirit than the mediocre imitator. "Sir Patrick Spens," one of the greatest songs (poems) ever written, was originally the product of a single creative genius. Today's best folklore-to-be, that is the most esthetically satisfying folklore which is working into tradition today, is that of such people as Woody Guthrie, Larry Gorman and such individual artists.

To a large number of observers, however, folklore is felt to be the same as popular culture. To another large number folklore derives directly from popular culture, with only a slight time lag. To them, today's popular culture is tomorrow's folklore. Both notions are gross and out of line.

Esthetically folk culture has two levels. There is superb folk art and deficient mediocre folk art. Esthetically folk art is more nearly akin to Elite art, despite the lack of sophistication that much folk art has, than to popular. Elite art has much that is inferior, as even the most prejudiced critic must admit. In motivation of artist, also, folk art is close to Elite, for like the Elite artist the truly accomplished folk artist values individualism and personal expression, he explores new forms and seeks new depths in expression and feeling. But there are at the same time workers in folklore who are mere imitators, just trying to get along—exactly like their counterparts in mass culture.

Thus all elements in our culture (or cultures) are closely related and are not mutually exclusive one from another. They constitute one long continuum. Perhaps the best metaphorical figure for all is that of a flattened ellipsis, or a lens. In the center, largest in bulk and easiest seen through is Popular Culture, which includes Mass Culture.

On either end of the lens are High and Folk Cultures, both looking fundamentally alike in many respects and both having a great deal in common, for both have keen direct vision and extensive peripheral insight and acumen. All four derive in many ways and to many degrees from one another, and the lines of demarcations between any two are indistinct and mobile.

Despite the obvious difficulty of arriving at a hard and fast definition of popular culture, it will probably be to our advantage—and a comfort to many who need one—to arrive at some viable though tentative understanding of how popular culture can be defined.

Two scholars who do attempt a definition, following George Santayana's broad distinctions between work and play, believe that "Popular Culture is really what people do when they are not working." This definition is both excessively general and overly exclusive, for it includes much that is "high" culture and leaves out many aspects that obviously belong to popular culture.

One serious scholar defines a total culture as "The body of intellectual and imaginative work which each generation receives" as its tradition. Basing our conclusion on this one, a viable definition for Popular Culture is all those elements of life which are not narrowly intellectual or creatively elitist and which are generally though not necessarily disseminated through the mass media, Popular Culture consists of the spoken and printed word, sounds, pictures, objects and artifacts.

"Popular Culture" thus embraces all levels of our society and culture other than the Elite—the "popular," "mass" and "folk." It includes most of the bewildering aspects of life that hammer us daily.

Such a definition, though perhaps umbrella-like in its comprehensiveness, provides the latitude needed at this point, it seems, for the serious scholar to study the world around him. Later, definitions may need to pare edges and change lighting and emphasis. But for the moment, inclusiveness is perhaps better than exclusiveness.

Bibliography

In the briefest bibliography possible I suggest the following references:

Gass, William H. "Even if by all the Oxen in the World," in Ray B. Browne, et al., *Frontiers of American Culture*. West Lafayette, PA: Purdue University Studies, 1968.

Hall, Stuart and Paddy Whannel. *The Popular Arts*. New York: Pantheon Books, 1964.

McLuhan, Marshall. *Understanding Media*. New York: McGraw-Hill, 1964.

_____. *War and Peace in the Global Village*. New York: McGraw-Hill, 1968.

Shapiro, Nat, and Nat Hentoff. *Hear Me Talkin' to Ya*. New York: Dover, 1955.

Sontag, Susan. *Against Interpretation*. New York: Farrar, Strauss, & Giroux, 1966.

Williams, Raymond. *Culture and Society: 1780–1950*. London: Chatto, & Winders, 1960.

_____. *The Long Revolution*. New York: Columbia University, 1961.

2

Popular Culture: New Notes Toward a Definition

Though the title implies a mere updating of the essay "Popular Culture: Notes Toward a Definition" this essay actually bears few similarities beyond the obvious one of attempting to define the term and its related concepts and applications.

Of special interest is Browne's fuller and clearer dealing with the weaker points of the earlier essay. Here he deals with "mass culture" and mass dissemination without the misleading lurch toward seeing all popular culture as part of the popular arts.

Intriguingly, Browne calls for an anthropologically styled "participant-observation" technique to properly engage in popular culture studies, yet doesn't name it as such. Also of note is the furtherance of his arguments for the democratic aspects of popular culture, and the final clarification (and admonition?) that popular culture studies are not intended to replace other academic investigations that prove their merit, but to exist alongside them.—The Editor

Popular Culture, in its simplest definition, is the way of life we inherit from the generations before us, use ourselves, and pass on to our followers. It is our attitudes, habits and actions: how we act and why we act the way we do; what we eat, wear; our buildings, roads and means of travel; our entertainments, sports; our politics, religion, medical practices; our beliefs and activities and what shapes and controls them. It is, in other words, the world we live in.

Popular culture is the culture of the people, of all the people, as distinguished from a select, small elite group. It is also the dominant culture of minorities—of ethnic, social, religious, or financial minorities—simply because their way of life is, by and large, not accepted into the elite culture of the dominant group. As the way of life of a people, popular culture has existed since the most primitive times, when it was simple and uncomplicated. It has obviously become more complex and sophisticated as means of communicating and ways of life have developed.

Although popular culture has existed as long as people have, the concentrated and widespread academic study of people's ways—even among anthropologists and sociologists—is a recent development. As such, today, of course, definitions differ somewhat as to what popular culture really is. In the recent past, many people have felt that popular culture is mass culture—that is, the common culture of the masses of people—and therefore it could develop only after the eighteenth century, when rapid means of producing the printed word came into being.

Though this attitude has some validity and appeal, it may be too narrow in concept and too short in time-span to be sufficiently comprehensive. The development of rapid means of printing and distribution led to a faster way of disseminating people's culture than had existed before, to be sure, and the very means of distribution increasingly created its own culture. But before this phenomenon people had had much culture in common; nowadays we call that "folk culture."

Folk culture traditionally had to a certain extent been individual and community oriented. Individual artisans and artists developed their own aspects of culture and folk community life evolved its own characteristics. Both aspects often were of necessity units unto themselves. After the eighteenth century, with the invention of movable type and rapid printing presses "folk culture" underwent some drastic changes. Wide and rapid dissemination of cultural phenomena forced former folk communities to become parts of a larger world, and mixing the cultures made them more similar. The development of machines to mass-produce thousands or millions of articles has had a dramatic and lasting influence. The means of dissemination always influences, or controls, the material being disseminated. Technology, of whatever degree of sophistication, holds our way of life in an iron grip. So, through the years, newspapers, magazines, radio, television and movies, as well as the numerous other means of communication, have demanded and worked best with a certain sameness in the material being communicated. This sameness created patterns of expectancy and understanding that appealed to a majority of the intended audience, all of which make dissemination easier and more profitable.

This is not to say, of course, that in this new mix of culture, folk life has disappeared. On the contrary, folk culture is still important — though on a modified scale — and remains very much alive. Folklorists recognize that old definitions of the field of their interests were too narrow and inflexible in the past and needed to be broadened, as indeed they have been.

Another conventional way to define popular culture is to distinguish among three areas of society — the elite, the mass and the folk. In such an arrangement, generally speaking, the elite and the folk each constitute roughly ten percent of society, each on opposite ends of the social and education line. Such a division leaves approximately 80 per cent of society for what many people call "mass" or "popular" culture. Such a distinction must be generalized and indeed might be somewhat artificial and arbitrary, since, in the anthropological sense of the term, virtually all people of a nation live in the same kind of life, are acted on by the same ways of behavior; they experience the same buildings, use the same kinds of transportation, hear the same music on radio, television or in public performances, see the same movies and television programs, attend the same sports events, eat at the same kinds of restaurants, etc. Thus Americans live an American way of life, English have an English way of life, Eskimos have their own way of life; though an alien looking down from another planet would clearly tend to group all people on Earth as living substantially the same kind of life. Many people like to view mass and popular culture as one and the same and as the massive section lost between elite and folk cultures. This large field of phenomena was possible only after the development of rapid means of disseminating culture such as the electronic media.

There is, of course, more to popular culture than that which is distributed by the electronic media, though they surely have a major impact. Popular culture consists of our patterns of thought and behavior, our educational system, what we study and why and how.

Traditionally cultures have been tiered according to degrees of sophistication, with the elite being on top and the folk on the bottom. Folklore scholars, however, finally tired of having their field of interest always relegated to the lowest, and inferior, level, and have quite properly insisted that all cultures draw from and feed into folk patterns. "Elite" culture is not "higher" and "superior" to folk; in fact, at least in an anthropological and scholarly sense, it is only different. We might alter the vertical hierarchy to a horizontal plane and thus demonstrate that neither is "superior" to the other but merely different, a more proper delineation. To a large extent, however, even this is too artificial because the solid boundaries between the "three" cultures seem to mark clear and distinct separations one from another, when in fact even the most casual observation of society reveals that there are not hard and fast lines separating one from the other; in fact all three — elite, popular and folk — exist pretty much at the same time in the same place (with noticeable shadings of differences). Perhaps the most revealing metaphor for culture is a flattened ellipse or a lens (the CBS logo is a good model) with elite and folk cultures on either end, both looking fundamentally alike in many ways and both having some characteristics in common. In the center, largest in bulk by far is popular culture, with no lines separating one from the other, only degrees of emphasis. Popular culture therefore consists of all the aspects of civilization that make up a way of life.

If people's popular culture consists of a total way of life, it would seem obvious that it is necessary that we understand this culture if we are to understand our country, our way of life, if we are to understand ourselves, if, in other words, we are to be "educated" in any sense of the word. The controversy of what constitutes a proper education is old and is yet very much unsettled, especially in these days when many people advocate a trip "back to basics." Socrates held to the injunction "Know thyself." Plato, following hard on Socrates' counsel, was all for educating out of the context of life, for dealing only in the ideal, for despising the common people — whom he called the oxen of the world — and their way of life. The Englishman Edmund Burke voiced the same attitude in the eighteenth-century. Burke, as every student of American history remembers, had been a friend of the American Revolution, but he condemned the French — and all the masses— as the "swinish multitude" when they tried to throw off their monarch's yoke. The American patriot Tom Paine condemned Burke's attitude and though it is still held by many this attitude has been gradually ground away throughout the history of this country. In fact, it seems obvious that the democratic way of life demands respect for and understanding of a total people's culture. *The Declaration of Independence* proclaimed the fact and the *Bill of Rights* guaranteed it.

Americans generally have always been a practical people, and most realize that one must train for life as we lead it. It is not proper for people to be educated for life as it might have been or might become, or as we wish ideally it were. One makes more progress toward improving the conditions of life if he recognizes where reality begins and sets out to work from that point, not from some idealized position where he is not and cannot ever be. Many Americans therefore think that the old Socratic injunction of "Know thyself," must be modified to read "Know yourself in your surroundings."

Commenting on the change in people's attitudes toward popular culture, Irving Wallace, present-day author of half a dozen bestselling novels and co-editor of, among various books, *The People's Almanac* (1976) and *The Book of Lists* (1977), observed, "The relationship between the critical community and the popular author has changed in recent years. Some critics are honest enough to respect public taste, or at least be curious about it and treat it seriously." Concerning his own purposes in writing, Wallace said, "I write to explore other human beings, the human condition, through my own psyche and within my own limitations."

Ross Macdonald, contemporary creator of the great detective Lew Archer, commented, somewhat on the same subject as Wallace's, on the value of popular culture in our society. "We learn to see reality through the popular arts we create and patronize. That's what they're for. That's why we love them." And Irving Wallace, again, attested to the power of the popular arts as model when he commented: "I was always going to be a writer. But if I ever faltered in my single-minded ambition, then surely there was popular art to influence me in my ambition and prop me up and carry me along."

The value of popular culture as a window to the human condition is timeless. Perhaps because it is less artful, less altered by the alchemy of the artist, popular culture is often a more truthful picture of what the people were thinking and doing at any given time than artistic creations are. In other words, a catalogue of what Athenians in Socrates' time were wearing, eating, drinking, joking about, how they were reacting to sports, their sex habits, their whole mode of life, might be more revealing of the real Athens than the philosophy of Socrates is. They surely would be more important. Realizing the value of these documents of everyday life, Thomas Jefferson commented "It is the duty of every good citizen to use all the opportunities which occur to him for preserving documents relating to the history of our country."

Jefferson might wisely have expanded his call to collect documents to include the preservation of all kinds of artifacts. If, for example, one wants to understand Shakespeare's plays fully, he studies outside the dramas, in what was going on in London at the time, the attitude of the people toward England's kings and queens, toward war, housing, poverty, foreigners, etc.

If one wants to understand eighteenth-century America he must read the old broadsides, sing the contemporary songs, investigate the wills and inventories of holdings, get as much into the lifestyle as possible, investigate all kinds of records.

In order to understand George Washington, for example, one needs to visit Mt. Vernon and while there study deeply the physical setting in which the man lived and worked: the house, the furniture, the geography of the surrounding houses, the slave culture, modes of transportation, distance, the music that was a part of the daily household. And the visitor must visit and examine the artifacts in the museum — the clothing, the trinkets, items of daily living; why, for example, was the set of dental equipment used on slaves' teeth composed of five iron instruments, probably made by the local blacksmith and easily bent, while Mr. Washington's set was of eight stainless steel instruments that probably could easily be used by dentists today? These artifacts tell us much, if only we learn to read and understand them, if we will listen to their stories.

If a picture is worth a thousand words, a museum is worth a million words, or a hundred books. And actually living the life — though the effort is to a large extent make-believe — is worth millions of words more. Thus one learns much from visiting restored historical communities and living museums and seeing how people actually dressed, behaved, talked in different times. Such communities are travels in time just like present-day travels in geography, and just as valuable.

In order to understand present day life, the place of the sports hero in our financial and cultural hierarchy, for example, obviously one must understand the setting. The weakness of many interpretations of life comes from the fact that the person doing the interpretation uses an artificial and half-complete setting.

Society cannot comfortably exist without heroes and heroines. The electronic media create and discard heroes so fast that they must always have new ones ready to be brought forward. A study of this need and process tells us much about ourselves. For example, on June 18, 1983, when Sally Ride became the first American woman astronaut she was flung into the heroic mold and immortality because America needed a female in their hall of heroes, at a time when heroes, especially women heroes, seemed to be fewer than they had been in the past. It will be interesting to see how Ride is built up and into what proportions and how long she will last. The electronic media create and burn out heroes and heroines rapidly. This is a process that we need to understand.

The public generally appreciates such an attitude about the value of understanding everyday things, though often the academic, the so-called intellectual, minimizes it because he or she is biased. For a long time intellectuals have been fond of quoting the old saying that one never went broke underestimating the intelligence of the American public. But is such a statement valid or is it the rankest snobbery? Is it for or against democracy? In America the answer obviously is of the greatest importance because it cuts to the heart of our political beliefs.

But one should not act under the false assumption that one's attitude toward the elite or the democratic should dictate whether or not the person wants to know about and understand all aspects of culture. One should always make a distinction between studying cultural phenomena in order to understand them and actually approving of or participating in them. For example, we do not have to engage in professional sports, or approve of them, in order to be interested in them or to want to understand their place in society; one does not even have to own a set to realize that television has a great impact on our lives, and to realize that he or she needs to comprehend this phenomenon. In understanding one does not have to love — or to hate. Understanding is the goal. Then one can shape one's life according to his or her likes or dislikes. But understanding is or should be requisite.

What, then, is the role of the intelligent and educated citizen in society? How does one start on the road to education? American education is, and perhaps always should be, in a state of crisis and consequently always debated. This means that we should try to understand, and then act. We should not be afraid to examine our assumptions. To this end Raymond Williams, a noted British critic, has stated:

> The human crisis is always a crisis of understanding; what we genuinely understand we can do.... There are ideas, and ways of thinking, with the seeds of life in them, and there are others, perhaps deep in our minds, with the seeds of general death. Our measure of success in recognizing these kinds, and in naming them making possible their common recognition, may be literally the measure of the future.

Toward better preparing the citizen for life, the critics, Stuart Hall and Paddy Whannel pointed out an important value in popular culture, aside from its enjoyable aspect:

> Perhaps the most significant connection between popular art and high art is to be seen in the way popular work helps the serious artist to focus the actual world, to draw upon common types, to sharpen his observations and to detach the large but hidden movements of society. New art forms frequently arise when profound modifications are taking place in social life and in the 'structure of feeling' in the society. Often this change is first recorded in popular work, and new popular themes and conventions are devised to deal with them, or to express them.

In other words, it could be argued that in the arts the forms and shapes, and ideas, that last, come up from the people, or at least last longest among them.

Lewis Mumford, one of the keener minds of our day, observed that education should be looked upon as a "lifelong transformation of the human personality, in which every aspect of life plays a part." In other words, these individuals, and many others like them, are saying that a person owes it to himself to develop his learning as much as possible, and this learning should include the popular culture.

Perhaps a word of caution might be necessary. Educators who insist that popular culture should be studied emphasize that it should be a supplement to not a substitute for the so-called classics of culture and civilization. Although for too long popular culture was excluded from the ordinary fare of education and should now be included, the more traditional materials—where their validity can be demonstrated and proved — should be retained. Popular culture should be studied to more nearly round out — to deepen and to enrich — at least portions of the more conventional curriculum. Education is too important to settle for anything less.

3

The Many Faces of American Culture:
The Long Push to Democracy

In this speech, Browne offers one of his most cogent explanations of his fundamental argument that popular culture is both an expression of democratic plurality and a disseminator of egalitarian ideals. Browne clarifies his points early on by discussing the reactions to both elite and popular arts and showing the shortcomings in only judging the elite arts as the only proper representations of cultural forms. Browne moves his analysis from art criticism to cultural critique, finding the need for applying aesthetic judgments to be limiting at best and often missing the point of the cultural expressions being evaluated. Browne then takes up the issue of commercial arts, bringing in an understanding of capitalist dynamics to his overall argument.

This approach is typical of much of Browne's work, and seems to have been overlooked by those who accuse him of merely "celebrating" popular culture. They fail to notice the deeper aspects of his work. Assuredly Browne doesn't develop, overtly or otherwise, his commentaries on democratic-capitalist culture along the lines of say, John Fiske or Jean Baudrillard. But we have Fiske and Baudrillard for that. In the latter part of the speech, Browne notes elite responses to media technology and chastises the elites for denigrating such forms, stating that they fear their use as democratizing forces. This is a topic he would return to in earnest in the coming decade.

The speech was printed (not actually published) in pamphlet form and received scant, if any, distribution beyond the BGSU campus. This allowed Browne to cannibalize and rework parts of it for several later articles and book chapters, the two most obvious being his well known "Popular Culture as the New Humanities" and "Popular Culture: Medicine for Illiteracy and Associated Ills" (included elsewhere in this collection). Of some interest is Browne's prediction that the mass media form that follows television will likely also follow the same general cultural patterns as both expresser and disseminator of democracy.— The Editor

The many faces of American Culture have remained essentially the same from colonial days to the present because they have always responded to and reflected life in this country. The seeds of American culture had been pretty well established by the time the Europeans settled down in this land; unfortunately, although it was difficult to sustain day by day, there had already begun to develop in Europe, and therefore in America, a break between everyday life and an "elite" which separated and made an artificial distinction between the two. This break had not really existed in Europe until the development of printing in the fifteenth century, but thereafter it grew and spread.

Before the fifteenth century (as Peter Burke's revealing book *Popular Culture and Early Modern Europe* has pointed out) there may have been different thrusts in European culture (in city and country, for example) but there was not a sharp break between the more sophisticated and the less sophisticated, between the well off and the poor, the politically strong and weak. That cleavage was to begin with the invention of printing and the resulting importance of the ability to read and write, and was to continue to grow until this day.

Before the fifteenth century the well-to-do and the poor were united by and in their largely oral culture. Though the upward mobility of the common people even then was limited, there was almost unlimited *downward* mobility. The aristocracy moved freely in the fairs, the circuses, the sports, the art objects, the daily lives of the poor. The poor and unprivileged, though they were not invited into the castles of the others, jostled them in public and did not pay much mind, did not grieve — generally — over their exclusion. They were somewhat content with their own culture.

But with the coming of printing, many poor people became aware of what they had been missing, and many of the privileged became nervous and defensive about what they had and wanted to protect. Though this feeling of defensiveness and alienation extended pretty much across the whole way of life, it was especially keen in the question of education and schooling because literacy in the medium of communication — access to the flow of information and to pleasure — brought with it power and freedom of choice. At this time, then, we generally agree began modern popular culture.

Two definitions are in order at this point. By "elite" culture I mean "minority" and exclusive culture, those aspects of life, which are self-proclaimed to be superior in taste, in manners, in aesthetics, in revealing the finer things of life. In the words of Matthew Arnold, the nineteenth century British poet and essayist who became the high priest of the elitists, culture is something only a few fortunate individuals can ever acquire: some people have it — generally by the gift of birth — but the majority — the Philistines, as he called such people — by definition do not: culture is, as Arnold called it, "acquainting ourselves with the best that has been known and said in the world."

By "popular culture" I do not mean the opposite of "elite" in any sense of the term. On the contrary, I mean an extension of it. I mean the arts and artifacts of culture that are created, used and perpetuated by the majority of people. The popular culture consists of those parts of our daily lives which a majority of us have inherited from the past and which we will use and, in turn, pass on to our children. The popular culture is the unconscious aspects of culture, the everyday way of life we lead, the way we work and play, eat and go hungry, conduct our lives while we are awake and dream when we are asleep. The popular culture consists of such items as books, magazines, movies, radio, music, television, architecture, automobiles, fast food industries, bumper stickers and thousands of other things. This culture is generally though not necessarily passed among us by the rapid — electronic — media. Most important, this popular culture is the voice and action of the people — their likes and dislikes, their way of life — and is therefore the voice and action of democracy. In this country it is the voice of America, which makes this country what it is, provides it with its strengths and weaknesses.

The elitists always insist that this popular culture is manipulated, the people are coerced, don't know what they like and will therefore take anything that is fed to them by the calculating media barons. But this attitude is demonstrably incorrect, as any observer of television pilots over any season will know. It can be illustrated, in fact, that there is no difference in the manipulation of the artifacts of popular culture and those of "elite" culture: only the instruments and styles are changed. "Elite" artifacts, like popular artifacts, are controlled by people with self-interests to serve. For example, Shakespeare would be largely forgotten and unused now but for the several groups who for their own reasons keep him in fashion all the time.

Society grows, as everyone should recognize, by rewriting its beliefs and points of view. Each generation must define the past in its own terms, and in so doing each generation re-evaluates the past. Whenever criticism feels the impact of an expanded or altered sensitivity (which often is tied in with a political attitude) it becomes shot through with ideological dispute, with determined champions on each side. In all aspects of existence, there must be movement if there is life. And the movement must be forward, not backward. But it is difficult to get the establishment to recognize the inevitability and desirability of forward movement. The establishment, particularly most members of the academic establishment, are aesthetic conservatives and hang on to the past as long as possible, and admit something new only after it has become accepted by virtually everybody else.

For example, if you had gone to Harvard University — or any other — in 1920 and stated that you wanted to study American literature, the smart-aleck answer you would have received from your professors would have been something like: "*Is* there any such thing?" The highly sensible American Studies movement now more than thirty years old throughout the country still frequently has to justify itself (at the University of California, Berkeley, for example). In many American universities now if you want to take courses in modern art or modern music, you will be told something like, "There is no such thing." In England, it is only recently that courses in any kind of literature written after the eighteenth century have been admitted as being worthy of study. And Cambridge University admitted its first sociologist to the faculty in 1969 — and he was on trial, to prove his worth or have the position eliminated, that after sociology had been a viable discipline for a hundred years.

Now avant-garde, "elite" arts, to be sure, are often creative and discover new ideas and new ways of expression. Sometimes these new ideas and modes of expression are worthwhile; sometimes they are merely different. But all too frequently the critics who try to explain the newest ideas are themselves old fashioned, conservative and work against the creators rather than for them. All you need to do to remember this point is think of the reception of the works of such people as Beethoven, Tchaikovsky, William Faulkner, Ernest Hemingway, Pablo Picasso, Frank Lloyd Wright and Milt Caniff.

The popular critic fails, therefore, to see how all the do-good "elite" critics of the past and present have really altered or "improved" the condition of the arts. The great American poet Walt Whitman once said that to have a great literature you must have a great audience, and he said further, "the proof of a poet is that his country absorbs him as affectionately as he has absorbed it." Apparently he was talking about *all* the people, not just the select few, since he always aspired to be the great poet of democracy. Concerning the "elite" critic a certain case could be made for a paraphrase of the old saw: critics are those persons who cannot create.

The popular critic — as distinguished from the "elite" critic — recognizes that it is just as dangerous to classify all minority, "elite," art as being meritorious and high-minded as it is to condemn all popular art as being empty and mindless. Not every elite critic of so-called "serious" art comes with heart and soul spotless, just as not every popular artist is out to rape the public. Both the "serious" and the popular artist are really each in his or her own way out to pin their names on the bulletin boards of history in the most lasting way they can.

The elite critics' insistence on the lack of aesthetic quality in popular culture represents a counter force, an anti–democratic vote, an attempt to return to the time when you could tell the difference between the quality of people by their language, their dress, where they were seen, whether they went to the opera house or the movie palace — when, in short, you *could* tell a book by its cover and a reader by the book he read. But this attitude represents an attempt to turn back a clock that does not move backward — social and aesthetic movements, for better or worse, drive forward.

On the basis of some very common-sense observations and assumptions, many critics, both elite and popular, are today modifying their attitudes toward the arts. Susan Sontag, for example, observed with much obvious reality: "One cheats oneself as a human being if one has respect only for the style [and the content, one might add] of high culture," and elsewhere she insists that "the function of criticism should be to show how a work of art is and what it is, even that it is what it is, rather than to show what it means."

Another critic, Roger Rollin, following hard on the Sontag thesis, under the amusing epigraph, "To evaluate is human, to explicate, divine," argued against any form of evaluation. To this critic the only real authority regarding beauty and excellence is not the critic but the people, especially in popular works of art. In popular literature, he points out; the rule is "one person-one vote." To him popular culture represents the triumph of the democratic aesthetic. Mark Twain, this critic might have pointed out, was proud of the fact that whereas his contemporary Henry James wrote his novels for a select few, he, Mark Twain, wrote for the millions.

But critics such as these, though they are bold in breaking away from the rules of the elite critics, are in fact not courageous enough. All admit that in reaction to aesthetics you are largely controlled by your training — you are what you have read, how you have been trained. Therefore these critics believe that though it should be downplayed or ignored there *is* a fundamental difference between elite and popular art. They really should go further and insist what they and everybody else knows deep down in his or her heart — not in the head or social attitude — that there is no fundamental difference between the two; the difference is merely one of degree.

All works of art — from the least pretentious popular work to the grandest minority accomplishment — differ only in intensity. All exist on a continuum that can perhaps be best described as a flattened ellipsis somewhat like the CBS logo. On the right end of the flattened ellipsis is folk art; on the left end (both politically and creatively) is so-called "serious" art. Between the two — occupying perhaps 80 percent of the scale — is popular art. Between any two of the three types there are not clear lines of distinction, only grey areas overlapping each other. One grows out of and merges into the other.

In all areas along this horizontal continuum there is a vertical scale of aesthetic accomplishment, since obviously some works are artistically more satisfying than others. Some folk creations are strong and effective; some are weak. In elite art there are some powerful statements and some weak and silly. Undoubtedly the largest range of strength and weakness lies in the popular area because there are far more attempts being made there. Much is weak; but much is strong. It is a grave mistake to assume that the creators of the popular arts achieve no worthwhile results. Many indeed do. Stephen Foster's songs to a large majority of Americans are more nearly immortal than Giovanni Pergolesi's. *Huckleberry Finn* will always be a more powerful book than Henry James' *The American* and *Uncle Tom's Cabin* will always be a more moving statement about the downtrodden than William Dean Howells' *Annie Kilburn*, which was dedicated to doing the same kind of thing.

The arts, aside from the beauty of experiencing them have always been held to do something for us, to pull us together, to explain the profundities of life, to make existence more meaningful.

Such is the function of the humanities at large. Let us expand our discussion to include the humanities as well as the arts. Popular culture is nowadays being equated with the "new humanities" because it is clear, at least to many observers, that the old concept of the humanities is as incomplete as the old definition of "aesthetics." The "new humanities" comprehends a definition of what the old humanities included and expands to embrace all aspects of the world around us—its mass media, entertainment, heroes, icons, rituals, psychology, religion and all other aspects of society. The "new humanists" believe that in a democracy the democratic institutions as well as the forces and artifacts of the ordinary people should be a main focus of attention and study.

Advocates of this position believe that continued acceptance of the statement of Plato (whom many elitists think of as a leading humanist) and the belief of like-minded individuals among us that the common people are the "oxen of the world" is intolerable.

Yet, though such terminology is discredited, the attitude is still held by many individuals whose opinions are highly regarded. For example, professor Maynard Mack of Yale University, remarked in an interview the ultimate elitist point of view: "The humanities," he said, "are not really something you can democratize. It's like democratizing surgery. Who wants someone picked off the streets to operate on him? Well, it's the same thing in the humanities."

The new humanists are all-inclusive in their interests because the humanities by definition has wide parameters and multiple purposes, paralleling and duplicating those of popular culture. Russel Nye, for example, states: "The study of popular culture, done seriously and with proper purpose and methodology, can open up new areas of evidence which can contribute greatly to what we know about the attitudes, ideas and values of a society at a given place or time; in so doing, we find a broader and deeper understanding of our society."

In studying and trying to understand a culture—drawing forth its humanities—the act of including the details in which the creator worked helps to explain and enrich the work, giving it in the real sense of the word the humanistic truth that it could not otherwise have. Many of the works of popular culture may not be pleasing, to be sure. Neither, for that matter, are many elite works. But in cultural studies aesthetic value is irrelevant—is beside the point. Aesthetic value must be looked upon as a pleasing bonus if it is present, but it is by no means necessary. In fact, sometimes, aesthetic value can be the cause of much danger. D.W. Griffith's movie *The Birth of a Nation* (1915), for example, became a dangerous movie, with overwhelmingly persuasive after-effects of racism because it was aesthetically pleasing. Present-day plantation novels, in the tradition of *Mandingo*, have no aesthetic value—to most people at least—yet obviously they satisfy some deep felt need of many people, which though displeasing to most of us is obviously of value to them. The question concerning the aesthetic value is, then, the total effect of the item itself—and its value far exceeds that of its A.Q.—aesthetic quotient.

The popular culture is the one that does most of the job of perpetuating a culture. Its impact was recognized by the late poet T.S. Eliot—surely one of the high priests of elite art—when he cried out against popular books: "I incline to come to the alarming conclusion," he wrote in *Essays Ancient and Modern*, "that it is just the literature that we read for 'amusement' or 'purely for pleasure' that may have the greatest ... least suspected ... earliest and most insidious influence upon us. Hence it is that the influence of popular novelists, and of popular plays of contemporary life, require to be scrutinized." Richard Hoggart, one of today's leading social observers of England, says, in a typical British understatement, "Literature at all levels has the unique capacity to increase our understanding of a culture."

The so-called works of amusement and pleasure, as Eliot referred to them, exert their overwhelming influence because all of us come into contact with them daily and to an irresistible extent. They present in simple and therefore usable ways the ideas of the time. Most creators of popular culture do in their own ways the most effective job they can under the circumstances. For example, Irving Wallace likes to tell of an interview he had with James Baldwin when he, Wallace, was writing his novel *The Man*. Baldwin wanted to know why a white man would be writing about a Black as President of the United States. Wallace replied that the subject of racial prejudice had worried him for a long time and he knew that in his work he could convince a hundred times more readers than Baldwin would ever reach. The message, to Wallace, was too important to leave in the hands of certain differently qualified people. Wallace's ideas were what we might call "noble." Sometimes popular writers' ideas are relatively unimportant, and many people are therefore inclined to look down upon them despite the fact that we all at least pay lip service to the notion that in order to live life most fully we need to include as much of it — the important and the relatively unimportant — as possible. Yet frequently we take seriously only what we have been told is great. As one observer remarked with real truth, many of us are not interested in ideas unless they come to us dressed in full war paint.

Actually in the seeming gap between what might be called "elite" and "popular" humanities there is no break whatsoever. Robert Coles, psychologist and Pulitzer Prize-winning author at Harvard, has remarked: "The humanities belong to no one kind of person; they are part of the lives of ordinary people, who have their own various ways of struggling for coherence, for a compelling faith, for social vision, for an ethical position, for a sense of historical perspective." Richard Hoggart, to whom I referred before, speaking in a larger context said essentially the same thing: "the closer study of mass society may make us have sad hearts at the supermarket, but at the same time it may produce an enhanced and tempered sense of humanity and humility, instead of the sense of superiority and separateness that our traditional training is likely to have encouraged."

Leslie Fiedler, one of the keenest critics in popular culture today, drives this thinking to its logical conclusion. He believes that popular culture can achieve perhaps its greatest challenge, that of bringing us all together again. The popular culture — or the new humanities — then, given its way, can unite us into a community somewhat similar to that which existed before people became separated by class, education, interests and desires. The strongest instrument for this happy joining together, despite what you think on the spur of the moment, will likely be television. I say this because television tends to promote *oral* culture, the oldest kind, as opposed to print culture, and with it a kind of community, which is much broader and more democratic than the world of print.

No one in the new humanities or popular culture would suggest that study of these phenomena replace the traditional courses in the humanities where they can be demonstrated to be valuable, where they can prove their worth. Nobody suggests that the study of popular culture blindly celebrate rather than analyze very keenly. Any other attitude would be non–intellectual and bound to defeat the purpose.

But on the other hand there is no question that it is important that the old ideas be tested and modified to incorporate new approaches, new definitions and new areas of subject matter. Otherwise the humanities — in all their possible ways — will be found misguided and inadequate to present day needs and potentialities. That means that there should be no sacred cows among the humanities, no areas that because they have been assumed valuable for years cannot be reexamined. Each one should be asked to revalidate itself, and if it cannot it should be retired. The classroom — and the research desk — is one place that cannot afford to become a museum of dead ideas and concepts.

The "elite" novel perhaps more than most other forms of the old humanities has in many instances followed the trend into inadequacy, widening the gap between it and the best-seller, which is what it was in the eighteenth century. Originally the novel was intended to tell an interesting story, to provide what we now would call a good read. The novel was originally a straightforward account of adventure. Some adventures were livelier than others and inevitably some accounts were more interesting, more given to include sex and more violence than others. But, regardless of what they did in addition to the original purpose, novels, like folktales before them and from which they grew, were meant to recount lively stories.

Now, of course, novels have been forced to do much more than that. They have become more complicated. In form and development they have come more and more to reflect the authors' private philosophies. They may have become more expressive of the complications of society and life in our world. But in so doing, "elite" novels, by and large, with some notable exceptions to be sure, have ceased to appeal to the general public because they have ceased speaking to that general public. They do not address themselves to the concerns of the mass public in terms that the people can understand. Thus they have abandoned one of their first principles.

It is no good to say that this is the fault of the general reader. The general reader is eager to buy and read books today, as the fact that there are 3,000 books published per month in the United States demonstrates. The fault lies with the authors who while serving their own purposes have abandoned those of the general public, in a public-be-damned attitude. The public-insofar as one can group such a large mass of people into one unit-is not the lowest common denominator but the *largest*. A strong case can be made for the argument that the elite author, in failing to write to the public is abandoning the purpose of the novel and in so doing is the cause of the so-called low quality of the popular novel. Abandoned people turn to any relief they can find. In fact, however, the accusations that the reading public are now of the lowest quality ever is simply an "elite" conspiracy to keep the public in their place: never in the past have there been so many readers of such high quality as there are today.

Perhaps it is not the accomplishments, or lack of them, of the democratic arts or the democratic humanities that disturb the elite critics today as much as the demands, the intentions and functions, placed upon all the arts. The attitude of the popular critics is perhaps best stated by Alan Gowans: "To know what art is, you must define what it does. You can define art only in terms of function. High art historically grew out of low art, and the functions of low art have remained unchanged throughout history." The function is to get something done — to convert the sinner, to record a hunt, to curry favor, to explicate the human form, to examine human experience, to sell soap or automobiles. Debating about aesthetic accomplishments without keeping these functions and purposes in mind is as fruitless as the old argument among Puritan ministers over the number of angels that could dance on the head of a pin.

Here, finally, is the point laid on the table unanaesthetized: what is the purpose of the arts and the various ways they are displayed? Are the arts to teach us more about life, and in so doing bring the human community together? Or are they things which because of the nature of the human being can be enjoyed only individually and privately, and perhaps through their speaking a common language work privately and thereby achieve a kind of community? There is no question that the arts—music, paintings, architecture, etc., speak a common language to the people who understand it. In the past this common language has been a kind of lingua franca—a universal language—to a select group—something like the aristocrats of pre–revolutionary Russia speaking French; or scholars speaking Latin instead of their native tongues. Being a common language the elite arts do to a certain extent bind a select, small number of people together, but more intellectually than emotionally. The binding is exclusive and excluding, not meaning to bring in outsiders.

One interesting thrust in this direction is the recent activity of Nelson Rockefeller before he died, an activity which many people did not approve of and perhaps did not really understand—establishment of the commercial company Nelson Rockefeller Collection, Inc. (30 Rockefeller Plaza, New York, 10020) to sell replicas of his private art collection. In the introduction to the second edition of the catalog of the pieces for sale, Rockefeller is quoted: "To want beautiful things is a very human instinct. It has been seen down through the ages in the aesthetic quality of objects created for religious purposes, and in objects to be taken into the afterworld." William J. Ronan, President of the selling company, added that Rockefeller's purpose in offering these reproductions for sale was "for others to share the enjoyment of living with beautiful objects." But notice the restrictions imposed upon spreading this enjoyment around. Frederic Remington's "Coming Through the Rye," a statue of four horsemen, "an extremely fine study of balance with only six legs as support," as the catalog describes it, is presented in a *Limited Edition of 75 individually numbered pieces* superbly reproduced in solid bronze by the 'lost wax' method and finished with meticulous care" (my italics); the price is $19,500. Other items are less limited, less attractive and less expensive. For example, one can buy a Weathervane Horse and Sulky, a "replica of an early American silhouette model, about 1900" for $275. For $225 one can buy a Dogon Horse and Rider, which has as its only claim to beauty its rarity and historical significance. So, in fact, these objects of beauty are made more valuable by having the Rockefeller cachet and association.

This commercial activity on the part of Rockefeller, Inc., put the art sellers community into a dither—those people who had nothing to do with the creation of the art, and who are in reality only people in the same business as those who sell soap, but they have an affected way of talking and a pretense of culture, whatever that is. These art sellers said that Rockefeller was cutting into their profit. Perhaps he was in the short run. But if one examines his inroads a little more closely, one will see that Rockefeller was doing the art dealers a great service, for he was bringing into the community of art buyers many people who in the past were not interested because they knew they could not bid against the veterans or the wealthy for ownership. So Rockefeller's move is going to have a ripple effect, which will be beneficial to the commercial aspects of the art community at large.

But there is a larger and much more interesting dynamic about Rockefeller's act which we should examine. What about those of us who cannot buy a reproduction running into the hundreds and thousands of dollars? We too would like to share in the beauty that Rockefeller enjoyed throughout life. Why not therefore a $10.00 reproduction? You might say that the stores are filled with plastic reproductions that sell for $1.98. The same store is stocked with reproductions of other prized works of art—often technically superior to the originals—that sell for $20.00 or $100.00. The would-be art hoarders are not satisfied with these reproductions because they are imperfect. Those of us who cannot afford the more expensive works would possibly appreciate finer reproductions too. No, the expensive reproduction is designed for a meaner and more exclusive purpose: to serve as a half-way art house that will let in some more people, who will bring their money with them, but at the same time will keep out many others. After all, royalty must admit a few commoners every once in a while to strengthen the blood and introduce new money. Princess Margaret of England married a photographer and Prince Rainier of Monaco married a pipe fitter's daughter. What Rockefeller really did — in addition perhaps to some good he was doing — was spread snobbery around a little more. Democratic snobbery, to be sure, but snobbery. We all like to have beauty around. But to have everybody enjoy it? That's spreading joy just a little bit too far. Beauty is uplifting, but being uplifted is pleasurable only if we are uplifted *above* other people.

Nowadays there is a great movement afoot to change the *image* of art, to make it appear more democratic but to stop short of democratizing it into bastardy. The philosophy among artists and art critics is that if an object is enjoyed by all there must be something weak and meretricious about it. One of the reasons for the new democratizing impulse is of course money — and the need for it. Art is simply too expensive for the elite alone to support. So they turn to their conventional bearers of this burden, the mass. Throughout history the poor — while they have not been allowed to experience and enjoy it — have subsidized the arts for the elite to relish. Now that the arts are getting too dear for the elite to support for themselves, the public is being called upon again to help out, or carry the donkey's share of the burden.

With the nation filled with hundreds of foundations, created by the wealthy for themselves, it would seem logical for the elite to appeal to these foundations for patronage, for financial assistance in their pursuit of the arts, and it would seem fitting for the foundations to respond in supporting their kind. To a certain extent, of course, the people do appeal and the foundations do respond. But within careful fiduciary guidelines, and there is never enough money to support all the thrusts in elite art. So the elite appeal to the greatest Foundation of them all (the Federal government), under the names, mainly, of the National Endowment for the Arts and the National Endowment for the Humanities. A large recipient of this patronage is collectively, under any of the numerous local channels, the Public Broadcasting Service, the television service parallel to the commercial networks and which spends this money it gets from the NEH and the NEA in developing broadcasts which are "superior" to those broadcast on commercial television and are therefore designed to "improve the tastes" of the general American public. Actually, there is little concern among the PBS people whether the public really does learn to appreciate these programs. The only thing needed to salve the conscience of the producers and appreciators of PBS programming is that the public *ought* to enjoy the programs if given the opportunity. With this rationalization, the U.S. Government is continually called upon to supply tax money taken from the American mass public to support the elite arts, which the elite patrons can not or will not support for themselves. Often these productions are duplicatory and unnecessary. For example, how can one justify yet another television production of the complete works of Shakespeare as was recently done when there are splendid productions already available? The answer lies of course in the need to stroke someone's ego about how he or she would produce Shakespeare, and to respond to the whim of the elite to see yet another version of the works.

In yet another — parallel — medium, what are the art museums doing these days to spread the arts to a larger community? Are they great educators and creators of pleasure, or are they really mainly mausoleums where people go to view corpses that are revered, like pickled cadavers? Is art, that is in Gowan's view, no longer doing its primary job? In short, is there a better way to market the work even if it is dead — than these managers are now utilizing?

Of course there are better ways — there are always better ways. First of all, it is very difficult for art museum directors not to capitalize on the things that they have the most money in and those that in the past were assumed to be the most attractive. That is what we called "signature art," that art which is produced by the famous people — the "masters" — which is recognizable by its style and subject, and which fellow directors and people on the boards of directors say is the most important. In many ways it is like kings comparing their castles or rich people comparing fortunes. The general public may or may not be interested in the two Van Goghs, one Rembrandt, three Brueghels and four Gauguins proudly displayed by an art gallery. Surely the average audience will not experience them as exquisitely as the owners do. So it might well be that the directors could get more people to come to their art museums — and thereby attract more money at the same time they were "doing good" — if they displayed their wares in somewhat more attractive ways. Perhaps not by signature of artist but by theme: something like "Scenes of Medieval Peasant Life," "Languorous Life in the Polynesians," "Views of the Christ Child and Mother," "Scenes of the Holy Land," "Most Effective Propaganda in Paintings," or something like that. If an individual does not go into art museums how is he or she going to know that Brueghel painted the liveliest and quaintest and most interesting pictures of peasant life?

Along this line two unfortunate commercials on television now appeal to one of the baser drives of society. One for the VW automobile features a bearded man in an art gallery. He purchases what the voice-over calls a picture and the bearded man condescendingly corrects the voice: "It's a painting, my good man," he says. When the same voice-over asks why the art connoisseur has bought a VW — one of the most widely bought automobiles in the U.S. — he is assured that it is an "original." "Why buy a copy when you can own an original?" the snob asks. The other disappointing commercial is about the Toledo Museum of Art. One of the local savings and loan companies has Hal Holbrook on television praising Toledo and the Art Museum because of its "signature" art. He says something like the museum has "two Van Goghs, two Gaugins, and one Rembrandt" (let's say, I do not remember the actual count). Now this treasure of ownership might impress the Director of the Cleveland Museum or the Cincinnati Museum. But what does it say to us on the street who have never been into an art museum, have never heard of these artists — but who have all kinds of potential for appreciating those things which the art people consider worthwhile and for having a pleasant time in a museum? Does Holbrook not say, in effect, that the public will not find displays of comic art and Saturday morning cartoons and street art and old people's art and Chicano art and the like in the Toledo Art Museum? These are the kinds of art that will bring in many new people — especially those who should be the primary target for broadening the base support. But with Holbrook's pitch they feel excluded.

There are many other ideas about how art should be displayed and vitalized and made more attractive. I suggest that the new wing of the National Art Gallery in Washington is doing an effective job. Though to some the building is, to be sure, rather forbidding, somehow this impact is overcome and people flock in to see new and interesting art displayed in fascinating and interesting ways. There's even an armored knight on horseback on the ground floor and a gigantic mobile circling around overhead. The people who work in this gallery have learned a lot from those who set up the displays in the Smithsonian Institution.

But the most effective display of art in the world today is probably that at the Georges Pompidou Centre in Paris. It is time for every director of an art museum to go to Paris. Not to the Louvre, but to the Pompidou Centre. This is a marvelous building turned inside out. The girders, pipes, escalators, everything that ordinarily belongs hidden inside a building is now outside. Something like the marvelous Gothic flying buttresses that grace Notre Dame and Westminster Abbey, and the bare girders of the George Washington Bridge across the Hudson in New York, and which have been criticized as being ugly.

The Centre in Paris was dreamed up by President Georges Pompidou in 1969 because he believed that so-called culture should be for the masses, that culture is lying in wait ready to "pounce," in his word, on the public if they are allowed to get close to it. Inside the Centre are displays of all kinds of art, modem, video, film, and even tattoo art. Just as the insides of the building are exposed on the outside, much of the art activity that traditionally used to go inside an art museum now goes on *outside* the Centre as it did in the Middle Ages around churches. In space reserved for them, for example, on any given day outside the Centre will be traditional French street performers, jugglers, mom-pop-daughter acrobats, mimes, people with performing dogs, spielers, etc. On a typical Sunday afternoon there will be up to twenty acts, with several thousand people wandering about, watching and putting francs in the performers' hats. *That* is getting people and art together!

The critics, of course, will not allow the people to have their arts. The Pompidou Centre has been criticized since its inception and especially since its opening. But critics wondered about the flying buttresses of Notre Dame and Westminster, and still think that the George Washington Bridge, with its exposed girders, is not finished. Such critics writing for the Rome *Vox Populi* in 100 A.D. undoubtedly would have backed the government but criticized the people who attended the circuses as lacking in aesthetic standards. All the Pompidou Centre has going for it is the people. By 1980 eleven million people have already been into the Centre, and the number now is at least 25,000 per day. Such figures should give the elite something to worry about.

They — and we — should think, further, more deeply, not superficially, about the two liveliest of the popular arts, movies and television. Undoubtedly the movies—film, if you prefer — represents a step toward one of the highest art forms, and television — properly understood and used — would represent the potentially highest art form known at this time. It is the potentially highest form because it is the most democratic, and being the most democratic — to follow Gowans' line of reasoning — it is the most susceptible to having to prove its value every day, to have to serve a purpose in order to survive. If it accomplishes nothing it cannot last.

Before anyone agrees with the elite critics that television has accomplished nothing and therefore probably should be killed off, think back on the crawling stages of other forms of communication. The novel, for example, an art form that began to flower in the eighteenth century in England, could be evaluated as having had a lot of action, sex and violence. Novels had, as someone has said, ODTA — one damned thing after another. For a hundred years this tradition persisted. Nowadays, of course, the artists working the novel form are likely to write *away* from the public, above our heads. In doing this they alienate us, refuse to allow us to read their works because we cannot understand them. In many ways contemporary elite novelists could be held responsible for much of the mass' so-called inability to read.

But one thing about the novel as an art form is clear. In order to improve its potential, the elite authors had to learn its nature, its vocabulary, its dynamics, and its potential. That took a long time. Today we know virtually nothing about the television set except where it is and how to turn it on. We have not learned even the grammar, the language, of television, much less its dynamics and aesthetics. Little wonder that we might be dissatisfied with it, that in fact it has fewer aesthetic attainments than we might like.

It would seem important then that we learn about it, that we make a determined effort to meet it halfway. The elitist critics are likely to call television a "wasteland," and we are likely then to infer that inasmuch as we despise and are too good for wastelands, we will not pay it any mind. But that is a great mistake. At a meeting of the National Opera Institute recently the main item on the agenda was to determine ways to make opera more popular than it is now, though it is in fact enjoying a rather phenomenal comeback in popularity. The director of one of the leading outdoor summer entertainment spas (Wolftrap, just outside Washington), a man who has the function of making opera live for the American people, said that he does not own a television set, cares nothing for it, in fact looks upon it as a plague. Such an attitude seems incredible in America at this time. How can one know America if he boycotts the single most influential medium of communication? I suggest that the Grand Ole Opry would have a great deal to teach Grand Opera.

Laverne and Shirley surely has not reached the highest peak in our scale of creating enjoyment. But the surest way to allow such shows to take over the TV screen, as has often been observed about politics and tyrants, is for the viewing public to become indifferent to the television screen.

Television is only the latest in a long line of technological developments for communication, which have been resisted on at least three levels throughout history. In the first place, people in charge of the world, the elite, have always resisted communication among any people but themselves, for communication might breed rebellion. The Catholic Church fought against it when there were suggestions that the Bible be translated into the vulgar tongues; Southern slave-owners banned slaves' congregating, etc. In the second place, the elite almost always resist any kind of technological improvement; they are afraid of it because they do not understand it, and they recognize that technology takes power out of the hands of the privileged. Few technological developments have threatened Europe quite so dramatically as the invention of printing did in the fifteenth century because with printing went education; as late as the eighteenth century the elite in England were protesting that it was all right to allow the hoi polloi to read but they should not be allowed to write because they would no longer be any good as servants. Thirdly, the elite always are the self-styled guardians of the standards of what is worthwhile and uplifting in the world; they always know what is best for the remainder of the people, as they have always known; therefore they do not cotton easily to new arbitrators of taste.

But television as the latest and potentially most permeating of the many media will present the many faces of American culture and will do so fully and effectively — even aesthetically, in the proper use of that word, perhaps not conventionally, but aesthetically. Television flashes before us the many aspects of American culture and the faces of the democratic arts. If anything is going to unite the nation — and all humanity — it will not be the art museum, not the elite novels, architecture, the so-called legitimate theater, not the conventional humanities and standard approaches to education. These have all been tried before, often at great length and expense of time and money. All too often these turn from, fly over the heads of or at best only obliquely glance at humanity. If anything binds humanity together it will be the arts and humanities that speak about, to and with the basic voice of the people. Television — or whatever forms it develops into— because it is the basic medium for the expression of democracy — might well be the medium for the dissemination of democracy.

The many faces of American culture may be chaotic, confusing and alarming now as they have always been — the face of any culture has always been strong, mobile and sometimes not what it appeared to be. But, to paraphrase Winston Churchill when he was talking about the weakness of democracy, they are still the best around.

4

The Humanities as Redefined through Popular Culture

At the core of Browne's understanding of the importance and validity of popular culture studies was the idea that popular culture expresses and disseminates democratic impulses. The popular arts, a subset as it were of popular culture, are, then, a key aspect of democracy and to belittle them is to belittle democracy itself.

This thinking led Browne to term popular culture and its scholarship "the new humanities" and defend it against those who negated and denied its value. This battle reached an apex of sorts during the 1980s as Browne responded to books and reports from Allan Bloom, William Bennett, E. D. Hirsch, and Lynne Cheney with mounting passion and at times, outright and justifiable indignation.

Browne published several articles on the topic in both major academic journals and special sub-discipline newsletters, drawing the core of the earliest efforts from his unpublished speech "The Many Faces of American Culture: The Long Push to Democracy" (included elsewhere in this collection). This piece has been created from two of the more comprehensive (and overlapping) articles to create a version that retains his larger points without replicating information included in other selections of this volume. The second article is, in fact, a partial reworking of the first, and both originally included adaptations of the aforementioned speech. In addition, specific responses Browne made to points from the works of Bloom, Bennett, Hirsch, and Cheney in particular, have been eliminated to maintain the coherency of his general argument and the consistency of this newly fused effort.

Browne notes that by necessity, the "new humanities" cannot be limited to creations of Western cultures but must properly be cross-cultural, trans-national and global. This concern became an increasing one throughout his later work.— The Editor

The winds of change that swept across America during the Sixties finally breezed through academia and blew the dust off some of the concepts of what constitutes the ideal educational curriculum, and in so doing demonstrated the importance of the study of popular culture for both the academic and the non–academic worlds. This discovery was needed because now perhaps for the first time on so large a scale both groups are coming to realize that, like it or not, the popular culture of America is the force that has overwhelming impact on shaping our lives. The so-called "elite" or "minority" culture may have some influence according to the degree it is brought to the people and made applicable to their everyday lives. But the popular culture is already *with* the people, a part of their everyday lives, speaking their language. It is therefore irresistibly influential. What it is, the way it works and its relation to the other humanities need to be understood if we are to appreciate its overwhelming influence in our lives.

The humanities as the football of political bias and self-interest generally continue to get redefined according to the political attitude running the show. Apparently not knowing or caring about real or objective definitions, the National Endowment for the Humanities, for example, the one institution in the United States that has a vital role in the humanities has always bent its definition to fit that of the chairman and the politician in charge of the White House.

Several administrations ago, Ronald Berman, as Chairman, was an avowed snob despite the fact that he had been the speechwriter for Spiro Agnew, who made much political hay railing against the effete elitists of the East Coast; Berman obviously pleased president Nixon, again in a strange way since Nixon was so strongly against the Eastern elite group. The next Chairman, Joseph Duffy, reflecting the political attitude of Jimmy Carter, tried to redefine the humanities in a somewhat different way. As a graduate of Yale University he had been trained into foreswearing his West Virginia coal-mining background, but he finally learned that there is no reason to find his childhood antithetical to a true meaning of the humanities. In his speech before the Congress at his nomination, Duffy said that he felt "There need be no issue of a separated elite as against popular participation" in the humanities. "The work of the humanistic conversation should by its nature be spread into every part and region of the country."

Chairman William J. Bennett, however, swung decidedly back to the elitist side. Mr. Bennett was either confused about proper definitions or depended entirely upon his own interpretations. For example, in a speech to the National Federation of State Humanities councils, he laid down four commandments. He allowed that "in pursuing the goal of fostering a better understanding of the humanities on the part of the public, there are boundaries that may not be crossed, no matter how imaginatively." Two of the commandments are paradoxical:

"You may not ignore the humanities."

"You may not trivialize the humanities."

To call efforts to broaden and modernize the humanities movements to trivialize them is a peculiar attitude that only an intellectual could take. These two commandments are mutually contradictory and they lead to negative and far-reaching results. For example, in 1984 the National Endowment for the Humanities called upon the academic community to study the Constitution and America in a Bicentennial Celebration. One would think that this interest in the impact of the Constitution upon American life would include all levels. But apparently not. The NEH Bicentennial Commission told one person who applied for a grant to hold a convention on the impact of the Constitution on American Popular Culture that this kind of material was not worthy of support; the people in Washington interested in the Constitution and this Bicentennial Celebration were Constitutional lawyers and serious historians, and they were not interested in the America of common people.

The fifty local state humanities councils that were created to bring the Humanities to the state level vary sharply among themselves in the matter of definitions and projects they encourage and support. Though confused by the signals that come from Washington they tend to be a little less elitist than the national office. All, however, both the Washington headquarters and the state offices are more elitist than the National Endowment for the Arts, though uninformed logic would tend to suggest that the NEA should be far more elitist than the NEH. Perhaps the political manipulations of the humanities, since the humanities are hard to define, are understandable, something we have to live with.

It is more difficult, however, to understand the attitudes of some academics in well-established disciplines and areas of study that at least profess interest in forming the cutting edge of thinking and innovation. Ideologically based and apparently thoroughly rationalized, the academic groups when off the mark can be mischievous. They often masquerade as "friends" to re-evaluated and relevant definitions when in fact they are antagonists and adhere to old, elitist and questionable definitions and attitudes that do the humanities much harm.

This attitude takes all kinds of turns in different directions, sometimes aided and abetted by the NEH and other foundations. For example the summer NEH seminars for "Humanities in the Schools: Programs for Teachers and Administrators" for 1984 contained disturbing aspects. The announcement — and remember this was for public school teachers — was pretentiously presented with the cover elaborately displaying quotations from Plato — in Greek — Cicero in Latin — and Thomas Jefferson. Roughly translated Plato's dictum says, "Knowledge depends on what you study," or perhaps more accurately, "If you don't understand what has gone before in context you remain uneducated." Cicero's statement says something like "Understand in context what happened before your time if you do not want to remain naive." Jefferson's quotation is the often used, "If a nation expects to be ignorant and free, in a state of civilization, it expects what never was and never will be." No one would disagree with the aptness of the quotations, though Plato, we should remember, was the elitist who referred to the common people of his time as "oxen," and the Greek and Latin phrases are pretentious for most public school teachers; they would surely have been more effective in English. But apparently the purpose of the humanities, at least as seen by the NEH, is to mystify and impress more than to enlighten and lead. And undoubtedly there have been people since the Romans, other than Jefferson, who had apt things to say about the humanities.

Further, some of us might well disagree with the NEH's definition of the humanities relevant for American school teachers and through them children of the 1980s as revealed in the seminars that were to be held in 1984, for example. Some of the subjects were "The English Heritage from Chaucer to Pope," "Shakespeare: The State of the Art," "Shakespeare in Production" and "An Institute on Homer's *Odyssey*." I would suggest that anybody outlining these courses as the most appropriate in the humanities for our public schools in that decade was going to have a hard time steering humanities programs between the Scylla and Charybdis of elitism and conservatism and would, deliberately or not, get lost, as Odysseus was lost, in the eastern Mediterranean of old and dead ideas.

That there were stirrings of discontent and questioning could be seen in various statements by directors of the state NEH groups. One of the more cogent was that of Alan J. Shusterman, who writing an essay called "Plain Folks and Fancy Reading" in *College English* pointed out the damage done by authors of so-called "signature" art in their willful effort to write away from its general public. His hesitant conclusion leaned toward an enlightened attitude about the new humanities: "Provided that a popular test is not made into an object for categorization or scorn, a skillful and unassuring teacher can use it to move to analysis of culture, dramatic method, historical analogues, or sometimes critical techniques." Such an attitude is surely a suggestion in the right direction.

As an antidote to such poison many critics of today, on the bases of some commonsense observations and assumptions, are modifying their attitudes toward the arts and culture.

The popular arts are more and more being equated with the humanities, or what could more properly be called "The New Humanities," as the realization grows that the conventional humanities have probably not succeeded in their function, and because acceptance of popular culture as the "New Humanities" arises from the ever-widening belief that in a democracy the democratic institutions, as well as the ordinary people, should be a main focus of attention and study. The humanities must include the arts. Historically, many academics as well as non–academies have looked upon the humanities and the study of a whole culture from an elite point of view. They have insisted that the humanities teach us how to live life most fully but have treated the humanities as though they were designed exclusively for the educationally and financially privileged and were to be denied to the ordinary taxpayer.

The "New Humanists" believe that this traditional elitist point of view is tunnel-visioned and myopic, and that it is misleading to study artistic creations as though the creators lived in a vacuum, oblivious to and unaffected by the society around them.

These "New Humanists" are or ought to be all-inclusive in their interests, then, because popular culture by definition has wide parameters and multiple purposes, and can comment on virtually every aspect of life.

The Popular Humanities do most of the job of perpetuating a culture, an attitude increasingly recognized by people of all esthetic bias. For example, Thomas Hoving, former executive director of the New York Metropolitan Museum of Art and chief editor of *Connoisseur* magazine, told Nancy Shulins, an AP Newsfeature writer, in an article dated March 11, 1984, "There's a role for it [popular culture], no question. It's not the culture I care much about. But if we had examples of it from Pericles' Athens, we'd certainly be better off."

The so-called works of amusement and pleasure, exert their overwhelming influence because all of us come unavoidably into contact with them daily. They present in simple and therefore usable ways the ideas of the time. Often the ideas are oversimplified and may be relatively unimportant singly and individually. We therefore are inclined to look down upon them, despite the fact that we all at least pay lip service to the hypothesis that in order to live most fully we need to include as much of life as possible. Yet we frequently concentrate on — or claim to be interested in — only what we call or have been told is the important.

The popular culture — or popular humanities— then, given their way, can unite us into a community which existed before people became separated by class, education, interests and desires. An especially appropriate example of this function might be television, with its completely democratic audience, which tends to relegate Gutenberg obsolete and to promote visual culture, the oldest kind, and with it an oral community which is broader and more democratic than the world of print, with its few but real limitations.

A voice to speak out on the need for a new look at education and for the humanities— and generalists— is Ernest L. Boyer, former U.S. Commissioner of Education, in "Toward a New Core Curriculum" (published in the *NEA Advocate*, April/May 1978). He comes down hard on those educationists who speak about "liberal versus vocational" education to the disparagement of the latter. "Education," he insists, "has always been a blend of inspiration and utility, but because of tradition, lethargy, ignorance and snobbery, mindless distinctions are made between what is vocationally legitimate and illegitimate." In a reversion to what must seem to many a dangerous respect of Ben Franklinism, Boyer insists that the work ethic should play a strong role in the true meaning of liberal education. His remarks obviously parallel and attack the assumed distinctions between "elite" and popular humanities.

With or without Boyer's emphasis on the work ethic, no one in the New Humanities would suggest that investigation of popular culture replace the traditional humanities where those can be demonstrated to be valuable, where they can prove their worth. Or that the study of popular phenomena and culture be blind in celebration rather than keen analysis. Such studies must deserve the same care and precision as any other area in the humanities. Any other attitude would be non–intellectual and bound to defeat the purpose of education.

To paraphrase Lincoln, the Elitists can fool some of the people all of the time and all of the people some of the time, but they cannot fool all the people all the time. As they try to fool society in general, the only ones they really fool are themselves. They are like the emperor who struts around making people think that his clothes are superior when in fact he is not wearing any. Although Elitists through time continually change their statements about their clothes, history always recognizes the fraud and convicts them of indecent exposure. The regrettable aspect of the process is that history moves slowly and is mainly accurate in retrospect only. The preachments of the elitist should be recognized contemporaneously for what they are. We cannot wait for the future to inscribe what we already know — that the elitists were pushing points of view out of self-interest and that these points of view represented generally only what they believed or pretended to believe; such nonsense surely did not represent a consensus.

We see then that the failure of the humanities to fulfill their full potential in the United States is clear. To a large extent that fault lies with the people involved, of course, because individuals seldom live up to all expectations. But to another degree the fault lies in definition, in goals the people want to attain.

The humanities must reach beyond the esthetics of the three handmaidens of conventional venue — literature, philosophy and history. Esthetics— even the "best that has been thought and said"— should be tested mainly or only on the questions of truth and value not only to the individual but also beyond that to humanity. Is the literature appropriate? Is the philosophy sensible? Is the history accurate? Validity rests not on whether something is beautiful, imaginative and self-creating but on whether it bears some resemblance to reality and whether it is applicable to humankind as a whole.

So, to many of us the humanities are more than beautiful and "true" statements. The humanities are those aspects of life that make us understand our society and ourselves. They are a philosophical attitude and an approach to thinking and behaving that interpret life in a human context. In other words, the humanities humanize life and living, make it more understandable and bearable and human. In the words of British critic Fred Inglis: "The humanities are the materials with which humanity gains knowledge of itself." There cannot be humanities without some kind of human compassion about the experiences of life, without some kind of "togetherness," or connectedness. If we understand our strengths and weaknesses and our role in the great scheme, then presumably we will have enough intelligence to develop a useful and helpful attitude and action toward our world. If we know the truth — the whole truth supposedly we will not only be free, but we might also behave sensibly. If we understand the humanities, we might be fully human.

The humanities are without time and limitations. They were important to the Romans, the Greeks before them and the Egyptians before them. But they are not and must not be merely historical statements. Today's humanities are far more important to us than those of the Romans are to us. Nobody should be content to view his or her present-day life through the ignorance, biases and prejudices of the past. One of the goals of education, especially in the humanities, is to develop a healthy — but not reverential — respect for the past while at the same time freeing one from the errors of the past.

The old saw these days is that unless one knows the past he will be condemned to reliving it. But the wisdom of the saw should be explicit enough to say that unless we understand — not just know — the past we will forever be chained by it. To paraphrase one of our wisest maxims, "Ye shall understand the past and that understanding shall make you free," and presumably wiser.

It is a grave error, as we see it, to believe, as Professor Allan Bloom says in his book *The Closing of the American Mind*, that our role is to fit ourselves into the world of the past. That is the action of an ostrich as he buries his head in the sand and turns his rear to the sun. We don't fit ourselves into Shakespeare's world. Surely if Shakespeare is to live today — should live, deserves to live — his works must be fitted into our world; otherwise he is merely a beautiful heirloom. It is as impossible to go back into history, as it is to fit the genie back into the bottle once it has escaped. The humanities are for the living, not the dead.

Increasingly the various media of education — the transmission of facts and attitudes and the development of thinking and reasoning — are broadening the base and raising the levels of understanding and appreciation of the humanities. Presumably, we are becoming more "civilized" — more humane — and maybe to a certain extent this is a result of our deepening understanding of the humanities. The humanities, if they do anything, erase the gap between the privileged and unprivileged classes in society.

The growth of the study and power of the humanities has lagged far behind the development of society. The fault lies not with the humanities but with the academics that profess them. While academics are forming committees to study the issue, the people are reaching far outside those three fields of academic departmentalization of literature, history and philosophy and far beyond the other traditional "good arts." They are reaching out into all aspects of the popular culture for their humanities and finding that all the arts — both "good" and otherwise — have the potential for enriching the lives of us all and, through us, society.

Every American owes it to themselves and their society to make a great effort, through formal or informal study, to understand the culture around him or her. They will discover that there are power brokers in elite culture just as in popular culture — most of us have little influence in shaping our culture. Studying the dynamics of culture, often the student will discover, if he can rid himself or herself of blind prejudice that much of the popular culture is to be appreciated, just as much of the elite is unappreciable.

Actually, of course, there is nothing new in studying popular culture, that is, the culture of the times. As the editors of the *Literary History of the United States* (1955) asserted: "Each generation must define the past in its own terms," as well as the present.

These days, specialty abounds. Medical doctors can no longer understand other doctors outside their areas of specialization. Sociologists can speak only to other specialists in a sub-category. Literary critics do not understand the jargon of a particular "school" of criticism no their own. But the humanities don't flourish in specialties — even among those who specialize in the humanities. The humanities grow in the world of generalities, in syntheses, in questions and answers raised about the purposes and ends — not necessarily in the miles of the road traveled in getting to the ends. But, just as every road consists of the miles separating one point from another, the particulars are ignored at peril.

The ends of the humanities are the whole humanities, not Western humanities, not Black humanities, not Eastern humanities or Women's humanities but total humanities. It is true that we are in the tradition of Western civilization and humanities; and undoubtedly, that tradition has many treasures that we should hold dear. But it is myopic and arrogant to assume that the tradition contains all that is needed for us to understand the humanities, no matter how far back we might go. People in the Western tradition are, after all, only a minority of humanity. Individuals throughout the world share in the hopes and aspirations of a common humanity, no matter how widely divergent our ways of living and achieving those goals seem at times to be. On this space ship Earth we all fly together or we all fall together.

Often we give credit to our ancestors' ways of life and wisdom that they could not possibly have had. Plato, our godfather, flourished in a slave society and as mentioned previously, despised democracy. To realize his shortcomings does not mean that we toss all of him out with the shortcomings; it merely means that we do not slavishly accept his wrong assumptions and incorrect conclusions. There can be no doubt that the amount of information on virtually all fronts that was available to the "giant humanists" of the past was not sufficient to allow them to come to irrefutable generalizations about everything. It is our duty to question everything they said and invalidate or revalidate their conclusions. If the classics still speak to us, then we should hear them. If their voice is no longer applicable, it should be ignored.

There is no question that it is imperative that the old concepts be tested and modified to incorporate new approaches, new definitions and new areas of subject matter. Otherwise the humanities—in all their ramifications—will prove misguided and generally inadequate to present-day needs and possibilities. Maybe it will be found that the "eternal truths" that the humanities are supposed to reveal have more effective spokespersons in sources that have not been recognized in the past.

Take, for example, the fact that there are some 50,000 separate titles of books published in the U.S. annually. Never before have so many books been read. In 1985 there were more than two billion copies of books printed — 400 percent of the number just forty years before. And that was in a society where ninety-eight of every one hundred homes had television. In total number most of those two billion were in popular culture. Which ought to tell the elitists something. And the elite should openly admit what they are actually doing — that is, reading the popular books for pleasure and edification. Just as they are watching television and participating in the other media for pleasure and edification. Sometimes they are bootlegging their enjoyment to themselves. But they fool only themselves, and perhaps the government. There is no need for the elite to dissemble and claim that popular books are the bane of civilization when they read those books and talk about them most of the time. The popular books are, instead, the blessing and the tool of democracy. They spread knowledge and encourage learning.

There can be no doubt that reading stimulates watching television, and that watching television encourages reading. People apparently do not like to live in a quiet, one-dimensional atmosphere. When they pick up a book or magazine to read, many automatically turn on the television set. Likewise, when they turn on the television set many automatically pick up something to read. Further, the television program is likely to stimulate reading in another way: One sees a television show and then gets hold of the book from which the show was made and reads it, just as often one will tune in a television show because the book from which it was made was enjoyable. British crime novelist Ruth Rendell tells how she has seen the television version of her works stimulate people to do all kinds of direct and collateral reading. The media are mutually dependent and supportive. Books, television and movies are only three kinds of media that are mutually helpful one of another.

This means that there should be no sacred domains among the old humanities; they should not be treasured as holy writ and, therefore, be immune to tests of value. They must periodically be asked to revalidate themselves, and if they cannot they must be retired until rejuvenated. Doubtless, many of the old workhorses should be given permanent sabbaticals. They have ceased to have value except as historical markers. The present-day classroom — and research desk — is the one place in society that cannot afford to become a museum of dead ideas and concepts.

Casting out the dead fish from our pond of living ideas is not condemnation of what people have done in the past. It does not invalidate anybody's life's work, anybody's literary or artistic loves, even anybody's evaluation of aesthetically commendable or contemptible materials. Rather, it is a call for intellectuals and other people interested in studying and understanding American life and culture, in its broadest and richest sense, to become broader-minded, more open-minded and less exclusive and excluding. Nobody says one has to approve of or like everything that goes on, just as no one has to approve of or like all the "great" works of the arts of the past or the present. Scientists, to our betterment, do not restrict their interests to the "good" things in life. It is foolish for us to pull an ostrich-like hiding of the head and be unaware of the winds that sweep our bodies while the thinking part is in the sand. Such an attitude is dangerous to one's own and the culture's well being, because in truth American culture continues to grow and develop in its own way pretty much irrespective of the intellectuals' approval or disapproval. It would behoove us to recognize that fact and to bring the humanities into the electronic age. The humanities must prepare us to think our way through the age of instant media.

It is undoubtedly a flaw of education to assume that the person who knows a lot of facts is educated. Such a person could do well on *Jeopardy*, but so could an encyclopedia that was trained to speak or a voice-motivated computer. The educated person is the person who has refused to be cloned, declined to be satisfied working with the lumber of facts that many educators have handed him, but has instead gone on to imagine and build new concepts and constructions.

The academic's tendency is to be rather open-minded while they do not know much and do not have much to defend. But as they get more and more specialized, they tend more and more to become proprietary and protective over what they know, apparently in developing such an attitude fulfilling a deep-felt need within themselves. Often, we turn off our listening button and switch on our broadcast button too soon. We learn to "profess" exclusively while we should still be learning what to profess. Such a one-way activity is indeed dangerous, for it is self-defeating. But academia persists in being, by and large in the humanities, the old nest of last year's ideas, not the place where new ideas are generated and welcomed in order to be tested and approved or cast out. Academia should generally use the library as the storehouse of old ideas, for there they need not do any harm. Archives are archives, and the classroom of new ideas ought to be something else entirely. We should never assume that we know something that has not been examined and validated. Academia should be the leading, not the trailing, edge of ideas.

We should remember that Josh Billings, one of our insightful humorists of the 19th century reminded us: "It ain't the things we don't know that makes such fools of us, but a whole lot of things that we know that ain't so." We should always keep an open mind about what are the valuable things we know and the worthwhile attitudes we hold. Otherwise, we insult our intelligence and jeopardize the natural and peaceful development of culture and mankind. The humanities, properly studied and understood, enrich immeasurably our journey and assist us in achieving literacy for all. They also assist us in another equally important way.

They help us recognize the false ways that are constantly placed alluringly before us, offering cure-alls and quick-fixes that society can ill afford to tolerate — much less encourage. The humanities are too important to leave in the hands of the charlatans.

Works Consulted, but Not Cited In-Text

Bloom, Allan. *The Closing of the American Mind*. New York: Simon and Schuster, 1987.
Inglis, Fred. *Popular Culture and Political Power*. Sussex: HarvesterWheatsheaf, 1988.
Spiller, Robert, Willard Thorp, Thomas H. Johnson, Henry Seidel Canby. *Literary History of the United States*. New York: Macmillan, 1953.

5

Popular Culture: Medicine for Illiteracy and Associated Educational Ills

Many scholars in and out of the popular culture studies movement addressed issues about education in a mass-mediated society, especially in the 1960s and 1970s. Browne addressed the topic in limited ways in aspects of several writings. The conservative mood of the Reagan era brought a call among some in government and higher education to revitalize the canon and erase the "mistakes" of the curriculum reform of the previous two decades. Many of those in the Popular Culture Studies movement, Browne included, saw this as an attempt to sweep away much that they had done.

In this essay Browne follows the tangent that a citizen must be literate and informed for a democracy to function. Yet study after study shows rising rates of illiteracy, as conventionally defined. For Browne, the standard composition-literacy definition is insufficient. A contemporary democratic culture requires literacy in various media, which he terms "mediacy."

Browne's thinking here is a clear outgrowth of his belief that popular culture is an expansion of the humanities as expressed by a complex plural democracy and shouldn't be limited to an approved elitist canon. Those defending the old ways are seen as being essentially elitist and therefore anti-democratic. Browne therefore calls on educators to rethink literacy as the ability to communicate within and across various media, and to use the shared popular culture as the way to stimulate a love for learning, and participation in the culture. Other forms of communication can be tied to the teaching of conventional composition-literacy. This would hopefully lead to a more informed and critically thinking person, and therefore a stronger democracy.— *The Editor*

Statistics on the rising tide of functional illiteracy in the United States are staggering. Some reports indicate 13 percent of Americans are not literate. Other figures state more precise numbers: 20–27 million Americans are "seriously illiterate," 40 million are "marginally illiterate" and 4 million adults are studying to learn to read and write. Even if all these figures are too high, on a personal level, illiteracy is crushing. Young people as well as older persons are intimidated by their illiteracy and the fact that the literate condescend to them. Sometimes the reaction is violent. Young people fight and kill when insulted about their illiteracy. British crime-writer Ruth Rendell centered one of her novels on a housekeeper who was illiterate and lashed out and murdered her employers because they kept leaving her notes that she could not read. Society, as well as the individual, is deeply and seriously wounded by the illiteracy of its citizens. Thomas Jefferson quite properly felt that a country couldn't have a democracy if its citizens were not literate.

In a world of such mischief created by illiteracy, it is time that educators turned to radical cures for this disease and its fellow-horsemen of a potential apocalypse, school dropouts, indifference to education and under-education (fade-outs) if they can be found. As many of us have been pointing out for years, such a radical cure is available in the educational value to be found in popular culture.

Popular culture is the practical — pragmatic — Humanities. So it can be used as a tool to assist us in education. It can be utilized in many ways to overcome illiteracy, to keep people in school, to encourage life-long learning and to energize our educational system and the materials we teach.

As a healthy preamble it can be used to counter the hocus-pocus of academia that presents literacy — and education in general — as magic that one can achieve only after a long and arduous investment of time and labor. This pretentiousness quite understandably puts many people off. The 1987 business of celebrating the Bicentennial of the U.S. Constitution is an excellent case in point. In one effort, the Commission on the Bicentennial Educational Grant Program solicited grant applications for "the development of instructional materials on the Constitution and Bill of Rights" for use in elementary and secondary schools because there is a "lack of citizen knowledge about the Constitution and American history." To correct this lack of knowledge, the Commission proposed funding institutes where thirty or more social science teachers would be taught by "two Constitutional scholars" giving a series of lectures and being aided by two "master teachers." Note the language: "two Constitutional scholars" and two "master teachers." Now everybody knows that words and labels are cheap and meaningless. But a great deal of harm can be done when a government agency is so pretentious that they set about teaching tax-paying citizens— not to mention public school teachers— about our governing document in such phony language. Paternalism does indeed die hard. Apparently the educators in Washington still did not want the people in this country to understand the Constitution on their own. It must be spoon-fed by Constitutional scholars and Constitutional historians. Perhaps it might be threatening to have people understand the Constitution rationally in the light and language of 1987. Undoubtedly the Constitution, like education in general, could profit by a little less pretentiousness surrounding it. That is, it should be viewed in its popular culture setting, in the setting of the people whose life it guides and controls.

Popular culture is the everyday lifeblood of the experiences and thinking of all of us: the daily, vernacular, common cultural environment around us all, the culture we inherit from our forebears, use throughout our lives and then pass on to our descendants. Popular culture is the television we watch, the movies we see, the fast food, or slow food, we eat, the clothes we wear, the music we sing and hear, the things we spend our money for, our attitude toward life. It is the whole society we live in, that which may or may not be distributed by the mass media. It is virtually our whole world.

Though popular culture is to many people the monster that has caused the problems of functional illiteracy and lack of interest in solid education in the first place, it is really — viewed disinterestedly — merely an environment, a force, a background and foreground and a means of communication and entertainment. It can and should be used as a key to open the possibilities of proficiency in the use of conventional language, especially by those whose use of the language of the media — the main disseminating force of popular culture — is very high but whose utilization of the printed word is generally weak and undeveloped.

The principle I am proposing is that pragmatically one begins with the known and proceeds to the unknown, that one uses what he/she already knows in order to learn something unknown. I propose that educators, recognizing this principle, use it in getting people of all degrees of proficiency and non–proficiency in the printed word to expand their capabilities.

That the popular culture around us is known, that it occupies most of the time of nearly all of us and that therefore properly channeled, it can be the single most powerful force to encourage and drive people toward a goal seems to go without saying. The sticking point will be in getting interested people on all levels of education to accept popular culture as a worthwhile and effective tool in teaching instead of as a distracting and weakening diversion, and in motivating them to act on this knowledge. In education, as elsewhere, we all need scapegoats to lay the blame on for faults we see in society and what we might secretly admit is our own failings to accomplish the jobs we would like to achieve. To paraphrase Lincoln, if we would make some progress in a task, we must first recognize the means by which the progress might be made, and then we should persevere in our goals. I suggest that we know that experience has taught us that in the teaching business we proceed from the known to the unknown, that we use every device we can in that teaching process, that the popular culture around us is well known, and that therefore we should use it as educational devices in promoting literacy and love of education and learning.

Popular culture is in fact being used successfully in many areas, especially among pre- and early-schoolers in the highly useful *Sesame Street* and *Mr. Rogers' Neighborhood*, and in numerous computer and non–computer children's games, which are teaching children vocabulary and simple sentences. It is also being used in the continued education of senior citizens. What is involved is basically the rudiments of communication. Once the basics have been established, the same principles should be used to build more vocabulary, more complicated sentences and more sophisticated communication. In other words, the popular culture can be used to establish the basics of communication and, as I shall argue later on, in the continued growth of literacy, sophisticated communication and to lure people into a love of learning and education. In other words, I am suggesting that popular culture can be a kind of textbook for beginners in all fields of learning. It can begin at the beginning. It can develop into all kinds of sophistication, and it can spur interest in every aspect of life and learning known to man and woman.

The beauty of using the popular culture is the motivation it provides if it is used as a spur to learning instead of an end in itself. Sometimes the tendency is to use the popular culture as a goal, as entertainment, but it is very easy to switch from entertainment to instruction, from passive acceptance of communication to participatory communication, if educators merely make the effort.

Some people in the television medium recognize this potential and are willing to put their money where their mouth is. Bill Moyers, for example, gave up a lucrative position with CBS and settled with PBS for one-tenth his CBS salary because he wanted to do more "think" pieces for television. As reported by the Associated Press, April 26, 1987, Moyers said, "Television is a wonderful medium for teaching, as Mister Rogers has proved, as Mac-Neil-Lehrer has proved, as any carefully crafted documentary proves. It's a wonderful medium for teaching." Moyers essentially summed up the educator's opinion when he said: "The world is endlessly fascinating, and journalists are beachcombers permitted on the shores of other people's ideas and experiences, and they're all around you."

The lure of popular culture to people is constantly brought to our attention.

Children spend more time watching television than they do in the classroom. Add to this all the extra time they spend absorbing popular music, eating, dressing, going to the movies, talking about all these activities, and you have most of every day of most people's lives. That is, popular culture is a constant classroom in which education can take place virtually eighteen hours a day. The trick is to make passing the time of our lives, of entertainment, into an educational exercise. All people like to be entertained. The literate and sophisticated want to be entertained, the illiterate want to be entertained. The entertainment of the literate does not differ much in kind from that of the illiterate, only in degree. Both kinds of people want desperately to communicate, and the communication of both does not differ in kind, only in "sophistication." Generally speaking, both have the same experiences in our everyday culture. They go to the same movies, watch the same television, sing the same songs, and share the eating and dressing experiences. We are all locked in the America of our day. It seems logical therefore that the literate and the illiterate use the experiences they share, the motivations they have in common, to bring both groups together in communication and shared American life.

We have always prided ourselves on being a practical people. America has always been the land of the tinkerer, the craftsman, and the people who can do things, build tall buildings, and develop faster means of communication. People have always developed skills because they have seen those skills as being practical and useful. The much-vaunted high literacy rate of the nineteenth century in America developed because people needed to communicate, wanted to develop a sense of community, longed to rise in the social and financial world, and realized that the proper way to accomplish those goals was through the leading communication medium of the time-the printed word.

Despite what may at times seem to be the contrary, Americans still want to communicate; they yearn to develop a sense of community, and they surely lust after social and fiscal upward mobility. Communication among people is more desperately needed today than it has ever been before. In a world that seems forever fragmenting into more and more islands of interest and abilities, people simply are yearning to find the ties that bind them together. Everybody is searching for bonding with other people.

Few people in the United States today are not able to understand and communicate in some of the various media of popular culture. Some cannot handle the printed word but can easily understand and use the various other symbols promulgated by the media. Since literacy is a term which applies only to an old-fashioned technology, we should expand the term to include the ability to understand and use the vocabularies and structures of other media, the symbols of communication such as television, radio, movies, popular music, rapping, jiving, fashions, vernacular architecture, fast foods, etc. That is, *literacy* should include literacy in the media, or *mediacy*.

One becomes proficient in the communication symbols because one needs to. So it has always been. In the folk community, people learned to communicate because it was necessary. They learned the visual media — home and community activities, farming, everyday needs and means— because they realized that the visual media contained elements that they needed to understand in order to get along.

It is likewise easily demonstrable to the populace at large today that they need to understand and be able to communicate the symbols used in everyday communication in media other than those in which the communication occurs. In our compartmentalized world, the media tend to create islands of in-groups, which can understand and communicate in a specific language without being able to communicate outside that particular group. Such people are *mediate*— that is, can understand the language of a particular medium — but may not be able to handle other languages and specifically not the printed word, the one language common to them all. Thus several "languages" may be requisite for communication.

The lure to be held out for people learning other languages of communication can be entirely pragmatic, selfish and self-serving. One gets along better and more easily in life, one gets farther ahead, one becomes happier if he/she understands and uses the dominant symbols of communication, which at this time happen to be the written word.

An excellent case in point was the ability of Americans to use the dominant means of communication in the middle of the nineteenth century. Although only 60 percent of adult Britons were literate in 1851, over 90 percent of America's white population was. There were many forces driving Americans toward literacy, the need for family cohesion, the church, schools, etc — but the main ones were, of course, private: ambition, loneliness, hunger for knowledge and self improvement. People did not learn to read and write primarily because they were told to. They learned because it was demonstrated to be for their personal benefit.

But for the past fifty years or so, it has not been demonstrable that the only — even the preferred — way of getting ahead in America is through the print medium. Technology has invented new means of one's surviving — even flourishing — and has provided people with choices. They could become literate or remain illiterate in the conventional medium yet still get ahead.

Many people have chosen illiteracy because the road to literacy in the conventional medium has seemed too difficult to accomplish. The seeming difficulty of achieving literacy in the printed word is, of course, an illusion, often created by people who for one reason or another thought and taught that it was difficult, in other words promulgated by people who themselves had an entirely false notion of what literacy is and does.

Literacy is a democratic tool available to and usable by all. It develops in and is expanded by the latest tools of democracy; that is the latest gadgets of technology. The printed word was, after all, printed by technology. Now there are other technological tools developed which promote different kinds of literacy, in other words *mediacy*. No longer is the printed word the key to survival. Television, movies, music, and all the other manifestations of the culture around us, are reestablishing an oral and visual culture in which literacy in the printed word is not absolutely necessary. Naturally the clash between the old and the new is traumatic.

What we have is one technology pushing out another and older technology, with the practitioners of the old clinging to it because they have not worked out a way to manage and manipulate the new. Practitioners of print literacy have reason to recognize the force of the new technology. The cost in emotional and financial terms to change from print technology to electronic technology will be staggering. It is hard to imagine a world that is visually and symbolically, and numbers, oriented, pretty much devoid of conventional printed words, depending on a different kind of mediacy. We can hardly imagine and cope with a world that uses the standard means of communication flashed on the computer screen. How can we even contemplate a world that virtually ignores the old forms of literacy? The answer is of course that the clash is made to seem more dangerous than it really is. There are around us several worlds of communication and all are compatible, all can be interfaced, can speak to one another. Scientists and mathematicians, musicians and medical doctors, operate in the worlds of symbols peculiar to their trade while at the same time living in the world of the printed word. But the mutual incomprehensibility among the several jargons creates areas of expertise, and one that suffers most is the area of composition-literacy.

It is a peculiar fallacy that has become almost a truism that says that educators in composition-literacy are the ones who are responsible for developing that competency because effective composition equals literacy, or that literacy comes only with artful composition. So other educational departments that use literacy as a tool in their communication often opt out of the teaching of literacy because they were not formally trained and therefore feel themselves not competent to teach and develop composition-literacy, a feeling of inadequacy historically promoted by composition teachers. Such teachers, having installed themselves as sovereign in the teaching of literacy, have pretty much shamed members of other literate groups into withholding their assistance. Professors of history, sociology, technology, dance, education, etc., may not be able to write sentences that please their colleagues in English departments, but they communicate. Responsibility for keeping English as the coin of the realm is theirs also. After all, their sons and daughters need to communicate. On Spaceship Earth we all communicate or we fly off course. But when the English departments try to enlist the assistance of their colleagues in other departments, often they are met with shrugs of the shoulders: Literacy is somebody else's problem.

To a real degree, the English departments have caused their own trouble.

Historically, teachers of composition-literacy have worked under the assumption that they are out to train people to craft well turned, grammatically correct and graceful sentences, paragraphs and essays. This attitude was built on the assumption that in order to recognize and appreciate great literature, one must be able to write "great" compositions. In other words one writes like the "masters," imitating them in style as well as thought.

Such reasoning is flawed from the beginning. In the first place there may be some correlation between the ability to write the well-crafted sentence and essay and the appreciation of "great" literature, but the relationship is vague and tenuous. The refutation is glaringly and embarrassingly self-evident; most literary scholars, who probe most deeply into the meanings of literature, write anything but the well crafted and graceful sentence and paragraph. They manage to communicate, but not much more.

Secondly, it is a misassumption to believe that literacy equals grace and charm in expression. Literacy-communication equals only the ability to string together a group of words that convey meaning. Teachers who do not admit this definition are doing themselves, their students and literacy a great disservice.

The purpose of all media is communication. Electronic media communicate very well. As a medium of communication, television is not a "vast wasteland" not a "boob tube," nor a "glass teat," as people have variously called it. Nor is the medium of rock music pornographic. Other manifestations of popular culture are not evil forces trying to destroy civilization merely for the riches of unprincipled people. Some people may use them for devious and dangerous purposes. But like computers, television and music, and other media, are merely means of communication that demand "literacy," that are perhaps more important than, and surely just as natural as, the printed word, and — worse yet to some people — will ultimately replace the printed word. In other words, the *mediacy* of the new media of communication will eventually replace that of the old. The guardians of the old-style "literacy" can go with the flow or be washed over by it.

Washed over by it they will be, provided the keepers of the conventional literacy do not realize the threat and adjust to it. There seem to be two choices: keepers of the conventional literacy can use the communication capabilities of the other media and in so doing maintain literacy for all people in the conventional printed word; or ignore and despise the more advanced electronic media and in so doing guarantee the continued erosion of conventional literacy in the present forms and eventually its disappearance or anachronistic status as a minority practice. It is conceivable that a hundred years from now — or even less—conventional literacy in language will have disappeared because it is no longer useful to the general public.

That is not to say, however, that users of the conventional literacy must capitulate to the new, even before it has arrived. On the contrary. But it should be to our interests to realize that the finest tool in the retention of the old form of literacy is in fact the very electronic media that might eventually replace it. That is, the best way to retain the old literacy is to use the popular media and the popular culturing they disseminate as a means of teaching it.

People interested in promoting written literacy should understand that experiencing anything gives a basis for communicating. Communication is analogical. One experiences something in one medium, becomes interested, and wishes to have similar experiences in other media. One "reads" something in television and turns to the medium of print in order to supplement his knowledge, excitement and enjoyment. Unfortunately, of course, one who is excited by television or some other electronic medium frequently is denied access to the treasures of the printed word because he does not understand it.

Here is where the promoter of written communication can take advantage of the media. All forms of communication in the modern vernacular world can be springboards for conventional literacy. The key is getting people to realize that the printed word is the common language — the *lingua franca* that they all need.

The electronic media provide access to and enrich the print medium. They open up myriads of opportunities to stimulate the mind and capabilities of students, which then can be translated into the print medium. Students respond to the stimuli provided by rock music, by questions of youth behavior as catalogued in the media, by questions of morality, ethics, teenage and adult behavior, by the symbolism in such American phenomena as the fast-food industry, shopping malls, rituals, icons and fetishes. Some of the most exciting and useful courses taught in high school and college level composition courses have been sports-oriented: the literature of sports, sports in American culture, the history of sports. The media fairly bulge every day with subjects that excite and invite the thoughtful student and teacher: the commercialization of Christmas, sex-education in public schools, combating the spread of AIDS, abortion, televangelism, the role of the elderly in society, pet therapy, the positive and negative images of television shows, etc. The Popular Culture Department of Bowling Green State University once ran a successful statewide writing contest among eleventh-grade high-school students on "Should Rock Lyrics be Censored?" Uncountable instructors in composition classes have always used current events and other popular culture subjects as topics for compositions. The range of stimulating topics is boundless.

One medium foolishly ignored is the comic book. Everyone knows that in Mexico, Central and South America, the People's Republic of China, and elsewhere, comics are used to teach reading and writing as well as political ideology. In Japan, according to a recent AP article, children, women and business executives read comics all the time. According to one expert, comics exert as much influence over school kids as school itself does. Increasingly comic books are being used to simplify and augment textbooks. How-to comic books are becoming more and more popular, covering all kinds of education and activities. Japan, like America, is a very visual-oriented society. With a claimed 100 percent literacy rate, does Japan know something about teaching literacy that we refuse to accept? It seems so. Let me give you an example.

At Bowling Green State University we created the Popular Culture Library and archive as much popular culture as we can. One of the largest collections is our comic book archive. Years ago when we were just getting started, a man from Toledo, Ohio called one day and said that he would like to contribute his collection of comic books to our archives. He brought down several thousand comics — a station wagon full. Six months later he brought down another thousand comics — a station wagon full. Six months later he brought down another thousand, and sometime later another large collection. Being curious about where he was getting his books, I asked him where he got them and why. His answer was very poignant — touching — and significant. He said that he worked for Toledo Edison as a lineman, and he simply liked to read. So he bought as many comic books as he could. Now I would suggest that in that man's simple statement lies the whole kernel of an American educational system: a person so desiring to read that he would spend all available cash for the opportunity. There lies the seed for education, and one of the media.

Providing access to literacy through these various media does not mean that anybody who teaches composition through the popular culture must undergo a shriveling of his own talents, his own life, his own tastes, if that is the result of such association, though I surely doubt that it is. The teacher should be able to maintain a distance between his private tastes and his professional ones. Using the various popular culture media merely means that in a democracy, one teaches from democratic premises, with democratic assumptions, from and through democratic media, for democratic ends. That means that the instructor should never be embarrassed by or condescending to the degree of literacy or illiteracy one finds or to the means of eradicating that illiteracy. Everybody has to begin sometime at the beginning.

All people, no matter how humble, have the democratic right to access to the valuable and useful experiences of the past and present in order to improve or make more enjoyable their own lives. They cannot, in our democracy, properly be denied the tools of access to those experiences.

Which, of course, brings up an informative parallel. Asian-American children are doing so well in schools and colleges that questions are being raised as to whether they are smarter than other American kids. The statistics are impressive: Asian-American kids usually score some 30 points higher than other Americans on the Scholastic Aptitude Test, 520 out of a possible 800. Although Asian Americans constitute only 2.1 percent of the American population, they make up 11 percent of the freshman class at Harvard; 18 percent at MIT; 25 percent at Berkeley. Does that mean that Asian-American kids are smarter than other American kids? Though the jury is still out on that verdict, there is every reason to believe that success depends more on motivation than native intelligence. Asian-American kids simply work harder. University of Michigan psychologist Harold W. Stevenson feels that "they work harder largely because they share a greater belief in the efficacy of hard work." Stevenson added: "Japanese mothers gave the strongest rating to the idea that anyone can do well if he studies hard." Stevenson might have added that parents know very well that if students do not succeed early they will be condemned to a life in which they never can achieve the highest goals in their society. In Japanese society, success is built from one of the three elite universities and one's capabilities to matriculate in one of these schools are fiercely competitive and established early. Chinese mothers strongly agree in this particular work ethic. A typical Stanford Chinese student's comment was: "In the Chinese family, education is very important because parents see it as the way to achieve. With that environment it's natural to study. My friends are that way too. It's not a chore. They know the benefits."

Are we to conclude from these statistics that all other American students are stupider than the Asian-Americans? That their parents are stupider? Hardly. The evidence demonstrates that the Asian Americans work harder. They are "merely entertained" less than the other American kids. So what should we do? Being realistic, we may as well confess that television and the other aspects of American entertainment and popular culture are not going away. One inalienable right that we are prepared to fight for is the "American Way" of life — and that way consists mainly of our popular culture. Since we are not going to put technology back into the undeveloped stage, why not use it to further our designs to create and promote conventional literacy? If Asian-American kids learn because their family tradition expects it of them, why don't we get the other American kids to learn because it is so easy and one uses the most enjoyable media to learn from, and because American society expects it of them? And rewards them for it. If the American way of life is so much fun, we should use it to learn to get even more fun out of it. The American way of life can become even more pleasurable and profitable for many more if educators use that means of pleasure and profit to promote literacy in the conventional forms.

Yet educators, people who presumably lead in the world of ideas, continue to face backwards, to remember the "good old days" when they were acquiring their wisdom and to teach wrong-headed ideas. Little wonder that American higher education is falling apart. For example, in 1987 Allan Bloom, professor in the Committee on Social Thought at the University of Chicago, published a book entitled *The Closing of the American Mind*. Picturing modernity as the enemy of the classics, and therefore of learning in particular, Bloom (*Chronicle of Higher Education*, May 6, 1987, p. 96) railed against television, "pop psychology," popular literature, and nearly everything else that was not written in the misty past. One of his guiding stars for "classics" was the works of Charles Dickens and the unforgettable characters that Dickens created. Apparently little did Bloom know that Dickens was the most "popular" writer of his day, turning out copy while the printer's devil leaned over his shoulder in order to make a living and avoid the debtors' prison. And Bloom, who curses stereotypical thinking, says that one of the great benefits of Dickens' writing is that his characters are "a complex set of experiences that enables one to say so simply, 'He is a Scrooge,'" etc. In other words although he uses other words, Bloom desires the ease and convenience of the stereotype, the very rib-cage of popular literature of today.

Bloom stumbles over other dangerous misassumptions about education. One is that democracy helped kill off education: "The democratization of the university helped dismantle its structure and caused it to lose its focus." These are the words of the enemy of the people and of education in general, not of one who understands what education is for. Bloom also voices poisonous nonsense when he thinks of the purpose of education: "The old teachers who loved Shakespeare or Austen or Donne, and whose only reward for teaching was the perpetuation of their taste, have all but disappeared," he complains. Prof. Bloom apparently forgets that Shakespeare's plays were written for the very practical purpose of making the author a living on the stage, and Austen's and Donne's had their practical purposes. But mainly Bloom's words reflect the mentality of Matthew Arnold of the nineteenth century and merely demonstrate that many academics instead of wanting to generate free and innovative thinking for their times want to clone themselves and the past. An educational system that wants merely to clone itself and its history is going to be condemned to reliving the past. The frightening thing about Bloom's thinking is that apparently it is honey to many other academic bees who see in it salvation for their troubles. But it is more likely a Siren's song lulling unwary academics into a mess of troubles because it preaches against use of all modern thinking and theories, and surely against popular culture as one of the tools of instruction, with working with what one has.

In using popular culture to promote literacy, sometimes instructors have to be understanding and work from very little. For example, if a student in "composition" would rather perform on his guitar, if he would rather sing a song than write an essay, he should be encouraged, and the performance should be accepted as a "composition." If an "essay" consisted of a collage of pictures of rock 'n' roll stars, it should be accepted. From these parallel beginnings, actual literacy in conventional language can be encouraged. The person who sang a rock song or performed on his guitar could be induced to talk about what he had done, and then urged to write down his thoughts for those people not in class. The person who pasted up the collage could be asked to form some kind of connection, historical or cultural, between the pictures, and thus in effect do some "writing" that would promote his literacy. Acceptance of the different language is useful in bridging the gap between the two or three media, and through acceptance students are assured that the instructor lives in and appreciates the world that they are concerned with. The communication, the empathy, and the understanding all form a two-way street, and two-way communication.

With these purposes and techniques in mind no plan should be too low to begin on, and no idea should be assumed to be above the reach of the print illiterate until it has been proved to be so. Many Americans may have difficulty with even the simplest words and sentences. But these people are not necessarily stupid or unteachable: they simply have not yet learned the art of language use, and they have not learned because for one reason or another they have not been properly motivated. To teach such people, educators need liberated and active minds looking for ideas of today and tomorrow what will excite and motivate the minds before them. The field of these ideas remains constantly present.

There is no reason for the American educator to think that he will have to stop using the media when he has accomplished literacy in the print medium, that the potentials are short-lived and soon exhausted. Functional literacy through the media is only a beginning. This accomplishment can be like a person holding a piece of candy just out of the reach of a hungry child. As the child crawls toward the candy, it can be pulled back continuously — until, in theory at least, the child has become an adult. The bon-bon of media education can likewise be continually pulled back until the learner is accomplished in advanced degrees of literacy and knowledge, until they are, in fact, what we might call "educated." Properly presented the entertainment of life is an unending source of knowledge and training.

The point is to realize the possibilities and to get to implementing them.

Illiteracy, dropouts, fade-outs (arrested learners) are problems that should be attacked directly, not obliquely. Thus on the matter of effective education in the United States, the Secretary of Education,* should be out on the streets of Detroit — and Washington and every community in the U.S. — asking dropouts and fade-outs and illiterates why they are not in the classroom. He or she should be concerned with the very basics of long-range education — that is, keeping students in classrooms long enough for them to learn, then teaching them something while they are there. The task is to get them into situations conducive to our purposes and goals. As everybody knows, the people are learning, but they may not be learning what we think is of primary importance. But there is no doubt that

---

*In the original version, Browne names the then-current Secretary of Education William Bennett at this point in the essay. — The Editor

the Prof. Blooms of academia can do a great amount of mischief if they continue to rely exclusively on the "classics" for wisdom and then do not understand them.

Academics are often uncomfortable in the presence of the multitude of ideas that the media and popular culture provide because they need the feeling of safety and assurance guaranteed by the old restrictions. Such people prefer the snugness found in the old forms of expression to the potentials latent in the new and unrestricted possibilities. Some see merit in the cliché being circulated by many of today's politicians of going "back to basics." Indeed there is much merit in the concept, other than the deceptive alliteration, provided we do not misremember what the basics are. The basics are age-old means of communication about the phenomena of life. The media of communication have been modernized and brought up to date every time the medium of communication has changed. When copying of texts by hand, one by one, gave way to rapid printing, the "basics" became tied to printing. When mechanical typewriters gave way to electric machines, nearly everybody happily changed machines and the "basics" underwent yet another technological advance.

Entertainment is also "basic" in nearly everybody's life; one of the primary drives which socialize society. Through the years the media entertainment have changed radically. Though many people like to cling to some aspects of the "old" entertainment, perhaps claiming that they are superior to the newfangled ones, most people have moved happily into the forms provided by the electronic media.

Society like technology in a literate world moves inexorably forward. But it moves along a trail that includes the past. In truth, popular culture *is* that past as well as its present. Popular culture has never left the basics it is the basics, the fundamentals, the everyday, and indeed it should be so used. It is only the technology of popular culture changes. Technological genies do not go back into bottles once they have been released. The practical and sensible thing, then, is for educators to realize the importance and opportunities of the technological society we live in and to utilize its equipment in the teaching of print literacy. The opportunities are great — and the penalties for failing are heavy and costly, too costly, in fact, for us to afford. Either we go with the media or they go without us.

So popular culture which on the one hand seems to be destroying conventional literacy is actually providing people with the greatest and easiest access to practical functional literacy, to the basics, to getting people to remain in school, and to luring people into continued education long after their formal years are finished, if we will only realize the opportunity and take advantage of it.

Never before have so many people had such easy access to so many means of getting to the top and fulfilling the American Dream of success. That these media are not utilized to develop mediacy and love of learning constitutes one of the great and needless shames of our country and our time. Utilization of popular culture in this way would not, of course, cure the whole trouble. The literacy and education provided might not be of the casebook variety and might not be conventional literacy and education. But it would be communication, it would be functional literacy, and it would keep the human mind busy on "worthwhile" subjects. There would, of course, still be many people who would not or could not become literate in the conventional sense, who would, for one reason or another, not be interested in learning and using the mind. Perhaps the illiterate and the half-educated, like the poor, will always be with us in certain numbers. But literacy builds on its own accomplishments, just as education feeds on education. Literacy breeds love of learning; education breeds more love of education, and of literacy. Learning through popular culture is no panacea. But this approach would surely help alleviate the problem of illiteracy, of dropouts and fade-outs and would provide bases for further development. Any assistance should be welcome and tried. After all, half of the American Dream is better than none —for individuals *and* for society.

Part Two

Clearing The Horizon

In time, the Popular Culture Studies movement had more or less earned and maintained a successful beachhead in academia, and the basic propositions of the field had been — again, more or less — established. Not surprisingly, Browne's concerns for the developing field changed. The previous section demonstrated some of this, as Browne's concern with expanding the concept of literacy was clearly tied to his understanding of electronic media and his broader understanding of the humanities as a field.

Browne eventually turned his thinking toward the problem of cultural aesthetics and what he saw as their misguided application. Stemming from elite culture, these narrow aesthetic principles were used to attack both popular culture and popular culture studies. Browne demonstrated the emptiness and folly of judging all expressions (artifacts, forms, etc.) of a complex plural democratic culture by the standards of one minority section of that culture.

Browne was also concerned that Popular Culture Studies, like American Studies before it, might become obsessed with a dogmatic devotion to an entrenched theoretical base or small collection of approved methodologies. Or, if not, be blown by the academic winds and flock to whatever theory-methodology happened to be the flavor of the month. Browne called for the field to maintain its broad-based, wide-ranging, inclusive approach in both subject matter and theory-methodology.

Browne was also concerned that due to the movement's origin in the U.S. and academic roots largely (though not exclusively) in American Studies, that Popular Culture Studies might become too provincial. He urged the field to become more global in its outlook and focus, and described strategies for it to do so.

6

Up from Elitism:
The Aesthetics of Popular Fiction

This provocatively titled article is a well-made case against the confining strictures and anti–democratic cultural standards that make up elite aesthetic judgments. The main argument uses popular literature as a means to demonstrate the falsely supposed "lesser aesthetic value" of popular culture and to argue for a wider understanding of the value of popular culture expressions. Browne lists and refutes six arguments against the worth of popular literature and calls for a new consideration of aesthetic principles and their applications.

Browne's tone is lightly polemical. He makes a handful of insightful volleys regarding popular culture and its elitist critics in a surprisingly casual manner as he mounts his attack on elitism. Some of his most intriguing points are deceptively presented as secondary concerns. The tactic works best in the first third of the article where Browne's stance of bemused irony regarding elitist aesthetics sometimes borders on the absurd in order to highlight the ultimate vacuousness of his opposition.—The Editor

> When Adam delved and Eve span
> Who was then the aesthetician?

The question of the aesthetics of popular fiction is tied in with many complex drives, most of which reflect humanity's apparent necessity to arrive at and maintain some kind of pecking order that places them above somebody else. Although snobbery, the feeling of superiority and inferiority — like death and the exploitation of the poor — has always been with us, it probably received its most famous and long-lasting boost in the person of the nineteenth-century British poet and essayist Matthew Arnold, who insisted that culture was something only a few fortunate individuals were born with or could ever achieve; some people had it while others did not; in definition, culture was the best thoughts of mankind most beautifully expressed.

Arnold's most articulate followers in our day have been such individuals as Dwight MacDonald, Edmund Wilson, Stanley Kauffmann, and William Gass, among many others. They base their thoughts on the philosophy of Plato, the political attitudes of Edmund Burke, and Ortega d'Casset, to name just a few. These critics insist that there is a great chasm between high and low culture — between highbrow, mid–brow, low-brow, or mass-brow, and I suppose, folk-brow (whatever one wants to call the brow hierarchy) and that as the gap gets larger, it is the role of the conscientious critic to fight to the death to save, resurrect, and revitalize the elite. Anything but elite culture — and strangely and romantically folk culture — is deplorable. Mass culture, popular culture, and the everyday culture of a large majority of people, is to the elite critic ignorant, visceral, mindless, cheap, tawdry, and driving to self-destruction while it drags civilization with it. Elite culture is to these people avant-garde and "intellectual." The attitude of these people can perhaps be correctly summed up in that of one of the high priests, F. R. Leavis, who wrote in a small pamphlet, *Mass Civilization and Minority Culture* (1930), that the small minority of proper critics in the world "constitute the consciousness of the race" and must save the world from "popular fiction" and other damning influences. "Art," he insisted, is "the storehouse of recorded values and in consequence there is a relationship between the quality of the individual's response to art and his general fitness for a humane existence."

Such an attitude is loaded with nonsense, of course, from the very basic assumption that the critic should arrogate the right to be the aesthetic conscience of the world. Further, the attitude is based on the assumption that critical attitudes are immutable and therefore aesthetic standards are unchangeable. Experience demonstrates continually the contrary. Yesterday's classic often is today's forgotten work — unless it is artificially kept alive in the classroom. And yesterday's elite critic is generally looked upon now as a historical curiosity, hard to understand even in a society of the past, which might have been freer to accept such pomposity as truth. Yesterday's bestseller — which was duly consigned to the dust heap by the elite critics— is often today's classic: Dickens' works, *Uncle Tom's Cabin, Gone with the Wind*, Dorothy L. Sayer's *The Circular Staircase*, Agatha Christie's *The Murder of Roger Ackroyd*, Jack Shaeffer's *Shane*, Graham Greene's *The Quiet American*, Wilkie Collins' *Moonstone*. The list goes on and on.

Leavis' attitude is filled with many other assumptions that are only half-truths. That it is only the "serious" work that is avant-garde is subject to many corrections. Although popular culture is undoubtedly the backbone of conservatism and maintains and furthers the status quo, it is sufficiently broad and amorphous as to allow and even encourage all kinds of newness. Leslie Fiedler is surely partially correct when he said that popular culture is revolutionary: there are the examples of American vaudeville, of George Gershwin, of the media of motion pictures and television, or of moveable type, for that matter. The assumption that elite culture is academic is a historical fact but not one to be proud of. A profound and deserved criticism of academia for the last hundred years has been that it was too "ivory towered" and unrealistic. Luckily within the last two decades the walls between the campus and the world have been gradually falling.

Perhaps the most obnoxious of the assumptions of the elite camp is their claim to "intellectuality." A strong case could easily be made that this attitude is as reasonable as the philosophy of Lewis Carroll's Mad Hatter and that the elite "intellectual" is deliberately trying to exploit those not counted in their numbers. The principles the "intellectuals" advocate are at best only pseudo-intellectual, and the attitudes they oppose represent a much more comprehensive, natural, and vital form of intelligence and therefore, in the true sense of the term, are much more "intellectual."[1]

Society grows, as everyone should recognize, by rewriting its credos and points of view. Literary criticism, although sluggish in changing, alters under the impact of new sensibilities and political and social attitudes. We are raucously in such a transition stage at the moment, for many critics and scholars today have shaken off the rusty grip of Matthew Arnold and his present-day apostles. They believe that there is something insidious and ultimately self-defeating in the anachronistic elitist point of view. It is out of date and intolerable. These people — whom for convenience I shall call popular critics— oppose the philosophy and even question the motives of the elite critics, who sound like Cassandra predicting the downfall of the American cultural republic of letters unless they alone are appointed the vestal virgins to protect it. Such royalist defenders of the old and privileged have always opposed anything that seemed to threaten their privileged status. They criticize and condemn, pointing out the way from the darkness of unaesthetic error into the light of great aesthetic achievement. But the popular critic suspects the motives of the elitist critic, feeling that some of the condemner's motives are, sometimes unconsciously, ulterior and meant to better his own reputation, demonstrate his own superiority, defend his position, or create some reason for the continuance of his job.

Further, the popular critic fails to see how all the elite critics of the past have really altered or "improved" the condition of the popular arts that they so savagely berate. Walt Whitman, and others in the formative years of American culture, cried out that in order to have a great literature a country must also have great critics. But it was the people he was primarily concerned with. Emerson and Thoreau were much more concerned with the everyday and common than with the exotic and pretentiously "superior." The popular critic believes that little purpose is served in condemning virtually every book that becomes popular, every art form that is widely applauded. The popular critic recognizes that it is as dangerous to classify all elite art as being meritorious and high-minded as condemning all popular art as being empty, crass, and mindless. Not every popular artist is out to rape the public, nor every elite critic to be a policeman protecting society.

In fact, there are just as many popular artists who are "serious" and popular writers serious about their writings. Jerome Kern was a conscientious artist about his music; Cole Porter was a dedicated and inspired craftsman. James Michener writes very thick books because he feels that the readers want and should have all the background he gives them. James Baldwin upbraided Irving Wallace, when he was writing *The Man*, for having the temerity to write about a black man. Wallace's explanation was that somebody ought to write about the subject of what would happen if a Black inadvertently became President of the United States and that he, Wallace, could reach millions more readers with this vital subject than Baldwin could. He surely was correct. And he was serious. Garry Trudeau is deeply concerned in "Doonesbury," Walt Kelly had a message in his comic strip "Pogo," even Al Capp was serious—very serious—in "L'il Abner."

As the elite critics have their high priests, the popular critics have theirs—among them Lionel Trilling, at his last and best, and Susan Sontag. In the latter's oft-quoted statement, "one cheats oneself as a human being if one has respect only for the style (and the content, one might interpose) of high culture," one gets the general rationale for the broadened perspectives. In explaining such a statement she says at another place, "the distinction between 'high' and 'low' (or 'mass' or 'popular') culture is based partly on an evaluation of the difference between unique and mass-produced objects." But she points out that such a distinction "in the light of contemporary practice in the arts ... appears extremely shallow. Many of the serious works of art of recent decades have a decidedly impersonal character. The work of art is reasserting its existence as 'object' (even as manufactured or mass produced object, drawing on the popular arts) rather than as 'individual personal expression.'" In yet another place she insists, "the problem of the 'two cultures' in short, rests upon an uneducated, uncontemporary grasp of our present cultural situation."[2]

This point of view is strengthened by David Madden, himself a creative writer of considerable force. Paralleling Sontag in her halfway departure from elitism, Madden feels that although there is a distinct and palpable difference between popular and elite culture—two modes that should remain unjoined—"the aesthetics of popular art ought to deal directly only with those components that may be considered part of the aesthetic experience." And Madden very carefully stresses that he and many other aestheticians believe that many "popular culture products can be termed beautiful." In fact in a most pregnant and far-reaching phrase, Madden suggests, "perhaps popular art comes closer than high art to art for art's sake.[3]

Another critic deeply concerned about the aesthetics of popular culture but not its misapplication is Roger Rollin. Elaborating on the Sontag thesis, under the ersatz epigraph "to evaluate is human, to explicate, divine," he argues against any form of evaluation. To Rollin the only real authority on beauty and excellence is not the critic but the people, especially in popular literature. In literature, he points out, the rule is "one person — one vote."[4] Popular culture represents the triumph of a democratic aesthetic, one Mark Twain approved of a hundred years ago when he insisted that he wrote for the millions whereas Henry James wrote for the privileged few. The insistence by elite critics on the lack of aesthetic quality in popular culture represents a counter force, an anti–democratic surge, a return to the time when you could tell the difference between the quality of people by their language, their dress, where they were seen, when, in short, you *could* tell a book by its cover and a reader by his book.

Such critics as Sontag, Madden, Rollin, and most others with the same bent, do not push their attitudes far enough. All admit that in the field of aesthetics you are largely controlled by your training — you are what you have read, how you have been trained, what you have seen and experienced. They *should* insist what they and everybody else deep down in his or her heart — not in the head or the controlled attitudes— knows: that there is no fundamental difference between the two, no more than there is a fundamental difference between a weak nag and Seattle Slew. Both are horses. One is merely faster and stronger than the other. But both move on four feet and eat hay. They differ from each other only in degree.

Likewise all works of art —from the lowliest popular work to the grandest "elite"— differ only in degree. All exist on a continuum that can perhaps be best described as a flattened ellipsis. On the right end is folk art; on the left end (both politically and creatively) is so-called "signature" (elite) art. Between the two— occupying perhaps 80 percent of the scale — is popular art. And between the various types there are only large gray areas, one merging into, growing out of, the other. In all areas along this horizontal continuum there is, of course, a vertical scale of "aesthetic" accomplishment. Some folk creations are strong and effective while some are weak and ineffective. In "elite" art there are some strong and some weak efforts. Undoubtedly the largest range of strength and weakness lies in the popular area. But it is a mistake to assume that the creators of the popular arts achieve no worthwhile standards and accomplishments. Many indeed do: "The Battle Hymn of the Republic" is more universally immortal in America than the 1812 Overture.

Alan Gowans, one of the profoundest art critics, insists, "to know what art is, you must define what it *does*. You can define art only in terms of function. High art historically grew out of low art, and the functions of low art have remained unchanged throughout history.[5] The function is to get something done — to convert the sinner, to explicate the human form, to sell soap. Debating about aesthetic accomplishments without keeping these functions and purposes honestly in the forefront is as bootless as arguing over the number of angels who can dance on the head of a pin. The popular artist is just as much a member of the human community as the elite artist — sometimes much more so. He is just as serious about where humanity is and where it is going. In truth, both, no matter how they state it, are only trying to pin their names to the bulletin boards of history. Though some are a little more honestly hedonistic than others and, capitalistically, agree with Irving Wallace when he says that he has been both poor and rich and the latter state is more comfortable. Few authors—even the most altruistic and idealistic—if given the choice would don the hair shirt and forego the creature comforts and ego satisfaction of being a popular writer. In all their dedication to "higher ideals," Henry David Thoreau complained about his poor sales of *Walden* and Nathaniel Hawthorne was plainly sexist in whining about the "damned scribbling women" whose works sold more widely than his own.

In evaluating the aesthetics of the popular novel we should remember the original purpose of this form of literature. In the seventeenth and eighteenth centuries the novel was designed to tell an interesting story, to provide the public with what we now call a good read. Insofar as it is useful today we should not forget that first principle. The early novel was a straightforward account of adventure. Of course some adventures were livelier than others and inevitably some accounts were more interestingly told than others were. But, regardless of what they did along the way, novels were originally meant to tell stories, to amuse, to provide entertainment. Now, of course, novels have been forced to do much more. They have become more complicated and intricate. As they have developed they have become more expressive of the individual author's philosophy and aims. They may have become more expressive and reflective of the complications of society and life in our world, but elite novels, by and large, with some notable exceptions, have ceased to appeal to the general public because they have ceased speaking *to* that public. They do not address themselves to the concerns of the mass public in terms that can be understood. Rather, elite novelists talk to other novelists, to academic classes, to elite critics, or only to God.

It is foolish to say that the breakdown between the elite novel and the reading public is the fault of the general reader. As everyone knows, there are a larger number of potential readers now than there has ever been. The fault lies with the authors, who while serving their own purposes have abandoned those of the general public. The public are not the lowest common denominator that critics like to call them, not Plato's "oxen of the world" nor Edmund Burke's "swinish multitude," but the *largest* common denominator. And a strong case could be made for the argument that the elite novelist, in failing to write to the general public, is the cause of the so-called low quality of the public's reading tastes, if they are low. The elite author has abandoned the reading public to serve his own purposes. He and the critics who support this abandonment explain that the author's purpose should be that of "probing reality," of developing new genres and forms, of pushing back the horizons of art, of exploring new realities. But they are supporting rather than justifying. The elite authors and critics have made a fetish of their own private goals.

In turning *from* the general reader, what are the elite creators giving up? What are the standards of the general public? The requirements of a bestseller include, among other things, timeliness, informativeness, understandability, formulaic structure and development, and enjoyment. There are, of course, various other qualities that get mixed in— oversimplification, sex and violence, wordiness—which encourage sales. But these qualities are generally present in elite books also, and since they are a part of life they are not deleterious except in the extreme—and extremity, like beauty, is often in the eye of the beholder. Sometimes the bestselling book oversimplifies life; but the innocence of elite authors sometimes is overwhelming. Often the bestselling book represents or pictures life in all its grubbiness and complications because the author does not have the artistic ability or the time to distort it. And in telling his or her story the popular novelist often does a much finer job than the elite critic will allow, as a few examples will indicate.

Jaws, by Peter Benchley (1974), went through at least ten printings in hard cover; it was the Book of the Month selection; there were a *Playboy* and a *Reader's Digest* condensed editions; and it has had some twenty printings in paperback. The *New York Magazine* critic called it "lean, all sinew, everything directed toward a climax that is implanted on the retina from the very first sentence."[6] The book was that. But was it only a super read? For those who look for the more "serious" purposes in life, *Jaws* was much more. It showed man engaged in an elemental and heroic struggle with nature, and it demonstrated a trait in human nature that we sometimes do not want revealed: that all of us—politicians, businessmen, everyday citizens, professors—will do almost anything for profit. In other words, to paraphrase President Coolidge, the business of America is advancing our own purposes.

Irving Wallace's *The Fan Club* (1974)—twenty-four weeks a best seller in cloth—was one of his unusual novels. It developed an idea in Wallace's mind, which through the years had kept taking more and more possession of his imagination. Once on a train ride from Boston to New York, Wallace overheard some trainmen in the sleeper talking about how they would give anything in the world to spend a night with Elizabeth Taylor. Wallace developed this idea in a novel in which he asked what if four men, acting out their fantasy, kidnapped a Hollywood sex goddess and raped her, assuming that she would eventually repay their violence with love. The idea is, of course, ridiculous, but not Wallace's investigating it because undoubtedly the concept lies just under the pubic hair of most men. The book was criticized for being both prurient and sexist, and many bookstores that could have made a lot of money in sales refused to sell it. The charges against the book were peculiar, for in fact it was neither prurient nor sexist when compared with, say, *Fear of Flying*. *The Fan Club* demonstrates how a woman—though a sex goddess and therefore in the minds of men presumably merely a "dumb blonde"—could outsmart four men, one of them a writer, and triumph, while three of the four were condemned to death and self-destruction. Stylistically, the book is wordy, as all of Wallace's novels are. But there are readers who have found Cooper, Dickens, Melville, and even Henry James, taking too long to tell their stories.

Perhaps more graceful and stronger, and more interesting, are the style and subject matter of Leon Uris, and more satisfying, his book *Trinity* (1976). In eight hundred pages Uris embroils readers so much in the reality and anguish of contemporary Ireland that their only regret when the book ends is that it finished so quickly. Even more gripping are Frederick Forsyth's book *The Dogs of War* (1974) and Robert Ludlum's *The Chancellor Manuscript* (1977), each one an example from a series by each author. Ludlum's thesis is that J. Edgar Hoover was killed by a group of high-minded and high-placed intellectuals who saw a dangerous threat in the actions of the head of the FBI. Popular critics have been almost unanimous in praising this latest creation by one of the most skillful creators of suspense in the business and in believing that the suspense novel is one of the most viable genres of our time. The book is in fact so complicated, so fast-paced, and so unrelenting as almost to break upon itself. If ever there was a book that a reader could not put down, it is this one.

Likewise compelling—though in other ways and for other reasons—was Alex Haley's *Roots,* which may turn out to be the most significant book in any class of this decade. Quotes on the cover called it "bold ... extraordinary ... a blockbuster.... One that will reach millions of people and alter the way we see ourselves" by *Newsweek*. "An instant classic.... A vital and permanent contribution to our literature" said the *Philadelphia Inquirer*. And "one of the most moving books I have ever read.... It sometimes brought me to tears, and to feelings too deep for tears.... A document of great worth 'true to the truth of the human heart,'" said *Los Angeles Times* book reviewer Robert Kirsch, one of the most affirmative and incisive critics of popular fiction.[7] *Roots* is not, of course, a novel, but its success says a great deal about the general reading public. And there is no question that when books— popular or otherwise — achieve the level of Haley's work or those of Ludlum or Uris or many others— and these are merely a few of many I could have chosen — then blanket criticism of the bestselling work is simply ill-advised and unfounded.

An examination of two genres— the spy and the detective — which rely more closely on the formula per se than the books we have been discussing in general, can be revealing. John Cawelti has discussed at great length how the bestselling novel depends on formula development.[8] Fiction, like virtually everything else in life, is based on the observation that most things are done according to a proved and workable plan, a formula. Financial success, academic advancement, military tactics, and television programs all work on proved techniques. In fiction, in its simplest form, the formula might dictate the development of a western novel: you get a frontier town that is being terrorized by a selfish banker or rancher, who uses hired guns to enforce his will against a group of townspeople who are too frightened to resist. Then you bring in a faster gun, preferably one who has discovered the futility of gun-violence, who fights for the townspeople. Then, when he has rid the environment of evil, he rides off into the sunset. Such a formula can be simple, or it can be complex (it can give you Zane Grey's *Riders of the Purple Sage* or Jack Shaeffer's *Shane)*. Often it relies more on *convention* (the old and established) than on *invention* (new ways of developing the idea), to use two of Cawelti's terms, but in the hands of masterful writers the formula achieves profound accomplishments.

John D. MacDonald is an excellent study in formulaic writing at its strictest. In writing about a hard-nosed detective, Travis McGee, who fights crime from his houseboat, *The Busted Flush*, in Florida, MacDonald in all eighteen of the novels is to a certain extent, perhaps a large extent, governed by the limitations of the formula. All are powerful and thoroughly readable. In addition MacDonald writes about half his books outside this formula, about various subjects though they hover around or work in detective-violence crime. One would think that these broader-based, less formulaic stories would be more successful. In fact, they *are* more interesting but less skillfully written. In other words, MacDonald seems to be torn by having interests and goals broader than the formulaic detective stories but lacking the skill to carry them off as effectively. With him, then, the formula, though it restricts his intellectual inquiry, brings out his greatest skill in development and writing. His predicament illustrates the dilemma of formula writing. It is easier to write simple formula novels than non–formulaic ones but it is more difficult to write *successful* formula novels than the non–formulaic. MacDonald is very much aware of the strain of trying to accomplish his goals within the formula. He thinks that Jacques Barzun's dictum that "anyone who attempts to improve on the mystery genre and make it a real novel suffers from bad judgment" is, in MacDonald's words, "probably right." MacDonald accepts the "strictures and limitations of the medium and then within the boundaries" tries to write of the "climate and times and places in which the action takes place." He finds it "easier to do this sort of thing in a medium where it is not all that customary than to do it" in the other novels he writes.[9]

Ross Macdonald, on the contrary, has found the formula more confining and constricting. Though most of his books center on the hardnosed, softhearted detective Lew Archer, Macdonald has never been content merely to be a writer of detective stories. He sets his tales in southern California because, as he says, this part of America represents most vividly the raw edge of American society, where civilization has pushed itself nearly into the sea, and in so doing has created problems that it may never be able to solve. But Macdonald has broken the mold of detective fiction and expanded his probing into something larger, as writers before him have done. Strangely enough, however, he has been severely criticized by the elite critics for being presumptuous and for trying to write something other than conventional detective fiction, as in *Sleeping Beauty*. But he continues to adhere to his definition of the detective story because it is the best medium, expanded as he enlarges it, for his probing into the working of the human condition.

Working around even more expanded formulas; Margaret Millar pursues her own purposes. She has written in the detective and in the gothic-psychological formulas, and mixed them. In so doing she has been less obvious to many readers and has failed to gain as wide a reading public as those authors do who work in discrete genres, but she has created powerful studies of people and culture aesthetically satisfying on every count.

Certain other formulaic authors approach their media with different purposes and different accomplishments. Graham Greene, for example, with a long line of spy novels to his credit, began by distinguishing between those works as "entertainment" and others he wanted to write as "art." Finally, however, he realized that there is no real distinction, that the formulaic form can carry his message as well as any other, and he dropped his effort to keep the two separate. Other authors have felt even stronger than Greene about the presumed limitations of formulaic stories, at least to begin with. Some have intended to use them as stepping-stones to something more aesthetically satisfying. Thus the English author of detective fiction P.D. James, whose favorite author is Jane Austen, and who, like Henry James, learned art by writing popular literature, began by looking upon her works as serious endeavors, and as a step to something else: "I saw the writing of detective fiction with its challenging disciplines, its inner tensions between plot, character, and atmosphere, and its necessary reliance on structure and form, as the best possible apprenticeship for a serious novelist." And she has maintained her respect for the form itself. Each of her books has been, in her words, "a landmark in [her] gradual realization that, despite the constraints of this fascinating genre, a mystery writer can hope to call herself a serious novelist."[10]

What are the differences between "serious" fiction and the popular novel? What are the shortcomings of this sort of book to the elite critic? Like so many other things, they are more apparent than real, more in the eye of the critic than in the material itself. The presumed deficiencies are several:

1. They do not possess any uplift and social purpose. Incorrect. Although many popular books are written merely to make money, on any subject and with the introduction of much sex and violence, if there is one ingredient that a majority of the works of popular literature have in common it is a response to and a catering to America's continued fascination with the puritanical insistence on improvement. As to the other types, many conventional classics have no moral purpose. *Tom Jones,* for example, merely shows that if you are a rake you yourself eventually get raked as your coals burn out.

2. They present life falsely and therefore mislead the reader. To a certain extent this observation is correct, but to another it is incorrect. All art is by definition a falsification of reality, even the works of the realists, the naturalists, and surrealists. John D. MacDonald, however, maintains—correctly—"fiction at its most entertaining, provides little hints, clues, nuances which aid us in our endless deciphering of ourselves."[11] Modern Gothics present a spooky, goosepimply side of life. But *Wuthering Heights* and *Jane Eyre,* both classics of "serious" literature, hardly present "real" life.

3. They are sheer fantasy. True, at times—thank goodness. *Watership Down* (1972) and *Shardick* (1974), both very popular novels by Richard Adams, may be ridiculous. But then also might be Tolkien's works and *Alice in Wonderland* and the movie *The Wizard of Oz*. But whose world has not been brightened by these works?

4. The books are sentimental. Correct. But so were the many novels of the eighteenth and nineteenth centuries; sometimes sentimentalism is falsely branded as dangerous and useless.

5. They explore no new territory and the style is only copycat. This is a dangerous charge to level at popular novels. Their first principle is to confirm experience, but it can easily be demonstrated that as Leslie Fiedler and T.S. Eliot recognized, popular fiction is highly and strongly subversive. Fiedler applauded this quality; Eliot strongly condemned it. In the world of the popular novel a little memory is a dangerous thing. The fact that one writer does what a predecessor has done is no reason for condemning the second work. Obviously if Peter Benchley in *Jaws* wanted to write a sea story about an elemental struggle between man and a sea monster it was better for him to choose a great white shark than a great white whale or a blue marlin. The fact that the reader remembers that the whale and the marlin have already been written about should not vitiate Benchley's story of the shark but instead should enrich it as *it* enriches the other stories. That the reader recognizes the style, and even that it is "weak" and not "serious" (whatever those charges mean) should not invalidate the story. Numerous kinds of stories use exactly the same kind of language, and sometimes it is flat. Would the bestseller be approved if all began with the words "Once upon a time" as fairy tales do, or "Now here's a story about" as many folk tales do?

6. That the bestseller is loosely written and therefore very long. Correct. Because popular books need to be timely and must be written and published rapidly, the author generally cannot be as much concerned with style and brevity as the author of more deliberate books can. On the other hand, some of the authors simply like to write. Michael Avallone, who has written over 184 novels of various kinds, insists that a professional author should be prepared to write any time and "should be able to write *anything*: garden seed catalogues, the Bible, or minutes of the Last Meeting." In an interview with Michael Barson he once claimed that he wrote a novel in a day and a half as a "rush job."[12] This obviously represents his philosophy and his modus operandi. Harold Robbins supposedly locks himself into a library and turns out a book in six weeks. Louis L'Amour, author of the most effective series of western books today (with sales running over 100 million copies) runs his manuscripts through the typewriter once, has his wife check them for consistency, and sends them off to the publisher. Yet no one could accuse L'Amour of not wanting to and of not succeeding in establishing a western dynasty (*The Starretts*) and, perhaps of not succeeding in his goal of rewriting and correcting western history in 100 volumes. Though Robbins' books are, and L'Amour's books are not, wordy, one can remember many verbose classics. *Moby Dick* and *Pierre* were condemned, and continue to be condemned, for their wordiness and for their purple rhetoric. And both *are* wordy and purple. People today who buy the bestsellers like quantity. They like long books because they want to spend hours and hours with them. Often it is not so much the story as it is simply the reading that fascinates these readers. Should we criticize that desire in a society that we condemn as functionally illiterate?

The condescension in our condemnation is apparent. And condescension is rampant.

Every college and university instructor has the horror story, which apparently has happened many times, about the assistant professor (always somebody other than the speaker) who spent an hour demonstrating that Joyce Kilmer's poem "Trees" was unrealistic and silly, utterly destroying its value in the eyes of his students. At the end of the hour, so the story goes, a student came up and said to the professor: "I wish you hadn't done that. 'Trees' was the only poem I knew and liked, and now you have destroyed it for me." Such is knowledge and wisdom. On the other hand, every author has anecdotes about how out there in the readers' world somebody appreciates his works. In an interview with Michael Barson, John Jakes, the author of, among many books, the Kent Family Chronicles, recounted the reception of Volume VIII, *The Americans,* and the announcement that the series would not be continued beyond that volume:

> I've really been astonished at the volume and the emotional intensity of the mail that has come in following the conclusion of the series.... I have letters from people who have stayed up all night, who have stayed up eighteen hours reading continuously. And I even have, I'm amazed to say, tearstained letters from ladies who cried as they finished the book, and immediately sat down to write a letter. A writer can ask for no more, no greater reward, than that kind of response.[13]

So, what can we conclude about bestsellers in general? It is indeed dangerous to generalize about them, for they are numerous and varied in subject matter and range of accomplishments. Some are less effective than others; some attempt little and accomplish less. However, some attempt much and achieve as much, or more than, more "acceptable" works by recognized "serious" authors.

Perhaps a new set of aesthetic criteria should be set up for this kind of book, or, more desirable, the old set should be made more flexible because we realize that the set of elite criteria currently being used by many critics and academics is inappropriate and prejudiced. If we used a different set of criteria, critics could more correctly and openly evaluate these books and weigh them on their own terms. Then all of us could read and enjoy them — where they are readable and enjoyable — without doing it clandestinely with the guilty feeling that we often suffer from. We would recognize that the old criteria no longer hold, if they ever did, and that those of us who claim to be scholars interested in the social and cultural milieu around us must read the popular books indiscriminately if we are to understand the motivations, psychology, forms of entertainment — in short, the culture — of the people around us, and therefore of ourselves.

This observation is nothing new. Well over a hundred years ago someone writing in *Blackwood's Edinburgh Magazine* recognized what is only becoming more and more obvious:

> Popular literature is a reflection of the period in which it flourishes— its active as well as its meditative life— its politics and its romance, and we rest assured that there is not a movement in it, not a force, not an atom of life which has not its counterpart in contemporary history.... Literature, in fact, now implies far more than it did before. It is now a complete representation of society.... It is to the historian what the dial-plate is to the time piece; it is a perfect index of the innumerable processes at work throughout the whole frame of society.[14]

Except in details, perhaps, the statement could not be more directly on the mark.

In the world of fiction if we reduced everything to a kind of creative *Fowl Farm* there would be some swans bedazzling us with their charm but undoubtedly there would be a much larger gaggle of geese. Perhaps they all, in their way, lay golden eggs of varying karat.

These eggs provide coin of the realm for virtually everyone and for everything—for the promotion of democracy, of literacy, of the development of aesthetic tastes, of the enriching culture. The only ones who do not pass these coins openly are the elite and they do not because in general they are content with their place in life—they have no new places to go on the new coinage. They do not want to come up.[15]

Notes

1. "Intellectual" critics are a paradoxical and at times self-contradictory lot insofar as they can be classified as being similar. Claiming to be avant-garde and wanting to discover and embrace the new and different, they often are terrified of anything new and different. For example at the first presentation of Tchaikovsky's ballet *Nutcracker Suite*, the critics were aghast at the concept and presentation, vowing that the work could never live; history has, of course, proved them wrong. In April 1961, *ABC's Wide World of Sports*, with host Jim McKay, was first aired on television. Critics felt that this new approach, utilizing new camera angles, close-up shots, and other new concepts, would never succeed. As soon as it did, the critics adopted the techniques. Examples of this side of the "intellectual" are legion.

2. A standard book on this subject is Susan Sontag, *Against Interpretation* (New York, 1961). Any chapter will give the gist of her opinions, but the first and last are the source of these quotes.

3. David Madden, "The Necessity for an Aesthetics of Popular Culture," *Journal of Popular Culture*, 7 (Summer, 1973), 1–13. The whole article merits close reading.

4. Roger B. Rollin. "Against Evaluation: The Role of the Critic of Popular Culture," *Journal of Popular Culture*, 9 (Summer, 1975), 355–65. Filled with irony and gentle humor, the whole article requires careful reading.

5. Alan Gowans, *The Unchanging Arts* (Philadelphia: Lippincott, 1971). This thesis pervades this book. For a clearer statement see Alan Gowans, *Learning to See* (Bowling Green: Popular Press, 1981).

6. The quote from *New York Magazine* and others were used on the cover and first page of the paperback edition as advertising.

7. These quotes emblazoned the cover and first page of the paperback edition as advertising copy. Such advertising, obviously, is effective.

8. John Cawelti, *The Six-Gun Mystique* (Bowling Green: Popular Press, 1970).

9. John D. MacDonald, "Introduction and Comment," *Clues*, 1 (Spring, 1980), 73–74.

10. Quoted in Earl F. Bargainnier, *10 Women of Mystery* (Bowling Green: Popular Press, 1981), p. 108.

11. *Clues*, 1 (Spring, 1980), 67.

12. Michael Barson, *The Paperback Novel* (Diss., Bowling Green State University, 1981), p. 89.

13. Barson, p. 96.

14. Eneas S. Dallas, "Popular Literature: The Periodical Press," *Blackwoods Edinburgh Magazine*, 85 (January, 1859), 96–97. My thanks to Russel B. Nye for bringing this apt quote to my attention.

15. The careful reader will have noticed that not once in this paper have I used words *good* or *bad* in evaluative terms. They are words which critics—and all moralists—freely use when approving of elite works and condemning those that they dislike. The words are obviously laden with ethical, moral, and religious connotations and are used with such intentions when not chosen carelessly and unconsciously. The fact that they flow unconsciously reveals how deeply they course through our nature. They should be banned from the critic's lexicon. More precise and appropriate terms must be found if we are to free ourselves from prejudice and to provide fair evaluation.

7

The Repressive Nature
of TV Esthetics Criticism

In this article Browne continues his critique of elitist esthetics, moving from print to electronic communication, using television to make his points. It is very much an elaboration on and continuation of his earlier "Up from Elitism" (included elsewhere in this collection.)

However, Browne clearly wants his arguments to apply to other mass media forms than merely TV; extending, we can reasonably assume, to those not yet existing but which follow similar cultural patterns, such as (in some ways, at least) the Internet. This is a point he makes in his 1977 speech "The Many Faces of American Culture" (also included elsewhere in this collection).

Television has changed as technology, as industry, and as social force since the article was written. But dated examples aside, Browne's larger points are still useful and illuminating.

In a captivating two-fold strategy, Browne argues for the less than "masterpiece" status of then-lauded TV shows, and defends the form of the much-maligned soap opera in a cogent section. Early on in the piece Browne is quick to remind readers that "TV" as it exists in the USA is not necessarily "TV" as it exists in other cultures and reminds them that TV is not really that old a medium and may well be in its cultural infancy. Later, in a somewhat provocative move growing out of his analysis of the soap opera form, Browne compares TV, as a medium, to talking or seeing — not to some other example of mass media.

But the true heart of this essay, and one of his strongest statements of the idea, is Browne's accusation of the attempt of elitist cultural forces and individuals continuing a centuries-long attempt to control the people at large. In order to challenge the elitist cultural hegemony informing the repression mentioned in the article's title, Browne calls upon some of his favorite sources here, but mostly in abbreviated form. To that end, they have not been omitted since the redundancies with other pieces in this collection are minor, and the damage done to this piece would be noticeable. — The Editor

In the last decade there has been much useful development in the study of television — what it is, how it works, its impact upon and interrelationship with culture in its broadest sense. We clearly understand that television is a unique medium, different from movies and radio in both forms of communication and entertainment. It is an intimate domestic form, which must be understood in its own technology, on its own terms, as an all-pervasive medium that occupies an important role in up to 99 percent of American homes—and increasingly in growing numbers of homes worldwide.

In the last ten years a lot of condescension and resulting nonsense have disappeared from television viewing and from critics' vocabulary. But there is still more than enough around to make it clear that the main purpose of TV criticism by the elitists among us is political and cultural repression, an effort to make it manifest that TV is a form basically inferior to the other and older forms and that people who watch and *appreciate* television are intellectually and socially inferior.

Although we may still get aggravated by the sameness and repetition of programs, by the overwhelming saturation of commercials, and although we may secretly half agree with the old remark of Newton Minnow that television can at times be a limited wasteland, most responsible critics who are not trying to grind their axes, nowadays do not think the desert covers even half the land and should therefore be abandoned to its own death. Television, like the two other media closest to it, talking and seeing, is too important and pervasive a part of our daily lives to be abandoned. Increasingly we recognize that television, like conversation, sights, books, movies, and all forms of communication and entertainment, can have its high spots but that many — perhaps most — programs will be run-of-the mill. But there is nothing unusual in such an observation. Most of life, most entertainment, is dull — at best mediocre. The Pasadena Rose Parade gets boring to most people long before it ends at noon. Imagine how dull it would become as everyday diet. The football Super Bowl can be borne once a year, but no more! The Boston Symphony performs for the same customers only once a week, and changes its program all the time. *War and Peace* can be read only every few years. Even the most rewarding theatrical performance should not exceed three hours without a break. Perhaps our human or cultural limitations are unfortunate. As all researchers know, the more one experiences some work of art or entertainment the more rewarding it becomes to experience it. But most of us are not compellingly interested in all of them eighteen to twenty hours a day.

We have learned how to accept and appreciate most of our art forms and means of communication. We can stay with them or walk away. But, as usual with the introduction of a new form of communication, we have expected too much from television. As we have always expected every medium of communication to be a panacea to all problems, we have assumed that TV, because of its time of introduction into society and because of the power of its instantness, will be the ultimate and final cure-all, will solve all our problems. We have demanded that it be as exciting and entertaining as Shakespeare, Henry James or *Gone with the Wind* for 18 hours a day seven days a week. We have also expected it to be educational — the best of all media, both entertaining and educational at the same time, like the rare stand-up comedian or exciting slide-lecturer, or production of *Hamlet*. We have mistakenly assumed that television should somehow be an animated book that as we flipped the pages the pictures and print would come alive in beauty and soul satisfaction.

But, contrary to our expectations, we have learned that television must be viewed as a small-screen box which gives us an intimate view in the privacy of our homes of material that can be instantly communicated; must, for various reasons, be designed for the *largest*, but not the lowest, possible viewing audience; that except for news programs, certain documentaries and some series the programs are going to be formulaic, self-contained units somewhat discrete from antecedent and following materials, but heavily dependent upon the genre and type in which it fits. All entertainment is aware of the rest of the world of entertainment around it, and to the extent that it can profit from borrowing from other elements and shows, it will do so. Thus there are many units and series picking up and developing the formula and convention in individual shows and in spin-offs of series. The various police shows follow pretty much the trail of the ones before it, *Dynasty* changes only the location and characters of *Dallas*, and one situation comedy is pretty much like the others before and around it. To that extent all of TV, like all radio and movies, is "artificial." But all art is artificial.[1] Not many of us know personally any Hamlets or Shanes, or even Hawkeyes. And none of us lives in the intensity of "naturalist" or "realistic" works of art — even of, in our world of poverty, say, John Steinbeck's *Grapes of Wrath*.

We have also learned that television must be accepted on its own terms. Television programs may be enjoyed for their own development, laughed at for their incidental humor, valued for what they teach (directly or indirectly) or prized for their own form and esthetic achievement. Sometimes we forget, however, that although television may be appreciated for any one or several of these qualities, it should be viewed for *all* of them at the same time and *more*. Just as TV is obviously in its infancy as far as technology content and art forms are concerned, we viewers are hardly more than toddlers in our appreciation of its full potential — for tomorrow and even for today. In a medium that is so new and complex as television is, we need to experience it more on a comparative and understanding basis, especially before we draw any negative inferences. In order to understand more of its potentialities we need to know more about what is going on in Canadian, European and Japanese television. Before we condemn American TV and praise English, for example, we should see enough of the latter to realize that *Masterpiece Theater*'s imports into this country are the top of a heap of a British diet that would drive most Americans to our game shows and soaps with wild enthusiasm and appreciation. And many of the "Masterpiece" programs are neither masterpieces nor theater, as only one example, PBS' offering of Nancy Mitford's work *Love in a Cold Climate* can powerfully attest. Only long-suffering Anglophiles can sit through that mistake. Before we are stunned by TV-analyst Gerbner's Violence Profile and think that violence on American TV is the cause of our national and social problems, we should realize that there are nearly half a hundred acts of violence occurring daily on Japanese television, apparently with minimal excitation to violence. Before we decide to burn pornography and pornographers we should get to know the role of pornography in the lives of the Japanese, who are very much like us in the technological world.

Before we reach our conclusions about educational TV we should see what is happening in China where the TV set has almost just been switched on and yet where new "Television Universities" enroll some 324,000 students— not many in so populous a nation, but an indication of an attitude and of things to come.

In television a little watching is a dangerous thing because it may lead one to erroneous conclusions. Unconsciously one may fail to realize that TV is only 35 years old* — by far the fastest developed medium in human history — and will therefore base one's conclusions too much on similar media — books, movies, etc. Before we arrive at the final and true means of evaluating TV, we need to develop new vocabularies, new attitudes, new methods and new insights. Otherwise one may be lead to faulty evaluations.

One may also be led to superficial conclusions. We are all by now familiar with John Cawelti's concept of convention and invention in the arts— of formula — of his notion that the popular arts depend more on convention than the elite arts which are more inventive and more different one from another.[2] Some popular entertainments use more sameness in their development, follow clear and obvious lines of development, are more formulaic, are more predictable. But we realize that such a description is not necessarily a condemnation

---

*Dating from the time of the article's original publication, Browne has chosen 1948 as the year of the birth of television. That year is indeed generally considered the year by when each of the major networks (Dumont, CBS, NBC) had committed their resources toward establishing television as the successor to radio as a mass public oriented commercial system. The process of television itself had been more or less perfected by 1930.— The Editor

just as its opposite — the inventive — is not necessarily praise. In America we have made a great to-do over the fresh, the unique, the different. We do not want to read a book or a story if we have read one like it before, we do not want to see a movie if we have seen a similar one. One of our favorite ways of dismissing something as worthless is saying, "It's just like…" when it fact it may merely *seem* to be like something else. We have made a fetish out of newness and differentness, and that is a superficial and self-depriving attitude.

Nothing is without precedent, as Francis Bacon observed three hundred years ago. All ideas, all art, all developments stand on the shoulders of antecedents. In so doing each lengthens its range of vision. All of us know more mediocre people than brilliant uniques. Life is that way. So is the formula. *On the surface* formulaic art may seem all the same, but that is really no reason for us to despise it. In fact, formula has a double-barreled effect. On the one hand it seems to blunt probing into newness, to homogenize into a sameness. But on the other, actually it is freeing and liberating, in the same way that the form of the short story, the sonnet, and the limerick is freeing. There is a strict formulaic form, for example, about the popular 32 bar song, but history demonstrates that apparently the variations are infinite. Not having to invent a new form, the authors who work in the accepted and proved forms can devote their time to subtleties that often — especially in TV — escape the viewer. That is why the formulaic show is appreciated in reruns. It's like instant replays in sports: the viewer sees and appreciates more the more often they see the event, for they see beyond the obvious and surface generalities.

The subtlety and complexity of the formulaic development is sometimes more apparent than at others. In the larger TV show it is at times well camouflaged. NBC's *Hill Street Blues*, for example, is so densely peopled, so richly orchestrated and fast moving that it has up to a dozen formulas working at any given time (philosopher cop, divorced but loving couple, nosy but public-spirited newswoman, father-figure head cop, dedicated cops on the streets, misfits but comradely patrolmen, reformed outlaws, etc.). As one watches and sorts out all these movements, he or she thinks they like the show. It is a kind of *Gone with the Wind* television cop show. NBC's *Nero Wolfe*, on the other hand, was not successful in 1980–81 in attracting a large audience because it was so narrowly developed and orchestrated that the general viewer failed to appreciate it. It was like a barbershop quartet, with a dedicated but limited audience. Obviously the authors and producers assumed that a large audience would be familiar with author Rex Stout's rather narrow formulaic development in his books about the eccentric detective, and if they had, the TV formula would have been rewarding — despite the fact that out of sheer necessity the lead character Nero Wolfe had been miscast in William Conrad. In this case lack of familiarity was undoubtedly unfortunate. More experience with the books would have made the TV show more familiar and the TV series, which was cancelled for the 1981–82 season more widely pleasurable.

The value of the formula is even less apparent and understood in soap operas, the subject of this focus section. There is a peculiar paradox in soap opera viewing. Those people who do not like them find them silly and revolting; those people who do watch do not need any explanation of why they watch them, and they *know* why they appreciate what they see.

In truth the soaps are much more complicated than they appear to be. Written to a loose formula of duplication of an affluent life style, which can be so deeply complicated in the traumas of life, generally involving young people as the dynamic instruments, they duplicate to a certain extent and in a certain way an aspect of life. They are slow moving, as life is. In fact at times, like life, they seem to be dedicated to going on for days and weeks with absolutely nothing happening but a lot of talking. Because they are so slow moving they increasingly try to introduce as much implied scandal, as much sex, as many different aspects of life or as much titillation as the traffic will bear. And every viewer apparently is going along with the new material. In fact one of the main reasons given by viewers for that addiction to the soaps is that they are "just like life."

The attraction of the soaps, their audience, their using materials as they do, should not surprise anyone. It has been properly said that the soaps are formless, that they are all middle, no beginning and no end. Dennis Porter quotes Aristotle on the drama of the soap opera: "If … as Aristotle so reasonably claimed, drama is the imitation of a human action that has a beginning, a middle, and an end, soap opera belongs to a separate genus that is entirely composed of an indefinitely expandable middle."[3] They are even more universal. You can tune in at any time on a program and no matter how many days, weeks or months you have missed you will in fact not have missed anything that cannot be caught up on in fifteen minutes. The characters are old friends and acquaintances, and it takes only a few minutes to get them to know them again. You can switch from one soap to another and will find the same kind of inactivity going on, the same kind of talk. All soaps consist of interchangeable parts.

These comments are not necessarily pejorative. The reason soaps are so popular is that they are more like conversation and gossip than any other type of program on television or anywhere else, more than on radio because you can *see* your fellow gossipers. Like daily conversation they form a kind of background to life, fascinating, but background, which people utilize as they go about their other daily functions— of ironing, reading, cleaning the house, playing games, or just watching. They are appreciated, especially the social and sexual innuendoes and scenes, because soaps are like a particular kind of conversation — gossip. The seamier side of life is the backbone of gossip. And soaps are the backbone of TV watching because they do not have to be attended to; people don't really *pay attention* to soaps because they don't have to. Soaps are generally entertainment air we breathe.

Like gossip they are not formless. Soaps in fact have as much form as the folk tale or fairy tale, which they strongly resemble. Each day's program could easily begin with "Once upon a time…" in form. And it surely could begin with "Once upon a time a prince and a princess…" for the level of affluence represented on the soaps is what everyone aspires to. Apparently no hard-working housewife or househusband or kid in college resents the fact that life on the soaps is unlike hers of his, that nobody on the soaps has a job or needs one (at worst, they have vocations), the women are always well dressed and at leisure, the doctors all pay house-calls, one can always get a plumber (even on weekends) to keep up the way of life, although such people are never seen. In fact the soaps are perhaps the prime statement now of the American Dream, the Ideal Social Security Life — a rich world of leisure and wealth where talk and life's traumas and sex are the only activities. The soaps are the ideal focus of people's projections of the ideal life, and are all safely under glass and cleansed. Watchers can view at a safe distance and with whatever detachment desired the agony and joy of life, projecting their feelings and empathy as much as they please, or remaining aloof and protected. They can enjoy as much as they please. Soaps are the Land of Cockaigne, the Big Rock Candy Mountain of present-day Americans. No wonder they are so attractive and people are so obsessed by them. No wonder that if one starts watching them, he or she is hooked. No wonder also those who do not watch the soaps condemn them so harshly. They represent a kind of life that the Elitists (those representing the Puritan work ethic) cannot abide because in Soapland, all people are affluent, leisured and equal — not leveled down, but leveled *up* to equality. All people are going to heaven; or *are already there*.

Often elite critics draw the analogy of TV with literature, with education rather than with entertainment. Although we like to analogize and although we tend to associate one art form with another, we should realize that TV is not literature. It is a medium of communication more nearly like talk or gossip than anything else. Literature, despite its advocates who insist that it is "serious," is also primarily designed for entertainment rather than education, but through another medium.

To take TV seriously one does not have to equate it with another form. And if we do we should not misassign roles to both. Although we have properly assigned the role of education to books, as at least a part of their possible use, and although the transmission of knowledge was an early role of books, they are not even primarily for education. Books are a medium of communication — to be used any and every way communication can be used — and *primarily* as a means of amusement and entertainment, as are theater, drama, ballet, opera, etc. There is every reason we should take our entertainment seriously — but not too seriously. It took Americans a hundred and fifty years to learn to play; it may take us another hundred to learn to enjoy play rather than to participate self-indulgently, or to get the critics to allow us to enjoy it. A Roper public opinion poll of June 18, 1981 indicated that TV is second only to the family as a source of enjoyment. Such an attitude is bound to excite cries of social and educational apocalypse among critics who see in such interest in TV the downfall of America.

Our inability to enjoy play perhaps parallels our shortsighted understanding of television. Horace Newcomb, one of our insightful TV critics, thinks, "our fears about television, no matter how healthy or well founded, have restricted the development of a critical climate for television."[4] He is surely correct. And this fear is aided and abetted by a more fundamental and deep-seated academic elitist complex, which has inhibited our appreciation of and development in TV as in all other esthetics.

Lawrence Laurent, in "Wanted: The Complete Television Critic," calls for the critic who will "Stand above the boiling turmoil while he plunges into every controversy as a social critic and guardian of standards."[5] Such a watchdog attitude, and such language, although half-liberated, is also half-imprisoned. Before one can guard standards they should know what they are, and one who is inclined to want to *guard* standards rather than *promote* them (whatever they are) may be a half-dangerous person. Often, to paraphrase the learned 18th century lexicographer Samuel Johnson, the cry of guarding standards is fundamentally a fight for privilege and power, a defensive position of the haves against the have-nots, so as not to have to divide the goodies. It is the defensive posture of the bluebloods, the bluestockings, the FFV, DAR and others against sharing with the masses or with the *nouveau riche* or rich media barons. Obviously it pays to be alert, for everybody to a certain extent is a fox in the henhouse, but the position and motivation of the elitists should be understood for what they are, no matter how subtle, so that they can be more efficiently countered, for regardless of whatever "good" they may promote they also are anchors which retard growth and advancement.

The elitists have justified and defended their position in the Western world since at least the days of Plato. It is interesting that Graecophiles have long insisted that the Athenian populace of Plato's day was so sophisticated that one could go down on the street and pick up a group of citizens at any time and have them march to the theater and put on a production of Aeschylus or Euripides. But paradoxically Graecophiles also agree with Plato when he called his contemporaries "oxen of the world." Plato, we should not forget, like most elitists, had a position to protect.

This *guarding standard* against the "canaille," as they were called in the French Revolution, the "Swinish Multitude" as Edmund Burke called them during the American Revolution and the "mass" as people call them today, has had many protagonists throughout Western history. In 17th century England, for example, when the illiterate asked to be taught to read and write, the privileged elite tried to deny them both skills because they felt that the ability to read and write would ruin people as servants. They were finally first allowed to learn to read because it was felt that as long as they could not write they could be kept as servants. Then, as now, it was felt that the pen was mightier than the eye.

The importance of entertainment as a means of subjugation could be illustrated a thousand times. For example, in England in 1760 there was presented a play named *High Life Below Stairs*, which was something like our TV drama, *Upstairs, Downstairs*. The purpose of the earlier play was to demonstrate the threat of giving common people the right to lead their own lives. "The whole play was a moralizing satire, showing servants extravagantly entertaining when their master was away, stealing from him while aping the manners of high society." And in the theater, "The whole race of domestic gentry … were in a rage at what they conceived would be their ruin" as presented by the play. But servants in the gallery at the presentation of the play bitterly resented the effort of the playwright to picture them as unredeemed and unredeemable, and hissed and groaned and threw handfuls of halfpence onto the stage. When this play was presented in Edinburgh, seventy footmen threatened to burn down the theater if the play went on. The gentlemen in the pit called out to them to be silent or that they otherwise would be turned out and never permitted to enter the playhouse again. At a meeting following the uproar over the presentation of the play, the gentlemen decided "The spirit of independence had to be crushed by making servants more dependent on their masters."[6] In much the same way elitists use esthetics today; these early British elitists were using entertainment to keep people out of the ring of enjoyment. Today the elitists tell the "mass" that what they like is "junk."

Through the years this proprietary and snobbish attitude through necessity has modified somewhat, but the reasons for its existence have lain under a dangerously thin appearance of democracy, never giving in, never abnegating its claim to the control of society, allowing the "popular" aspects of entertainment—letting the mob have their circuses and hippodromes—but always insisting that the elitists with their superior tastes are protecting the mass from themselves.

The nineteenth century British poet and essayist Matthew Arnold, who dreamed of a golden era when culture was considered to be the best thoughts of mankind most beautifully expressed, has had his latter-day followers in America. Perhaps one of the most blatant was the high priest Englishman F.R. Leavis who wrote in a small pamphlet, *Mass Civilization and Minority Culture* (1930) that the small minority of proper critics in the world "Constitute the consciousness of the race" and must save the world from "popular fiction" and other damning influences. "Art," he insisted, is "the storehouse of recorded values and in consequence there is a relationship between the quality of the individual's response to art and his general fitness for a humane existence." T.S. Eliot feared that "popular literature" was the most powerful and pernicious and long-lasting influence of all. If he were alive today he would surely have discovered that television is infinitely more pervasive and powerful.

It is hard to imagine that such anachronistic and unreal attitudes still prevail among intelligent people, but they do—and widely. The cry of standards tends to restrain us all, undoubtedly inhibiting or preventing the production of much powerful and enjoyable art.

The otherwise perceptive critic Robert Warshow, in dealing with the question, was hoisted upon his own petard. In talking about the movies he led himself up an unfortunately golden path: "I have not brought Henry James to the movies or the movies to Henry James, but I hope that I have shown that the man who goes to the movies is the same as the man who reads Henry James."[7] Warshow was wrong: they are not the same man or woman, and never will be. To think that they are or to wish that they were is in fact imputing an importance to James that he never had and never deserved, and insulting the people by telling them that they should strive to rise to Henry James. Most viewers of movies and television would agree with Mark Twain that James was writing for the few and should be left to those who want him.

Most of the people who watch TV do not read James' novels and did not care for the recent PBS production of James' books. In such a work as the TV production of *The Golden Bowl*, for example, there was so little life that the director had to introduce a Greek-like chorus to interpret the inactivity. H.L. Mencken was certainly correct in believing that James suffered from looking to the Old World instead of the American West, the Frontier, for models of life. James is not grist for the TV mills. James belongs not to commercial television or even to the Public Broadcasting System, where although they are billed as "Masterpiece Theatre," the finest productions are of popular works, such as Neville Shute's *A Town Like Alice*, or "The Duchess of Duke Street." James belongs in a small theater for a small audience. The James mentality if it got around too widely could kill all popular art, especially television! And that move must be resisted.

Humanity has always resisted the bogus cry of standards imposed upon them by the privileged. In 1381 in England John Ball used anonymous lines of poetry to speak to the unwashed in Wat Tyler's rebellion and protest against privilege:

> When Adam delved and Eve span
> Who was then a gentleman?

Throughout American history the masses — the people who supported the theater and all kinds of entertainment — rebelled against being told what they should like. In the 1840s, for example, the uninhibited working-class audiences used lusty cheers and catcalls to force off the stage the material they did not like and to invite on that which they approved. A democratically inclined reviewer of the time felt that this was precisely as it should be. An author in the New York *Mirror*, March 9, 1833, applauded this assertion of "rights": "It is the American people who support the theatre, and this being the case, the people have an undoubted right to see and applaud who they please and we trust their right will never be relinquished. No Never!"[8]

During the last half of the nineteenth century, when thousands of immigrants were pouring into this country and making it look "un-American," the Americans who had come somewhat earlier, with apparent highest motives, insisted that the immigrants dress, eat, talk, sing, furnish their houses, use wallpaper like that of other Americans,' and otherwise become "Americanized." In the 1920s when these and similar immigrants and working-people preferred the cheap nickelodeons to the more expensive legitimate stage, the guardians of American standards tried to dissuade them by condemning the entertainment form. The privileged — those in power — never give up trying to maintain their positions. They try to take enjoyment out of entertainment by calling everything the underprivileged like inferior.

TV is obviously the most powerful distributor of entertainment-education developed so far. It is the greatest democratizer of the arts. It is not leveling down but *up*. It is mixing all the arts and showing that virtually all can be enjoyed by nearly everybody. Roger Rollin, a critic of real perception, insists half-seriously that the only real authority on esthetics is not the critic but the people. In the popular arts, he states, the rule is "one person — one vote."[9] In fact, Rollin should have been quite serious. The people will have their way. The elitists have always tried to control the media because they know that privileged people to maintain their control must control the means of communication. They tried in music, books, newspapers, movies, and now television. But they have lost in all media. The people who pay the producer will call the production.

TV is not raising or lowering standards. Standards, like beauty, have always been merely what people say they are; there never has been an absolute standard or esthetic; they are artificial and fluid. Television is merely broadening and enriching standards. To a certain extent this is because most critics are becoming more humane and more human in their understanding and evaluation of the popular arts, especially television. But mainly it is because the viewing public is having less and less to do with the critics. The public does their own thinking and allows the critics to talk to one another. They do not represent the consensus point of view. The critics, therefore, because they are losing their constituency and therefore their means of financial — and ego — support are running after the people trying to agree with them.

Still there is a legitimate place for the critic if he or she can locate it and find it comfortable and tenable. "Everyone their own critic," although not a new dictum, is not a bad rule of thumb. But we need a word to substitute for *critic*, which unfortunately still has negative overtones. *Evaluator* might be a more useful term. Any TV esthetics, or esthetics for any arts, must be protected from the phony ones imposed from the outside, by people who have selfish purposes to serve. We should insist that esthetics be natural, humane, and that they be for culture in the large, the *popular* sense. Perhaps the words of Robert Coles, psychologist and Pulitzer Prize winning author, should be engraved on the TV set and typewriter of every critic: "The humanities [and esthetics] belong to no one kind of person; they are part of the lives of ordinary people, who have their own various ways of struggling for coherence, for a compelling faith, for social vision, for an ethical position, for a sense of historical perspective."[10]

We may be approaching that state in America. If so it may well be because TV led the way into a human, loose, sensible esthetic sharply different from and superior to that held in this country before the full impact of television burst the restraining cords that repressed esthetics and allowed privilege to manipulate the media to their own advantage.

Notes

1. Often life imitates art but art never replicates life; at best it can merely suggest and intensify.
2. Developed first in his book *The Six-Gun Mystique* (Bowling Green, Ohio: Popular Press, 1970).
3. Dennis Porter, "Soap Time: Thoughts on a Commodity Art Form," *College English*, April 1977, p. 783.
4. Horace Newcomb, *Television: The Critical View*, 2nd ed. (New York: Oxford, 1979), p. xv.
5. Quoted in Newcomb, p. xvi.
6. Alan Ereira, *The People's England* (London and Boston: Routledge & Kegan Paul, 1981), p. 4.1.
7. Quoted in Newcomb, p. xx.
8. Quoted in Francis Hodge, *Yankee Theatre: The Image of America on the Stage, 1825–1950* (Austin, Texas, 1964).

9. *Journal of Popular Culture*, 9:2 Fall 1975, 335–365.

10. *Editor's Note*: The original publication includes the citation marker but omits the citation itself. It is likely Robert Coles, *The Mind's Fate: Ways of Seeing Psychiatry and Psychoanalysis* (Boston: Atlantic Monthly, 1975).

8

The Face of the Hero in Democracy*

Browne's interest in the "hero" extends from his early considerations of folklore and literature. In literature he wrote numerous times about the figure of the hero. Early in his career he paid special attention to concept of hero as it applied to key works by Melville and Twain. Later, he turned his attention to the hero as a more general and iconic cultural figure, contributing to and editing multiple volumes on the subject. Simultaneously he was considering the heroic aspects of the detective in popular crime fiction, also writing extensively on that subject, an interest that culminated again in multiple volumes.

Throughout his work, Browne was intrigued by the seeming paradox of the role of the hero in a democracy. In an egalitarian system that is based on equality, why do we need to set heroes above us? Is that why so many American genre fiction heroes, such as the cowboy-gunman and the hard-boiled detective, exist on the fringes of society, with no real place within it, somehow both "of" and "apart from"? And what of the masked vigilante heroes such as the Lone Ranger, Batman, Spider-Man, etc.?

This essay is edited from two pieces, an article and a book chapter, where Browne turns his investigations to the role of the hero, both fictional and real, in American democracy. After an early brief nod to Joseph Campbell, Browne takes on the distinction between actual heroes and celebrities in a mass-media culture, concluding that the differences are merely of degree and not of kind. Note the interesting McLuhanistic digression in this section.

After explicating the standard idea that a culture gets the heroes it needs, Browne puts for the intriguing idea that a mature democracy may not need heroes at all—at least not as conventionally defined. As he develops his explanations, Browne echoes the ideas of anthropologist Leslie White, opting for a sort of cultural determinism, if the culture needs something, it will have it, and the "great heroes" are the vessels used by the culture. Browne's argument then arrives at the point where the people of a mature democratic culture, instead of creating heroic projections, are able to function without them.

Heroes serve as models and leaders of people and nations because they reflect the projection of the consensus of the dreams, fantasies, and self-evaluations and needs of individuals and of society itself. Heroes like a lens concentrate the power of people, of a nation and serve as the muscle for the movement and development of a people, which they epitomize. In a simple society such as that reflected in the *Epic of Gilgamesh* (3,000 B.C.) or the Greeks' Odysseus, they are simple and straightforward, tending, in the words of Joseph Campbell, to be "monomyths," serving definite and clear purposes in society.

In more complicated societies, however, heroes wear many faces because of their many

*Professor Roger Rollin and I independently arrived at virtually the same conclusions about the status and development of the modern hero as discussed in the early parts of this essay.— Ray Browne

responses to the numerous needs of individuals, groups of people and national purposes. As the needs get more complicated, so too do the heroes; as people get more sophisticated the heroes become less modeled on the conventional demi-gods of the past, less clear-cut and obvious.

In a volatile and swiftly moving society like the present, heroes undergo rapid transformation, frequently developing in ways and for purposes not immediately apparent. Contemporary American heroes, existing in a highly technological society and driven by the electronics of mass communication, change quickly. But they are no less genuine and serve no less an important purpose than their counterparts of old.

In our day the hero still has the conventional body and soul of his predecessors, still serves the mythological purpose of helping to explain ourselves to ourselves and helps us maintain a stability and national purpose, but appears in different guises. The hero, as outlined by Northrop Frye, Freud, Jung, Lord Raglan, and dozens of others, has developed the thousand faces, as recorded by Joseph Campbell, into *thousands* of faces, and the number is growing. These are genuine heroes, as useful as those of old. They are not so stable, so formulaic, so stereotyped as those of conventional mythological proportions of old, but they are essentially the old heroes tailored to suit different peoples. Gods can live only by filling the needs of the society they serve; otherwise they become relics, useful only in studies of origins and the past. They cannot serve living purposes for the living.

To a large extent, naturally, modern heroes are developments, though not inventions, of the technological media simply because the media are our present-day means of communication. To many observers the media create *celebrities* not *heroes*. Daniel Boorstin, an elitist negative evaluator of the media, feels the hero was a being who achieved something, the celebrity merely a name. As he cleverly phrases it: "The hero was a big man; the celebrity is a big name." Elaborating on the celebrity, Boorstin says: "The celebrity is a person who is known for his well-knownness."[1] The tense in Boorstin's verb is significant. Apparently he feels that, as the Bible says, there were giants in the earth in the old days but there can be none in our time.

There is, of course, some validity in the observation, but it has its limitations. The hero-celebrity schism is more the tool of the phrasemaker than of actuality. It is something like the unfortunate term "fake-lore" that folklorist Richard M. Dorson coined early in his career to try to distinguish between genuine and "specious" folklore (folklore being of the people, "fakelore" a commercialization of the genuine article) and remained trapped by the term for most of his academic life though in his later years he admitted that the difference, insofar as there is one, is not similar to his distinction and far more subtle. The difference between the hero and the celebrity is largely artificial except in definition. Both exist on a continuum, and there are much of both in each. True, most heroes have done something, something perhaps even "heroic" in the old sense of the word. But not all. Contrary to Boorstin's assertion not all heroes have done something, or even exist. Paul Bunyan, for instance, patron saint of loggers, and especially of people who are not loggers, has been for over half a century the hero of woodsmen. Giant in size, boisterous, independent, generally indifferent to the niceties of logging, Bunyan epitomized what people think is the spirit of the logger. But he never existed. Created by a logging company in Westwood, California, because the management needed a logo, Bunyan, because he was needed by the folklore of the loggers, assumed mythological proportions, no matter what his origins. Other heroes have their proportions puffed by the popular media. Abraham Lincoln, surely one of our greatest heroes, was created partially through the "mass media" of his day: the dime-books, the songsters, the joke books, the burlesque books, newspapers, and every form of popular culture. The hero almost always stands on a platform of his own making or that created by others, often of dissembling and deceit.

Most heroes, it goes without saying, have done less than they have received credit for — regardless of their time of action. An excellent case in point was Johnny Appleseed (John Chapman), patron saint and hero of the Ohio Valley in the nineteenth century. Johnny was heroized for having walked from one end of the Ohio Valley to the other distributing what the people needed most — material to read, conversation and gossip and apple trees. Born and raised in Fort Wayne, Indiana, Johnny worked in a fruit nursery and apparently did sell apple trees. But he hardly planted the Valley by tossing apple seeds hither and yon as he wandered about like a scholar-benefactor of old since apple trees are not planted from seed. Johnny Appleseed did not quite fill the role that mythologizers created for him.

All heroes are more the products of "press agents" than of their own actions. Likewise, many celebrities have accomplished *more* than their press agents and negative commentators will allow them to get credit for. Nineteenth-century Davy Crockett is a good illustration. Despite the fact that he was largely a product of slick East Coast puffery he was a real hero to Tennesseans and frontiersmen and to the millions who have known the story of the fall of the Alamo. In the 1970s and 1980s, Alan Alda was a celebrity for his role in the television show *M*A*S*H* but a hero to many individuals because of his stand against the insanity of war. Billie Newman (Linda Kelsey), the very modest and quiet female star reporter of the television production *The Lou Grant Show*, assumed heroic proportions to many people who saw her as a leader in women's fight to attain equal rights.

In the argument over the proper media for the development of the hero, it is hardly realistic to ask that heroes be self-developed. The *true* hero, is, presumably, too much interested with being heroic to publicize himself, and often his acts of heroism are too private and unnoticed ever to be known by anyone. There are, to paraphrase the English poet Thomas Grey, many heroes "born to blush unseen and waste their sweetness on the desert air." For example, Lenny Skutnik, the government worker who happened along in January 1982 when the Air Florida airplane which had just taken off from the Washington National airport plunged into the Potomac and dived in to save a woman who was obviously drowning, would have gone unnoticed had not television cameras been there and wanted to turn him into a celebrity; Skutnik was embarrassed and felt that the media were making too much of his somewhat involuntary act of heroism. Chances are had the media not been present Skutnik would have received a brief and evanescent recognition by the people present, would probably have been discussed for a few days by the witnessing people, might even possibly have had a song written about him or a tale told about him, but his exploit would have received limited circulation. The media, however, made him known to everyone and in so doing, although they may have burned out the hero himself, made his heroic deed a part of American life, re-stating one of the fundamental principles of American mythology — that Americans are unselfish, willing to give to, or even to die for, other people.

Romantics and folklorists (especially library romantics and folklorists) think that heroism is circulated exclusively by word of mouth. Such an attitude is hardly tenable. Heroes have always been created by the media available at the time. If the operating medium is the bard around the campfire talking or singing of the deeds of someone on the hunt, that is the existing form of mass communication. If it is the illustrated manuscript of pre–movable type days, that is the means of communication. If it is the newspaper or the dime novel — or the TV camera — that is the means of mass communication. If it is today's gossip, then that is the means of communication. The main difference among all the media is one of intensity. Some burn cool and relaxed; some are hot and hurried. In the cool media the hero takes a long time developing and therefore can last a long time because his fire, never very hot, remains banked and can be drawn forth when needed. In the hotter media the life expectancy is much shorter. The hero serves his purpose and is then passed over, being left in the minds and hearts of the populace if he merits it, for a newer model. The media do not destroy so much as they just pass over. Like the eighteenth century deistic belief of God as creator who wound a cosmic clock and then sat back to see it unwind, they create and then move on.

Conventional definitions of the hero as necessarily demi-god are based on very little faith in the people the hero serves. They assume that the hero cannot survive in the light of reality in a democratic and technological society. There is, of course, a lot of hocus-pocus and mystery about the role of the hero. It is axiomatic that the more ignorant the society, the more heroic the hero. The needs of society demand and often want less than full revelation of the facts about the hero. No doubt had there been news media present when Odysseus returned to Ithaca from his odyssey, newsmen would have told him that it was poor navigating to spend ten years wandering around in the small lake of the eastern Mediterranean, and they would have suspected that his adventures among the unnatural creatures and gods and goddesses for ten years were merely an excuse to stay away from home. But had they searched around for background and in-depth interpretation they would have been able to confirm that the voyage, meaning more than it seemed, was symbolic and mythological and therefore *true*. More actuality about the voyage would not have destroyed its meaning but it would have made it less elevated, and greater circulation might have terminated its importance sooner, though it would not have negated its importance. In our own history, for example, Thomas Jefferson's stature as American hero has not been diminished, except among some of the Jefferson-cultists, by Fawn Brodie's revelation that he had a long-time affair with Sally Hemings, his slave, and had several children by her. America's Camelot of the early 1960s may have been strengthened not weakened in the long run by more closely associating it with the mythological world of King Arthur, through the revelations that John F. Kennedy, like Lancelot of old, had his Guineveres traipsing up and down the backstairs of the White House. And probably the late President Lyndon B. Johnson will withstand the revelations of his biographer, Robert Caro, that he was far less than a perfect man.

To assume that the people of a modern, technologized nation are too simple minded, too thoughtless to be able to appreciate a hero, warts and all, is to underestimate both the importance of the hero and the intelligence of the people. In an advanced civilized nation there is less room for and patience with the misty, part fake-phony hero, the anthropological culture hero of the past, because there is less dependence placed on him, people have less need for demi-gods. The kind of hero that is still needed — the down-to-earth, realistic role model — still serves contemporary society. To serve society, the individual needs to be known. The people in their slow but ultimate wisdom will recognize the difference between the heroic and the well-knownness and distinguish between the hero and the mere celebrity. And the hero will benefit.

Sometimes the media instead of casting too much light, cast too little, instead of over-exploiting, they under exploit. For example, Henry Ford, who along with Thomas A. Edison was the hero of the first half of the twentieth century, suffered from underexposure on at least one point. In explaining what he thought was the proper presentation of history, Ford said that if history were not a record of the common, instead of the elite, aspects of life, it was incorrect and therefore, in the words that were picked up by everyone, "history is bunk." Quoted out of context, he was thought an ignoramus, when in fact had his full attitude and statement been publicized he would have been celebrated and become more heroic because he was merely stating what was felt by many people and groups (the Italian Futurists, for example, who believed that art ought to brought out of the museums and given back to the people). Annoyed with the exclusive and therefore false interpretation of elite historians, Ford created Greenfield Village in Dearborn, Michigan, and demonstrated his (now recognized as a proper and useful) view of a enlightened way to record and study history.

Heroes, somewhat like fads though of longer life, come and go. They are "in" and they are "out." They are "national" in influence or local. The Puritans of New England are not much revered these days; sometimes one has to remind the untutored of the greatness of Benjamin Franklin; and only the specialist knows of the heroic exploits of Israel Potter during the Revolutionary War.

But the hero, even the transient heroes, still represent on a passing or eternal scale, a star in the distance, bigger than life and bright enough to attract imitation. They still serve as chinning bars on which are exercised the hopes and aspirations of individuals, groups and nations.

Heroes can by nature be either conservative or radical; can serve as havens of refuge or as sharp swords to draw the blood of progress. As stereotype and formula they have two edges, the drag edge and the cutting edge. Both serve useful purposes as counterbalancing weights to keep the pendulum of society from running amok and swinging too far either way.

Therefore at present, although they might be somewhat obscured by the glare of different types, there still exist many of the old heroes— Lincoln, Kennedy, FDR, Walter Reuther, and the like. But especially in the 1960s and 1970s a people tired of the old created new heroes: Elvis Presley, the Beatles, Jane Fonda, and particularly Martin Luther King, Jr., and many others. They were the new image of the role of America in the world at a time when people, goaded by the frustration of the war in Vietnam and fired by a genuine feeling of outrage at the immorality of war, demanded change. The old heroes tended to represent invalid ways of looking at things, of models for behavior.

The heroes of change have tended to become less important than they had been in more rebellious times. Heroes, as well as celebrities, suffer the vagaries of becoming anachronistic, and the energies that drove those in the 60s and 70s and the people supporting them, for better or worse, are burned out and banked. Society is indifferent to the supposed injustices, which articulated the heroes of those two earlier decades. Now, instead, people seem to have other purposes, other goals, and the heroes must correspondingly change. For example, in the early 1980s there was a rebirth of political, economic and religious conservatism of the right wing, more pragmatic and less idealistic than of old.

Heroes come in different sizes at different stages in a nation's development. When a nation is admittedly young and naive, heroes stand ten feet tall. But when the people are more advanced, more sophisticated, more cynical, they like their heroes more of their own size — or at times even the reverse scale of anti–heroism. In the more sophisticated societies the heroes serve more as only role models.

In the world today different societies still have various mythologies and heroes, all very strange to people of other groups. If it is true in the present world, where, despite the obvious vast differences among societies, there are fewer major differences than there have been in the history of mankind, try to imagine how vastly and unrecognizably different the mythologies and heroes have been throughout history. The wonders that Marco Polo saw on his trip to Cathay pale into sameness when one considers the differences throughout history. Obviously heroes had many faces.

It is unrealistic then to imagine that the heroes and mythologies of old have not had to be stretched mightily and completely modernized, to make them serve the needs of the present, when technology has made the world more different now from anything of the past than at any other time in history. Heroes and heroines have thousands of faces. With the obvious changes in the function and appearances of heroes and heroines, it seems clear that it is time to change and modernize definitions. Failure to do is being unrealistic and blind to the function of the form in society.

What then, might we expect from the face, form, and function of the American hero to be? If we are correct in our assessment that as societies change, so do their heroes, we may also be correct in asserting that the historical definition of the role of heroes is out of date in our democracy, or perhaps one day may be.

A democracy grows beyond the need for the conventional hero. Historically the hero has been a servant of the people, has tried to wrest privilege from the powerful and give it to the powerless. For example, Prometheus stole fire from Zeus and gave it to the people. Dionysius gave civilization to people through wine. Thus the hero, the hero-god, was created to help mankind escape the restrictions imposed by human nature. Historically and culturally, heroes and heroines have encouraged the development of mankind. They have been used as chinning bars on which people can strengthen their spirits and their culture, raise themselves above their environs so that they can see farther and escape those who seem to be holding them down and back.

Although heroes have always seemed to be held in high repute, above and superior to the common body of mankind, actually they have played a somewhat different role. They have occupied the position that Confucius's wise monarch should have occupied, of being, though superior, the wise servant of the people, although the hero has been wiser than the good monarch and often has served a much greater role.

The hero has known that his power flowed from recognition by the people and that therefore he had to serve them. Thus, though the hero has stood with his head in the clouds, his hands have been working for the good of mankind.

In a curious and seemingly paradoxical way the heroes have always been inferior to the people they served and subject to the people's granting of status and power. Heroes exist only so long as the people grant them superiority; vote them into office if you like. Once that license has been withdrawn, the heroes lose their power, their recognition, and their status. They become historical references and has-beens.

That's extraordinarily important. In their role then as stepladder, heroes have allowed mankind to climb toward something, and to feel superior to them; at the same time the heroes serve as a means by which a superior force descends to the world of humankind.

Up to a certain stage in a nation's development this two-way traffic is important. Growing boys and girls and growing nations apparently need role models, people and heroes they can look up to and emulate.

In such roles heroes and heroines serve useful purposes. But in the life of every person and nation there should come a time when these models of emulation should no longer be needed, should in fact act to inhibit and stifle rather than to develop.

When their rite of passage has been accomplished, people need to put away their youth and their immaturity. As one line from a certain good book said, "When I was a child I spake as a child, I acted as a child. But when I became an adult I put away childish things." In other words, heroes and superheroes, heroines and superheroines are really kid stuff and should hold no place in a properly educated and mature democracy.

A properly educated and mature democracy has no need for and no use for heroes and heroines. The people are able to stand on their own two feet and face reality, not try to hide their faces in nostalgia and make-believe and stand in the tracks and the shadow of superior people.

Theoretically, at least, a properly educated and mature democracy should not fear the present and the future and is not ravaged by emotional stress and anxiety. In fact, one could say axiomatically that the degree to which a people fear the present and the future is the degree to which they cater to heroes and heroines.

A culture can tyrannize itself and tie itself down with this use of heroes and heroines. But there's a far greater and more terrifying purpose that heroes and heroines serve. They can be party to the abuse of people. That is, the power brokers in society, the sophisticates who are, as they think, superior to all the heroic forces, are glad to use and abuse the concept and reputation and terrifying forces of heroes to manipulate the people who still believe in them.

The concept and device are age-old. People not subject to the power of certain ideas and forces, those who stand safely outside, use the assumed power of the force to keep in bondage those people who still believe in it.

The practice is as old and vicious as selling snake oil, a useless mixture sold as medicine. The mere naming of the snake oil and the ingredients make it magic by implication. So what's in a name? Everything. All the power and magic that people will allow to be forced into it; the more richly resonant the name can be made, the more it can be used and abused.

In addition to the rich resonance, names are endowed with the power of the abbreviated symbol. Originally, names, like those wonderful forty-word titles of books in the eighteenth century, were often comprehensive and revealing summaries. But people nowadays like short names and short titles. And just as brevity is the soul of wit, it is also the smoke and mirrors of disguise, deception, and abuse. Names are wrappers that can surround all kinds of poison, of flags, which can signal all kinds of misinformation. Often outside forces manipulate these names and symbols for their own purposes. Personal names, especially those that resonate with power and have echoed through the corridors of time, encrust themselves with magic and innuendo and become the most awesome and misleading of all.

In fact, we can safely say that every name, especially those of heroes, is loaded with pseudo-facts, outright falsifications, and the potential for corruption. People generally don't live up to the potential in their names. Names breed exaggeration and abuse.

So the concept of the hero in all societies is filled with make-believe, no matter how useful that make-believe might be, and is fraught with the potential of self-serving abuse. In a well-educated and mature democracy, the concept should be recognized for what it is and discontinued, as being no longer needed. If the concept of hero is needed, then the mantle should be placed where it belongs. Not on the shoulders of single individuals, but on the real heroes, the people. Heroes don't make history; they don't move mountains. People do the moving and the naming, but heroes get the credit.

It is particularly distressing to have history load all the glory, almost never the infamy, of so-called great events on the shoulders of individuals who generally don't deserve it. It is imperative that we move the bit players to center stage. They are the heroes. The nominal stars are only the players.

Let me give you two examples, safely from ancient history. Those of us who make heroes of the warlords who caused the building of the Great Wall of China turn history and reason upside down and shake out the wrong conclusions. It is said that every stone laid in the Great Wall cost the life of one worker. Some people are recognizing that credit, if that is the word, for the wall must be spread among those who physically built it, not the ones who sat in their castles and ordered it. For example, the editors of the book *Popular Culture in Late Imperial China* say, "The emphasis on the elite in Chinese history has led to grave distortions in our visions of Chinese history and culture, distortions that can only be remedied by serious systematic study of the world beyond the boundaries of the ruling class."

Let's take another example, which because of its opulence and wealth has become everybody's favorite during the last couple of decades, the pharaoh Tutankhamen. Tutankhamen apparently lived a short life of tyranny and opulence, and he was not the hero of his age. His tomb and the symbols of tyranny and robbery surrounding his sarcophagus do not make him a hero of ours. That has been done by the elitist archaeologists of today who when they open a tomb run for the gold. They are interested in the opulent and golden symbols of power and wealth. But gold ornaments do not cover the true heroes. The heroes, on the contrary, were the thousands of workers whom he exploited for his own glory, those people who endured the shifting sands of time and died in the process. Today there are at least four thousand mummies of Tutankhamen's contemporaries extant, in the sand surrounding the Egyptian pyramids. From x-rays of the mummies we can tell the number of children the women had, the diseases everybody suffered from, the food they ate, the causes of death. Often only Egyptologists and mummologists are interested in those nondescript mummies. But those thousands, not Tutankhamen, are the real heroes of the day. They should have precedence over Tutankhamen as the real heroic people of the time.

In our own country and especially in our own time, we should be careful how we place the mantle of heroics on individuals. Individuals are less creators of their age than they are creations of and spokesman for that age; if Thomas Paine had not written *Common Sense*, somebody else would have and stated the same principles. If Thomas A. Edison had not developed the electric light somebody else would have — in fact, Nikola Tesla did so when Edison refused the use of his patents. People were hopping all around the skies when Charles Lindbergh flew solo to Paris.

To admit these facts is not to diminish the feat of the individual, but only to put it in perspective. Heroes are as often pushed forward by the wave of events, as they are creators of the waves. Thus, in our chronicles and descriptions of heroes, we should be careful to give credit where credit is due, to recognize the proper heroes.

If I were looking for a title to properly describe the heroes of the American Civil War, for example, I would not choose the title *Lincoln Agonistes*. A better title would be *The Civil War and Lincoln*. But an even better one would be *The People of America During the Civil War*. There must be even more encompassing titles which would knit together the ragged edges of truth and reality. It is, I think, improper and perhaps dangerously erroneous to put the spotlight only on Lincoln, no matter how great his accomplishment in holding the nation together.

Thus, we should do away with the station of individual hero and heroine with its superiority and inferiority. For in every hierarchy there is a "lowerarchy" which tiers people into layers of importance and unimportance. At its silliest, the notion of the hierarchy leads to royal watching. At its best it provides an incentive for everybody to climb the ladder. But there is no excuse for the rungs of the ladder somehow to be reserved for the strong and powerful.

The concept of hero is large and strong enough for all to become heroic in mind and spirit, if not in wealth and fame. And I am convinced, again I emphasize, that in a properly educated and mature America, there would be no need of heroes and superheroes. The concept is contrary to the things we Americans as a nation must hold dear and desirable. The ultimate conclusion, of course, is that in a properly educated and mature America, we wouldn't be studying heroes except as historical subjects. In America the study of heroes is properly a historical subject rather than one for people looking into the future.

As historians we should study in a context of re-created life. We should re-create the life and culture in which the heroes and heroines existed. Otherwise we are in many ways distorting and misrepresenting the whole concept of heroes. Like Lincoln I'll stick with the people rather than the academics, the intellectuals, who often create papier-mâché heroes that don't last long or use criteria that are too subtle and unreal. The people, on the other hand, collectively know what they want. We hear warnings that people should not be allowed to create their own heroes; they know not what they do, what they need. But their concepts, their movements, their institutions are no worse or weaker than the intellectuals', whose may be high-sounding but surely lack the legitimization of consensus— and consensus is the backbone of creation and perpetuation of heroes and the concepts of heroes.

All heroes are figures of fantasy. The only hero who is not a figure of fantasy is that person who sees somebody in trouble, relieves him of that trouble, and then goes silently on his way. We never know the event. It is never recorded. We never know the name of the hero. Recall the earlier example of Lenny Skutnik and how he might not have been known had the media not been present.

Now, it seems that most people who do an extraordinary deed call a press conference. That's the way heroes are created and live these days. And ultimately the heroes' purposes are ulterior, used for their ego or for self-aggrandizement. If we are going to have heroes in their proper place in a democratic society, sooner or later we need to get to the point where the press is so wise that when the person who does a heroic deed calls a press conference nobody comes. The press doesn't need the copy and we the public do not need the news. The force of the concept of heroism is recognized and taken for granted. Therefore we do not need it individualized and demonstrated.

The names of individuals, although they are easy to put in the pantheon and remember, don't identify the true heroes. The heroes are the forces that alter, change, keep together, animate, make us Americans, or whatever. They are the dynamics that remain heroic and are the result of the forces, which American cultures create and direct. They are the subjects we should study. And we forget the named individuals since they are merely the incarnations of the forces. If on the road to the generalizing of heroes into concepts one studies the individuals, then those individuals can only be properly studied in deep and full context, as nameplates on the forces.

As we read about the lives of heroes around us maybe we see some growing sophistication in the development of our individual heroes and heroines and of the cultures in which they live. If so, perhaps, just perhaps, they demonstrate that American society is weaning itself from the need for heroes, and in so doing illustrating that society can get along without them.

Perhaps, just perhaps, we are moving toward being so properly and sufficiently educated and mature that heroes are, or sooner or later will, become unnecessary in our society. Perhaps.

Notes

1. Daniel J. Boorstin, *The Image: A Guide to Pseudo, Events in America* (New York: Atheneum, 1977), pp. 57, 61.

9

The Theory-Methodology Complex: The Critics' Jabberwock

This article has its roots in the speech Browne presented at a special conference given at Bowling Green State University to honor him in 1992 at the time of his retirement from teaching. Browne had been accused of being "anti–theory" but as this piece makes clear, he was actually against the idea of latching on to some particular theory as the solution to all scholarly needs. Rather, Browne argues for an eclectic and pragmatic approach, the researcher freely picking and choosing what is most useful to the problem or issue at hand.

As something of a valedictory moment to an audience of supporters, Browne allows himself to review what he sees as the key tenets of the Popular Culture Studies movement's formative strengths, while warning against possible pitfalls if they are erroneously "outgrown." At one point, Browne reaches back to his own academic roots and fuses folklore studies and literary studies to exemplify a "non–theoretical" method of studying an element of popular culture. Relaxed among his peers, Browne sprinkles his dry, whimsical humor throughout the piece to joyous effect, including at least one well-known in-joke among PCA members, thereby making the effort into a pleasurable admonition.— The Editor

We are faced with the crucial question of the future of Popular Culture Studies. History demonstrates that, like family dynasties that in three generations go from rags to riches and back to rags, academic ideas and organizations go through three stages before they wither and fade away or continue to transform themselves with the needs of their undertaking. Surely Popular Culture Studies, the *Journal of Popular Culture*, and the Popular Culture Association should take caution and learn from the lessons of history. The three stages are revolution, conformity, and bureaucracy (ossification and decline).

The study of Popular Culture, at least in this era, began in a revolutionary time in a blaze of fire and heat in 1969. We were not, of course, as new and without precedent as we might have thought. Nineteenth-century American thinkers like Emerson and Thoreau had long before counseled Americans to cast aside foolish theories and methodologies as hobgoblins of little academic minds and invent our own wheels. Some academics— Vernon Louis Parrington and A.O. Lovejoy, to name only two— had demonstrated the value of studying new materials in new ways. Those of us who were interested in their intent (though not necessarily in their conclusions) saw the value in their kind of work and were determined to use the insight gained from their conclusions but not to follow them slavishly.

One thing we had learned was a useful application of our predecessors and colleagues' scholarship. George Santayana — or somebody — once observed that we all must remember the past or be forced to repeat it. We knew that one must do more than remember the past in order to benefit from any lessons it might teach — one must understand the past. We must be freed from what historian Calvin Luther Martin calls "history's hammerlock on our imagination." I would want to be also freed from scholarship's hammerlock on our imagination.

Scholars like to be disciples, as they like to have their own disciples. We like to clone our students, just as we have cloned ourselves after our imagined heroic predecessors. In so doing we potentially stunt what potential for creative scholarship we might have in the narrow confines of our predecessors' incomplete thinking and stifle whatever new contributions we might make. As much as I dislike invoking the shadow of past giants, it is pertinent to paraphrase one of them in saying that unexamined scholarship is not worth relying on. One of the more obvious examples of unanalyzed scholarship is our slavishly bringing ourselves to the Classics, to see our undeveloped brain eaten away every day by the vulture of unimaginative scholarship cowardice. We like to think that the Greeks experienced and thought about all the generalities ever to be faced by humankind. We like to believe that in ancient Greece one could go to the barbershop and saloons of Athens and pick up actors to play in Euripides' and Aeschylus's plays. Perhaps so. But our intellectual god of the time, Plato, who advocated a slave society, felt his fellow Greeks were riffraff and hated the democracy. Aristotle could not have known the complexities of the natural universe and if he knew all there is to be known about rhetoric, as many moderns feel, then a lot of researchers have wasted a lot of ink and paper in searching for new realities.

What this means is that academics often commit themselves to others' ideas long before they have thought for themselves. Lovejoy in *The Great Chain of Being* (1936) reminded us that we are not interested in ideas unless they come to us dressed in the most extravagant war paint. Ideas have to have been endorsed by the elite establishment before we can use them comfortably and continue to sift through their ashes long after they have been proved obvious nonsense. Many humanities scholars agree with Alan Gowans that every artifact is a microcosm that, properly read, can reveal a whole society. But artifacts of the past are bound to speak of the past. Historic cadavers and relics of the past, as relics of the past, should be left to archeologists and forensic scientists. But as voices of the past, teaching us of the past and the continuity with the present and the future, the relics can be as fresh as yesterday's testimonials.

Through the years Popular Culture scholars have tried to avoid the hammerlock of theories and methodologies in their approach to studying everyday life. We recognize that scholarship in American studies— some of us at least recognize it — may have hit its peak in theory and methodology when Henry Nash Smith suggested in the *American Quarterly* in 1957 that American Studies does not have, cannot find, and could not benefit from a single theory and methodology. To remind you he said "collaboration among men working from within existing academic disciplines but attempting to widen the bounds imposed by conventional methods of enquiry" might well be the best. He wanted to be entirely pragmatic about any new approaches. "A new method," he said, "will have to come piecemeal, through a kind of ... opportunism, in the course of daily struggles with our various tasks." From this, I take it, daily struggles would rule out highly esoteric and irrelevant theories and methodologies that titillated no one but academics.

So far only a few American Popular Culture scholars have been lured off the ship by the call of the sirens of the misty Edenic island. The bent finger of structuralism has seduced only a few, though we all know countless manifestoes, which announced that Structuralism is the key to all truth and understanding. Few have fallen for deconstruction, modernism, post–modernism, etc. and only a diminishing number of conservatives cling to the wisdom

of Karl Marx in the face of the collapse of the Soviet empire. It may be Stalinism that col-
lapsed, not Marxism, as many critics contend; but the sad thing is that it might really be
only academia that teeters on the edge. All the rest of us know that the rich and powerful
exploit the poor and the weak, the ethnic groups, African-Americans, women, and nation-
ality pockets. We have all observed that academic institutions and churches all take from
the poor in order to strengthen their positions. We have done it ourselves. So it is difficult
to understand why we must follow "authority" that tells us what we already know. It is
difficult to understand how academics spend all their time splitting the hairs of theories
and methodologies and then defending those pieces if we did not understand that by and
large academics have nothing better to do—and perhaps our talents are most appropriate
for doing and then defending the silly. Our talents are more appropriate for separation than
for binding together, for specializing than for generalizing, for arguing over definitions, for
example, of the meaning of the Humanities than for seeing the obvious and trying to understand the pieces when all have been put together. The current battle between the conservative
national Endowment of the Humanities and its allies and the relatively more "liberal," that
is "modern," Modern Language Association is an excellent case in point. The view presented
by these organizations was at first to discover and define the future but has now become a
bastion to define that, which is past.

Conservative Matthew Arnold, as nearly all of us agree, used poetry as an escape and
as a test of culture to prove himself superior to most other people. To him, learning was
only negatively pleasurable. Lynne Cheney, chairman of the NEH, because she did a Ph.D.
dissertation on Arnold, seems unable to shake his ghost from the cobwebs of her mind. To
her, the very last thing that learning literacy should be is fun. People, as we know, will do
anything to rationalize and justify their prejudices. Everybody has always known that we
do the jobs best that we enjoy doing and we learn most easily when learning is fun. *Mr.
Rogers' Neighborhood* and *Sesame Street* have demonstrated for a whole generation that fun
is the opening key to learning and literacy. Now book chains are practicing what mom-
and-pop bookstores have known all along; people like to browse and have fun in bookstores.
Now the chains are encouraging people to browse. According to *Newsweek* (May 18, 1992),
Barnes and Noble now have 17 of these "destination stores" as they are called, Crown has
16, Bookstop, 44 and Waldenbooks plans 20. The new statistics about book reading in America and literacy contradict many prejudices of conservative critics like Lynne Cheney,
William Bennett, and Allan Bloom, who like to maintain their superiority by keeping the
masses illiterate in reputation and fact. According to a *Newsweek* survey, 81 percent of adults
asked said they had read a book in the last year. Reading is the preferred leisure-time activity
of 25 percent of adult Americans; TV is preferred by 19 percent. Last year Americans spent
$7.9 billion for books according to the *Newsweek* survey, $21 billion according to an AP
report, while Americans going to the movies spent only $4.9 billion. Sales of children's
books more than doubled from 1985–91. Contrary to the prejudices and hopes of many,
romances and best sellers do not head the list of American's sales. Some stores report poetry,
business books, and cookbooks lead the lists and demonstrate that learning and the pleasure
of learning should not be kept from people. If learning and literacy can be made relevant,
people will be pleased to overcome their illiteracy.

In searching for the truth, we seem unable to do anything but nitpick and modify. In
a praised new book, for example, the author Colin Falck points out how Ferdinand de Saus-
sure's theories, "On whose insights into the nature of signs and language the greater part
of the French and American literary theory of the past two decades has rather perilously

come to depend" (4), must be modified or changed if we are to come to the real truth. Who has that real truth? Well, Falck himself, of course. The "true Post-Modernism," he says, must be based on the realization that poetry and prose (literature) of the heart reveal the reality of true life. Have we heard that song before? I think so. Theories and methodologies cancel one another out. What goes around comes around. The more theories and methodologies change, the more they remain the same. Always the newest faddish theory rides again, dressed in newly washed feathers.

We must ask ourselves where all this academic dust is leading us and who is seeding the gold mines in order to sell them. Many of us think that academic activity in the Humanities is generally a sophisticated parlor game that is leading us into irrelevancy and uselessness. Such an attitude has naturally been one of the objects of criticism and scorn by those theorists who have taken time off from reading the activity going on the heads of pins and excoriated those who are not so engaged. There is still a lot of conflict between what Jonathan Swift called the Big Endians and Little Endians. But the pendulum is swinging away from theorists and methodologists despite the newly coined crop that springs up around us yearly. Cambridge University, those of you who read *Newsweek* (May 18, 1992) will remember, just awarded an honorary doctorate of letters to Jacques Derrida, so-called father of the theory of deconstructionism — but only after a heated debate. One professor of philosophy, Hugh Mellor, echoed what many of us have thought all along in saying that Derrida "has to write more and more obscurely to disguise the fact that he has nothing to say." Unfortunately, many of the rest of us fall into the same charade.

The Chronicle of Higher Education, which seems to be a bellwether for trends in academia, has recently run articles, especially by historians, who are decrying blind dependence on theories and methodologies. In an article entitled "Debate Among Historians Signals Waning Influence of 'Discourse Theory' Outside Literary Studies," for example, by Linda Gordon, Professor of History, University of Wisconsin, Milwaukee, the *Chronicle* quotes her as saying "Post-structuralists or not ... intellectuals are in a position of very substantial irrelevance today" (April 22, 1992: A6). Another historian, Steven Watts, professor at the University of Missouri at Columbia, insightfully calls for the same kind of slouching off academic irrelevance: "A commitment to public engagement — the civic, cultural criticism once practiced by intellectuals... — rather than intellectual gamesmanship would dampen poststructuralist elitism and help to fuse sophisticated theory with practical politics. In the political world of the late 20th century, which already is decentered, anything less would be dangerously deconstructive" (*Chronicle*, April 29, 1992: 92 Point of View). Sad but true that these are historians instructing cultural and literary critics in the realities of life. Who blunted the cutting edge of the cultural critics who had worthwhile agendas? And who continues to blunt those edges?

Not the scholars of Popular Culture Studies! We are more inclined to search with people who are dealing with other persons and other materials— in the thousand and one phenomena that constitute the realities of life. We are concerned with the areas that make up the materials advertised in the posters of our annual meetings and those represented in the publications by our scholars.

Not basing our whole point of view and theory and methodology on one approach, we can more easily shift gears and see other points of approach and view.

The leading blunters seem still to be British theoreticians who are driven by Marxism, classism, and the newest manifestations of evil in the world. For example, John Clarke tries hard to modify Marxist theory to square with the world, as it exists around us. Many other

methods are needed to deal with the rise of feminism, ethnic studies, nationalism, homophobia, etc., all of which are worthy fields of inquiry. Perhaps Clarke identifies the greatest
enemy of scholarship when he admits in his book that his effort in the book is an "attempt
to stake out my own political and intellectual commitments in relation to those of others,
to translate gut reactions into something I can communicate" (177). The drive to spread
"gut reactions" into signs that are bound in territoriality is dangerous. The personal pronoun
"I" and the arrogance that props it up might be the greatest single deterrent to proper scholarship that exists today. If people were not so slogan-conscious, so intent on building personal reputations, so determined to burn a moment in the limelight of public approval,
then perhaps a humanistic scholarship might develop and prosper.

What alternative, you might ask, do I propose? Among all these negative bites, what
positive programs do I suggest? It will hardly surprise you to hear that I continue to advocate
what might be termed the BGSU approach of general approaches to both specifics and generalities. The general approach allows flexibility to encompass all approaches to all areas
and to work most effectively with one of the most important, if not all of them, the Humanities. If there is one aspect of our culture that almost everybody recognizes as in dire need
of being rejuvenated, it is the Humanities. We as a society are increasingly microchipped
into a world of electronics and sciences. Many of us feel the barrenness and incompleteness
of such a world. The National Endowment for the Humanities is, obviously, a natural advocate for the revitalization of the Humanities. So are many other forces. Unfortunately, many
are trying to reanimate a dying body instead of revitalizing it by the infusion of new blood.

The Humanities are perhaps the single most important and useful cultural philosophy
driving societies and human actions. They oppose greed and lust and unbridled individual
rapacity. They drive toward what is good and necessary in society. To let the Humanities
languish is to deprive life of the major beneficial living force in — or capable of being introduced into— society today. They are the human elements that make us more than mere
animals. As such they include virtually every aspect of our society, far more than the conventional Humanities scholar is inclined to encompass—for example, architecture, outdoor
entertainment, tourism, archeology, iconography, ethnicity, nationalism, feminism, law,
environment, and religion. The list goes on and on to cover the living world.

Popular Culture is the voice of this world, spoken in a thousand languages. Popular
Culture Studies are therefore the New Humanities, intended to take up all the subjects
singly and collectively and bring some order and understanding to the seeming chaos.

The Humanities are, therefore, obviously international. Marshall Fishwick recently
asked the question, "Can the Humanities, being generally Eurocentric, cross the Pacific?"
He might more properly have asked if they can cross the Himalayas and the Sahara, as well
as the Panama Canal. The answer is a clear affirmative. And an imperative. They had better
become a communications satellite high in unprejudiced space that receives, stores, decodes,
and beams back to earth those elements, which allow us to live together down here.

To aid in this worldwide understanding, we must of course study the Humanities
internationally and comparatively. No longer is American scholarship defensibly a continent
mentality. It is a world mentality.

There are undoubtedly many ways to study the Humanities on a worldwide approach.
One effective way I would suggest is through a system that was pioneered years ago by the
Finnish folklorist Antti Arne and further developed by the American folklorist Stith Thomp-
son. In 1910 Arne observed that there are similarities in folk narratives around the world.
In order to study these narratives comparatively he called the similarities types. For example,

the type known as the stick-fast type he found current in 17 countries around the world. In the U.S. this story is best illustrated in the Uncle Remus Tar-Baby story, where Br'er Rabbit slaps Tar Baby with one foot after the other for insolence and in so doing gets his paws stuck on the tar baby's body. In the 17 countries around the world where this type is found, in several instances there is no tar or resin available, thus leaving open the question of how the story would be credible and useful. Obviously the story has a meaning above and beyond its motif and this meaning probably lies in its micro-motifs.

Though this typing is useful for comparative study of folktales around the world, Stith Thompson realized that it is too broad and general to be most effective. He needed greater detail for analysis. He found this greater detail by dividing the types into motifs. As he explained his reasoning: (If) an attempt is made to reduce the traditional narrative material of the whole earth to order it must be by means of a classification of single motifs—those details out of which full-fledged narratives are composed. Thus a type is divisible into motifs, the smallest unit of a narrative. Jan Brunvand, another folklorist, suggested that a motif might describe something, an object, a marvelous animal, a concept, action, character, or structural quality.

These categorizations of Thompson and Brunvand are helpful. The fact is, however, that a motif cannot be identified as the smallest unit that describes something. A description is an adjective, a synonym, a parallel or a symbol. A giant, for example, is not a motif, but gigantism is; a thief is not a motif, though a theft is. Thus a motif must be understood not as a description but as a unit in a work that generates some kind of action—physical or mental response. A haunted house, for example, or "hauntedness," a loaded gun, or "loadedness," is a motif because each generates some kind of response and is responsible for some kind of action in the person who experiences the phenomenon.

Though types and motifs are both useful in helping one understand the phenomena of life, they are too general to be most effective. They are like labels on containers of material rather than individual listings of the enclosed items. There are all kinds of loaded guns, for example; in order for the mere listing of a loaded gun to be most useful in narrative analysis, the loaded gun must be described in greater detail. For instance, what caliber gun? Women fire smaller caliber guns, macho males use the .45, police officers the .38 special, mass killers use the machine gun, and cocaine dealers currently use rapid-fire guns. Equally important is the location in which a gun is used. The revolver used at the O.K. Corral or carried by Gregory Peck in the movie *Gunfighter* is quite a different gun from that strapped to Billy the Kid or the cocaine-dealing punk on the streets of Detroit. The .22 caliber pistol carried by a woman on the streets of New York City for her own protection is quite a different motif from that of a hired assassin stalking the streets of London waiting for a chance to kill some government employee.

All these differences are significant. Though they all constitute the motif of the loaded gun, they should be broken down into micromotifs so that their true nature and purpose can be expressed. Each micromotif has its own distinct characteristics and develops along its own lines with a consequent beginning, middle, and end. Each micromotif directs the development of its own individualized constituents.

An excellent example of the needed breakdown of the motifs into micromotifs can be found in the ever-popular Dashiell Hammett novel *The Maltese Falcon*. The story's formula is, of course, the Private Investigator detective fiction. Within that formula there are several motifs: the magic symbol as a lure to crime (the bird); one man's revenge for the murder of a friend/colleague; a beautiful woman as a sex symbol, etc. The several motifs are developed in some 150 micromotifs, which set this book off from all others in the genre and from all others Hammett wrote.

These micromotifs range throughout the activities of life. For example; a quiet, shy voice reveals innocence; smoking a cigarette reveals nervousness; curious onlookers gawk at the scene of a crime; a cheap clock shows time in a slum; Sam Spade keeps the police in the dark; the police (power) try to coerce Spade; glancing at a watch reveals impatience; Effie envies Iva's body; Sam spreads newspapers around the bed before sleeping to protect himself; a foreigner depicts evil; the several [found] in the quoted passage below. One example can suffice for illustration of the development of a micromotif in a narrative.

The novel opens in Sam Spade's office, with Sam sitting in his swivel chair behind his oaken desk; it must be oaken because the chair the customer sits in is "the oaken armchair beside his desk," which is immediately referred to next as merely the "chair's wooden seat." Historically the oak tree has denoted fertility and sexuality. This scene, set against a background of potential fertility, becomes charged with sexuality as Miss Wonderly (one of the many names used by Brigid O'Shaunnessy) walks in for her interview with Spade:

> She advanced slowly, with tentative steps, looking at Spade with cobalt-blue eyes that were both shy and probing. She was tall and pliantly slender, without angularity anywhere. Her body was erect and high-breasted, her legs long, her hands and feet narrow. She wore two shades of blue that had been selected because of her eyes. The hair curling from under her blue hat was darkly red, her full lips more brightly red. White teeth glistened in the crescent her timid smile made.

Spade obviously responds to her sensuality, but he is primarily the professional, putting professional ethics above sensual pleasure. His office is the place for business, not pleasure. He is currently sleeping with Miles Archer's wife, Iva, but even in that relationship he puts business before pleasure. Miles Archer, however, is the opposite and is used for contrast. Archer puts pleasure before professional ethics. When Wonderly suggests somebody follow her and her companion later in the night, it is Archer who wants the tailing job because he sees potential sexual pleasure in the encounter. For his lecherous attitude he is killed.

Throughout the novel Spade remains the professional. At the end, he forces the law to take its course with Brigid O'Shaunnessy. She had killed Miles, had murdered and stolen, and was prepared to commit any crime in order to get and keep the jewel-laden falcon. At the end, she parades sex before Spade and promises him a life of sensual pleasure, but Spade does not hesitate a moment. He remains professional and calls the police: "I won't play the sap for you," he tells Brigid.

At the last scene of the novel, Spade has returned on Monday morning to his office, to the micromotif of the oaken desk and setting. He finds Effie, his secretary, sitting in his swivel chair behind his oaken desk. She immediately jumps up as he enters. The scene is again still-charged with sexuality. Sam puts his arm around Effie and begins to fondle her. But she resists, saying "But don't touch me now — not now." The scene is interrupted with the reappearance of Iva, who has always been Effie's rival. Earlier in the book Sam had told Iva that she should not come to the office — it was not good form. Now she has returned to reintroduce illicit sex into the scene.

But Sam again turns professional and it is the oaken desk that is the micromotif that develops this single most important element of the book. Sam puts professionalism above personal pleasure and the revealing micromotif is the oaken desk, his generating power that holds his duty, his office, and his moral code in place. The book ends with the simple but totally revealing short paragraph; "Spade, looking at his desk, nodded almost imperceptibly, 'Yes,' he said and shivered. 'Well, send her in.'" The micromotif of the oaken desk and the office has tied the book together. It made Sam the person he is and the novel and powerful statement it is. Without the micromotif, obviously the power would not be there. The oaken desk and chairs are a micromotif, not a symbol, since they drive the action; it is not something that symbolizes the action. It powers the action. Without understanding this micromotif the reader and critic can never fully understand the dynamics of the book.

If this micromotif approach to the study of culture has any merit, it should be added to the numerous approaches that other people could suggest that are free of restricting ideologies, theories, and methodologies, which together might drive toward useful approaches and results. With these I assume we have come to the second stage of our development — the present — and are smack up against several facts that should give us cause for caution.

In the present stage of a developing academic discipline such as Popular Culture, there usually emerge certain attitudes which must be viewed askance: a self-awareness, a self-justification, an inward-looking examination, an ossification, a self-indulgence with what a group is doing, a kind of virus if you will, which draws a community inward, writes its laws and patterns of behavior, and is more inclined to send signals of self-righteousness than to be in constant communication with the outside and still learning, a self-sustaining bureaucracy whose only end is self-perpetuation. The attitude affects the immediate and distant future of Popular Culture Studies in at least two ways. Let us look at two of these assertions:

1. The first suspicious "law" is that "mature" academic organizations need theories and methodologies. This conventional attitude is an apple with a rotten core, at least in the study of the Humanities and Social Sciences. There is no reason why the motivations, which drove an organization in its initial exploratory stages, should not continue to drive it in its more "mature" days. Popular Culture Studies began as an organization of rebellion, devoted to enlarging cultural and Humanities studies as much as possible. That goal has not yet been achieved. We might be on the verge of suggesting the parameters of such studies. But we are far from having developed all areas and subjects within those parameters. In fact, we may be merely developing our second wind in the struggle.

The recent 25th annual meeting of the PCA in Philadelphia may be a useful reference. Several participants volunteered the comment that the organization may have finally achieved its twin goals; highest quality presentations and informal pleasurable atmosphere — no jealous criticism one of another, no envy, only a spirit of helpfulness. They also remarked that at no other scholarly group that they belonged to could there be an informal dance on a Thursday night, right in the midst of the "serious" presentations. Interesting observations, but hardly new. That is where we began 25 years ago. Unfortunately, somewhere along the way we might have wandered from the broad and inclusive path. But hopefully we have found it again.

2. A second bit of misguided advice is that Popular Culture Studies must decide on areas of concern and quit being all things to all people. The fear is, perhaps, that the open mind is the empty head.

Such constricting advice is anathema to the guiding philosophy of Popular Culture Studies. The initial drive grew from the realization that popular, that is, everyday, cultures cover virtually every aspect of life, suffuse the media, influence and shape every aspect of life. The more democratic the society the stronger the influence. Not to recognize this is to close one's eye to aspects of culture, which continue to grow in recognition and importance:

ethnicity, nationalism, feminism, homophobia, regionalism, ecology, animal rights and life rights. Popular Culture Studies are the only discipline to welcome all seemingly distinct and unrelated areas and to demonstrate the interrelatedness of all. Popular Culture Studies should continue to be dedicated to the understanding of all aspects of life. No matter how strongly elitists deny the validity of Popular Culture Studies, discerning people understand that not to recognize the irresistible power of Popular Culture in a democracy is to deny reality and often to delay the development of the obvious, often at great costs. What I have been saying about Popular Culture Studies in general applies equally to two other of our several thrusts: the Popular Culture Association and the *Journal of Popular Culture*.

On the former let me say a word or two. We have always tried to keep the PCA as catholic and open as possible. We have constantly not only reached out to touch everybody but have always welcomed the reverse trend and invited everyone to come to us. Somewhere along the line Peter Rollins suggested that we have Area Chairs to cover as many areas as possible. Through the years we must have had at least 150 areas of interest, sometimes with many people interested, sometimes with only a few. As new areas have developed, some others have languished. At the recent 25th annual meeting we had 125 areas. For the next one in Las Vegas we have several new ones, as we have advertised in the *Chronicle of Higher Education*, to try to bring in people we have never attracted before. In that effort, which by the way was first recognized as being perhaps fruitful by Felicia Campbell, UNLV, we are already meeting people we have never before seen.

On the *Journal of Popular Culture* let me say another word. When I first began collecting papers for the JPC in 1967 none of us knew what we were doing. Russ Nye, Carl Bode, David Anderson, Marshall Fishwick, John Cawelti and dozens of others had to scrape around among their papers and friends to find manuscripts. Through the years JPC has had some 8,000 papers submitted and some 900 published. We no longer have to scratch around to find papers. Nowadays we get on average two submitted papers every day. That's five or six hundred a year — out of which we are going to publish at most 50. We are so exclusive we are about to become elite and respectable! We will continue to accept the strongest papers on the widest range of subjects possible. We are still trying to comprehend the subject.

So I end my anatomy of Popular Culture Studies with a smile, confidence, and some apprehension. Our accomplishments have been considerable but we are vulnerable — not only to outsiders but also to ourselves. As we have been warned many times, students of Popular Culture Studies, like those people interested in democracy, need to be constantly vigilant, for foes are continually around us. As someone observed some time ago, we have seen the enemy and sometimes he is us. So we need to keep bouncing our vigilance off the satellites above us that might eventually unite all people. We have achieved maturity and the only thing scholars of Popular Culture Studies need fear as they march into the 21st century is timidity and conformity and the Theory-Methodology Complex.

You do not want the drummers you march to, to begin to beat out the common rhythm. You can remain independent, I'm sure. After all, any journal that can publish and any Association that can take seriously an essay on "The Significance of 'Mother' Pillows in American History and Culture" and then publish further research on the subject can rest assured they have imagination and courage! They can widely skirt at least some of the dangers that lie ahead. They can at least minimize their ego as they step up to and through the looking glass and see behind it the theory-methodology Jabberwock that tries to reduce us all. To paraphrase one of the most noteworthy admonitions by Lewis Carroll that should be tattooed on the wrist of all scholars and critics:

Beware theory-methodology, my son and daughter!
The jaws that bite, the claws that carg!
Beware the Jubjub bird, and shun as you oughter
The Frumious, brumious critjarg!

With confidence in our adhering to that caution I think we need not worry about going back to scholarly rags in the next generation. In fact, our wardrobe grows richer and more varied every day.

Works Cited

American Quarterly 9 (Summer 1957): 207.

Brunvand, Jan. *The Study of American Folklore: An Introduction.* New York: W.W. Norton, 1968.

Chronicle of Higher Education 22 Apr. 1992: A6.

Chronicle of Higher Education "Point of View." 29 Apr. 1992.

Clarke, John. *New Times and Old Enemies: Essays on Cultural Studies and America.* New York: Harper Collins, 1992, 177.

Falck, Colin. *Myth, Truth and Literature: Towards a True Post-Modernism.* Cambridge: Cambridge University Press, 1992.

Martin, Calvin Luther. *In the Spirit of the Earth: Rethinking History and Time.* Baltimore: Johns Hopkins University Press, 1992.

Thompson, Stith. *Motif-Index of Folk-Literature: A Classification of Narrative Elements in Folktales, Ballads, Myths, Fables, Medieval Romances, Exampla, Fabliaux, Jest-Books and Local Legends.* Rev. and enlarged. Bloomington: Indiana University Press, 1966.

10

Internationalizing Popular Culture Studies

This freewheeling yet pointed essay, like several of Browne's later works of calculated polemics, is more of an opinion-editorial than a traditional academic article, as readers will note. Browne affirms that contemporary electronic communications have altered the cultural landscapes considerably, and declares that applying the canonized standards and approaches of Western academia and culture is no longer a viable comparative research strategy, if indeed it ever truly was.

The urgency of Browne's statements spills out in wide-ranging metaphors early in the essay, before he shifts gears to illustrate his points with a summation of then-current global issues. He then turns, more gently though no less urgently, to his lambasting of the old order by discussing the potential richness of internationalized popular culture studies through such cultural phenomena as tourism, bumper stickers, and fashion. A droll attack on the canon via the vagaries of the fine-art world (similar to his 1977 speech elsewhere in this collection) concludes with another reference to Lewis Carroll, tying this article to his previous one on the theory-methodology "jabberwock" from the year before.—The Editor

John Cawelti has properly suggested that, in order for Popular Culture Studies to progress in the desired way, we need to expand our perspective, internationalizing them and becoming "increasingly sophisticated about the intricacies and complexities of multi-culturalism." And we need to blend that sophistication into greater understanding of multi-nationalistic, ethnic, linguistic, cultish and religious deterministic thrusts into society. We are at a crossroads in Popular Culture Studies and at the opening of several new highway chains. Fred Casmir, editor of the new book *Communication in Eastern Europe: The Role of History, Culture and New Media in Contemporary Conflicts* (Mahway: Lawrence Erlbaum Associates, 1995, 320) urgently outlines some of the problem: "If we are to reach [national] agreement," he says, "we need to learn to talk to each other, to accept and deal effectively with diversity, and we must build and use new models of human cooperation in which communication is not merely a technique, but a central ethical concern." On the computers of cultures, it is becoming perfectly clear, the lights are flashing all over the screen, alerting us to a sense of urgency in the Humanities and social sciences and the need for certain realizations.

The first thing we need to realize is that the heavy hand of an established canon of subjects to be learned and taught must be lifted. A canon of Popular Culture Studies is a controlling device that those in traditional power circles impose upon the rest of us. Their purpose is to control the present and the future by dictating which aspects of past are important. Such a canon is not altogether intentionally malicious. It maintains continuity and orderly succession. But it needs to be considered changeable as societies develop. Like all human conditions, the canon needs to be susceptible to development and change. Canonists need to desire improvement when change does not improve.

To paraphrase Abraham Lincoln in another crisis, if we can understand where the Humanities and social sciences are now and where they ought to be going, perhaps we can prepare for the future no matter where it tends. Academics especially should be concerned, for as Humanities critic Gerald Graf properly says, the university is popular culture, and as academics we should understand our world and the real world if we are going to teach and research those worlds effectively.

What is said about Popular Culture Studies should also be said about American Culture Studies and the national studies of all other nations because America and other countries are now increasingly parts of the large mosaic of the world and because they are all part of world popular culture.

Perhaps first we should clarify what Popular Culture Studies entail. There are more areas than some of us care to recognize or admit. Many of us think too narrowly. For example, the editor of a recent book on comparative culture (*Handbook of Chinese Popular Culture*, edited by Wu Dingbo and Patrick D. Murphy, Greenwood, 1994, 7) says that "Popular culture helps people observe and understand society," when, in fact, popular culture is that society. Such an observation is like saying that water helps fish understand their environment when water IS that environment.

Another scholar apparently misunderstands the term. In his recent book *The Art of Democracy: A Concise History of Popular Culture in the United States* (Monthly Review Press, 1996, 13), the author, Jim Cullen, says: "The focus of the book will be on mass-produced texts (a term that encompasses novels and periodicals, as well as plays, films, television shows, and other media) intended for large audiences to enjoy in their spare time." If we continue to look on popular culture as the culture of entertainment of large groups of people, we are walking the primrose path, and no wonder other scholars say we don't know what we're talking about. Often we don't.

Popular culture is the everyday culture of a group, large or small, of people. It is far more than entertainment, the electronic media, folk life, fast foods, fashions, Wall Street, the church, the educational system or the government. It is the way of life in which and by which most people in any society live. In a democracy like the United States, it is the voice of the people — their practices, likes and dislikes — the lifeblood of their daily existence. The popular culture is the voice of democracy, democracy speaking and acting, the seedbed in which democracy grows. Popular culture in all cultures — from the most authoritarian to the most democratic — democratizes society and makes democracy truly democratic. It is the everyday world around us: the mass media, entertainments, diversions; it is our heroes, icons, rituals, everyday actions, psychology and religion — our total life pictures. It is the way of life we inherit, practice, and modify as we please and then pass on to our descendants. It is what we do while we are awake and how we do it; it is the dreams we dream while asleep as well as where, when and how we sleep.

Obviously, then, since there are many manifestations of people's behavior dictated by race, history, custom, gender, age, locality and group-size conditions, popular culture actually consists of many overlapping and interworking cultures, like scales on a fish. The only way to talk of a singular popular culture is to realize that it is a mixture of many small and large cultures, which are controlled by elements smaller than and different from the large national picture.

In the United States, for example, the many races of people and their histories and cultures from around the world who have poured into this country over the past two centuries have brought their many elements of cultures and added them to the dominant Protestant Western European base. So the culture of the United States today is a broader stirring both vertically and laterally of all the people who today make up our society. It would have been completely different if this continent had been discovered and the country colonized and developed west to east instead of east to west, by Asians instead of Europeans, or south to north instead of north to south, by Catholic cultures instead of Protestant. The same basic human needs would have been present but their traditional and current development would have been different in expression and degree. Culture developments are driven by and develop within the needs and constraints of a people. They grow in directions and to degrees allowed by the physical, mental and emotional attitudes.

Popular culture is the total of nearly all elements of life, and that total equals more than the sum of its parts. It has no relationship to quantity or numbers of accessibility. Lawrence Levine's observation that popular culture is "culture that is widely accessible and widely accessed; widely disseminated, and widely viewed or heard or read" is wide of the mark, too deeply tied to the concept that popular culture is only electronic development of the old and narrow concept of what constitutes folklore ("The Folklore of Industrial Society: Popular Culture and Its Audience," *American Historical Review*, 97 (December 1992): 1373). Believing as Levine does is like saying that Washington, DC. is just a modern classical Rome, or, for that matter, that a citizen of our nation's capital is a cave man in a different environment. Such a belief is too simple. Human nature has changed little through thousands of years but the details of expressing it have changed radically. Some of the popular culture most important to small groups is of necessity limited in circulation and usage, just as that important to larger groups is more widespread.

At times it, and a record of its history, is of vital importance. Think, for example, how enlightening it would be to us if some worker slaving away on the Egyptian pyramids had taken the time to draw a picture of workers lifting one of the great rocks to its place on the structure. A vital chapter in Egyptian life and human development would have been written in that one picture.

The more an element of popular culture influences or controls a segment of society, the more important it becomes. It is more important in small groups— simple societies— than in large. Popular culture has nothing to do with popularity in the sense of number of people engaged in it. That kind of popularity has only to do with how widely something is used. Popular culture also has nothing to do with quality, though at times we might wish it did. Popular culture is the lifestyle and lifeblood of groups— large or small — of people.

In 1995 there are an estimated 327 languages and dialects being spoken in the United States. The smallest ethnic and nationalistic, cultish or religious group using one of those languages or dialects lives in and by their everyday culture; it is that culture that identifies the people and makes them cohere as a part of the large culture of the United States. The dominant popular culture is like a patchwork quilt made up of many different parts. This large quilt then covers the many smaller groups. In such societies, then, citizens must speak several cultural languages, those of their own — and similar groups— and that of the dominant culture.

One indication of the complexity of a national culture can be seen in just one manifestation by looking at it as an inverted pyramid or extended triangle on a horizontal plane. The United States as a nation has many cultures. So, too, in a kind of shrinkage to an American region, does the U.S. "South." So, too, does a state in the South, say Alabama, and a region in that state. For example, during the Civil War, Winston County opposed Secession and threatened to set up an independent state; surely in many ways Winston County differed from the surrounding counties and still does. Reducing further the size of a geographical unit we recognize that a city or town in Alabama differs from all others. So, too, does a family and even an individual in that community. Usually a family's or individual's culture is conventional in most ways, though at times it might be eccentric. But it is always to one degree or another the reflection of the individuals and their joint behaviors. With the persons, the culture is always to one degree or another individual and personal. In our time, when the rights of the individual are being stressed, the personal unit of culture is becoming more and more important.

Further, popular culture has nothing to do with so-called quality, with the "good and beautiful" in life as distinguished from those elements which are not considered good or beautiful. Some aspects of culture are beneficial and enjoyable, some seem to be destructive and nasty. Popular culture, especially in a republic like the United States, and in most other countries around the world that are driving toward democracy, is the total way of life and means of life, for better or worse, desired or undesired.

Popular culture in many instances is distributed by the mass media, but other, more old-fashioned media like habit, the "grapevine," gossip, imitation, observation and indifference are much more powerful controls. In popular culture, though at times we feel powerful forces beyond our control dictate it, eventually the people control it. Though a movie, for example, may get strong official approval or condemnation, it is word-of-mouth reviews that make or break it. The approving or disapproving glance and its supporting verbal comments control our culture. We vote at the ballot box but also with our feet and pocketbooks, and when we walk away from or fail to support an element or our popular culture sooner or later it will become inconsequential or disappear.

Popular culture studies are scholarly examinations of those everyday cultures, liked or disliked, approved or disapproved. Academic analyses of all such phenomena, of American culture studies, or studies of other national culture, should be carried on comparatively, whether approved or disapproved. Life goes on with or without academic approval. But we can hardly consider letting it go along without our understanding.

With that assumption, then, we need to think of the most effective ways to get at an understanding of the dynamics of culture. In the first place, we must discontinue our thinking that the age-old practice of starting at the top and working down, of generalizing — often from too little data — is the proper procedure.

One can and is likely to prove any thesis that he or she wants proved. The trick is in the points sought. While understanding the whole performance, the result we want ultimately, we must realize that wholes are made up of parts. Sometimes the whole is more than the sum of its parts, sometimes less. But the parts are the important elements. A giant building with dramatically beautiful walls can be far more impressive than it would be without the covering. But the beams and struts—the millions of parts that make up the structure—are more integral than the siding. It is important not to lose the forest in the trees. But the value of a rain forest lies in the collective items in every square yard on the ground as well as in the canopy. A book is more than the title.

The devil, as politicians are saying these days, is in the details. But as usual they confuse and obfuscate. The devil, on the contrary, is in the generalizations. The details contain angels. The genie of generalizations is impossible to put back into the bottle once it is verbalized and released. The only thing that can be done is follow the released genie and hope that, though error crushed to earth will rise again, as Carl Bode used to delight in saying, sometimes it can be stamped out.

Generalizations, like stereotypes, are fraught with potential error and danger. As soon as one learns something about the subject, he sees that the generalization is only partially correct if at all. We have all had the experience of learning ourselves out of error and misassumptions. Our increasing knowledge of fellow animals is an excellent case in point. Sharks, we are slowly learning, are not the threat to humans that we have thought for ages. In fact, they are less dangerous to people than hippopotamuses are. Further, we are finally coming to realize just how intelligent the "dumb" animals are. Makes one wonder what animals are the slow learners. Yet we study and change our minds in all areas of life; that's what study is all about. Wynton Marsalis, Director of Jazz at Lincoln Center and one of the best jazz trumpeters alive, for example, said that he had no respect for Louis Armstrong as jazz trumpeter until he learned about him. Now, to Marsalis, Armstrong was one of the greatest trumpeters of all time and his, Marsalis', model.

We must realize, then, that truth wears many faces and they are always changing. There is no such thing as absolute history, for example, but many histories. Even the word history is suspect and being challenged by her story by women. And apparently there is no such thing as fact, since the biggest lies and misunderstandings in Washington and the world these days are always prefaced with the words, "The fact is...."

There is also no such thing as the culture of a people. There are many cultures. The total culture of a nation, a collective people, is like a river. There are many currents and movements in the general flow. The force and directions change. Sometimes the current cuts in one direction, sometimes another. Sometimes elements of the land are abandoned and sloughs develop. Some cultures flourish and then fade, some hang on apparently forever. Though all roads do not continue to lead to Rome, Rome is still important in the world. The sun now sets on the British Empire but British culture still abounds. New cultural forces have arisen and rise every day. Two of the imperatives of popular culture studies are 1) realizing that culture studies must be international and comparative, and 2) understanding the cultures not only in generalities but also in details.

First, a word or two on internationalizing Popular Culture Studies. We are in the midst of the most rapid change in world cultures that has ever been experienced because we are on the frontier of a world in which there are no political or culture borders. Both are infiltrated electronically. So-called First World countries are being subjected to powerful strains which, if not properly handled, might tear them apart. So-called Second and Third World countries are being pushed and pulled through cyberspace at a speed and to a destination that are bewildering. They are having the electronic world forced upon them that bypasses the usual sequence of development. These forces are driving toward more power to the people. If the people of all countries are to develop their political and cultural power constructively, they must understand what is happening.

We have long said that unless people understand their history they will be forced to repeat it. Now we must also say that unless people understand the forces driving their present-day life they cannot control them. A people who do not understand their power might well run amok. As academics we must understand these potentials and the real sense of urgency driving them.

For centuries, people have realized that culture knows no geographical boundaries. For 1,000 years the Chinese felt their culture superior to all others and tried to keep others out by building a Great Wall. But people and their cultures move. An excellent case in point is the current dynamics of cultures in the United States. In this country, more than a million legal immigrants and perhaps more than that number of illegal immigrants leaven the cultures yearly. We now have more than 200 different sets of cultures conflicting more or less with one another. Immigrants take their cultures with them when they immigrate and often try to set them up as more or less distinct and independent. Take, for example, the many "Little" communities we have in cities through the world: "Little Tokyo," "Little China," "Little Korea." Americans, when they settle in other countries, conspicuously and assertively remain American. Can a nation survive when it consists of more than 200 little nations and languages asserting their desires for cultural equality, as is occurring in the United States today?

Europe is putting that question to the test. In France, in a recent poll, two out of three people admitted to burning with racist feeling. On the Continent, non–Europeans number 25 million, 6 percent of the population. Native Europeans see the immigrants as financial and cultural threats. The Canadian Broadcasting Corporation has just cut off 2½ hours daily of prime time American network TV programming in order to protect its own culture. Maybe all such felt threats are admissions of weakness and insecurity. CBC's effort to keep American TV programs out of Canada, when 90 percent of Canadians live within 100 miles of the border and get American broadcasts from American cities, is doomed to failure.

The irony of the CBC action is that, at the same time they are trying to move outside the American-controlled media zone, the Canadians are fighting against Quebec's doing the same thing of moving outside the Canadian cultural sphere of influence. By a paper-thin majority, Quebec has just voted not to separate from Canada and become a country and culture of its own. Just how the Quebecois planned to survive more strongly outside the Federation but still subjected to the strong English cultures of Canada and the U.S. is not clear. Some people conjectured that the new country of Quebec would want to become a state of the United States. And so separate from American culture! Isolation might delay cultural and political changes, but it is surely folly for the Quebecois to think that they can hide behind a Great Wall of Quebec and protect their cultures against the onslaught of the strong English-speaking cultures around them. Laws and isolation do not save cultures. Other forces — internal and external — shape ways of life.

The most effective way to protect a culture is to validate it, by making it alive and vital. The Canadian Broadcasting Corporation might well cut out a niche for itself by devoting more of its time to Canadian productions in both English and French and running those at the same time that Canadians are given their choice between American broadcasts and those at home. As developing nations face the same seeming onslaught of English-transmitted culture they might well recognize that their chances of survival as cultural entities depends not on blacking out the stronger culture but in making their own stronger and thus providing more attractive competition.

Another way to bring continued life to a culture is through Popular Culture Studies; the active and determined enlightened analysis of a culture's culture with its strengths and weaknesses thoroughly understood. Although such studies cannot juvenate a culture, Popular Culture Studies can validate a culture by making the academic community aware of and appreciative of a culture and, through academia's influence on government and the public, make the public proud and retentive of its own culture. Academia has always worked toward maintaining cultural status quo. In the past the strains on that purpose were less severe than they are now as cultures come into conflict more dramatically and dangerously.

Popular Culture Studies should and can be one of the very useful lubricants in conflicts that explode all over the world.

Conflicts in and resolutions of conflicts in culture between some countries and inside some societies will be peaceful, in others somewhat agitated or catastrophic. The French culture of Quebec is not going quietly to its grave. The transition in such countries as Bosnia-Herzegovina and Russia-Chechnya, in 1996, is world threatening. Pressure of great intensity is building up in China in all areas. Take, for example, music. In the face of the move to Westernize at least portions of the culture, a Chinese commission on music has decided that there is too much Western symphonic music being played and recommended that it be replaced by Chinese folk music. In a recent book, *China Popular Culture* (New Press, 1995), the author, Jianying Zha, asserts that the popular culture in China over a long period may effect more changes than the political protests that resulted in the 1989 massacre in Tiananmen Square. She should not have hesitated in her prediction. The voice — and the feet and music and pocketbook — of the people are the machines that ultimately effect most change. They pay the piper and eventually quite literally call the tune, even in the world of symphonic music, one of the bastions of elitism. Today symphony orchestras have great trouble supporting themselves. The National Endowment of the Arts and the National Endowment for the Humanities have had to drastically cut back on subventions, and private individual contributions are down 25 percent. Orchestras have had to turn to corporate funding, and corporations are demanding modifications in programs to make them more widely appreciated. Now we have programs that blend kinds of music, which in the past would have been considered incompatible: Beethoven and the Beatles, Grieg and the Grateful Dead. Orchestras and their leaders will do anything to keep their jobs. We have Keith Lockhart, Director of the Boston Pops, willing, he says, to conduct in a Batman suit or from a Dracula coffin if necessary. Further, definitions of concert quality music are changing. "We needed to change the impression that an orchestra is a bunch of stuffed shirts playing dead white European composers for almost dead white American audiences," confessed Joe Kluger, Executive Director of the Philadelphia Symphony Orchestra (*Wall Street Journal*, Jan. 8, 1996, A4).

The inevitable changes are sometimes revolutionary but generally are evolutionary. McDonald's, Coke, Pepsi and Pizza Hut are located around the world. In Southern France each summer there is a reenactment of the shoot-out at the OK Corral (with the bad guys being Vietnamese!). A few hundred miles north, Germans dressed like the participants sit around watching American westerns. For years Spaghetti Westerns, made in Italy, were popular throughout Europe and the U.S. Today around the world most of the movies and TV programs being watched were filmed in America and India.

Reverse cultural flow is common. Today, Americans turn the Karaoke TV channel from Singapore off their Japanese TV sets, dress in French, Italian or Chinese clothes, drive off in their Swedish car, drink German beer and French wine, scowl under French noir gloom, stay up all night to buy the latest release of early Beatles songs and make Princess Di their heroine. We elect a Japanese baseball pitcher, Hideo Nomo, as Rookie of the Year in the National Baseball League. In London every Saturday morning, thousands of Indians gather to watch the soap opera *Mahabharata* in order to hold on to the remnants of Indian culture that they still need and enjoy. What is going on?!

What's going on is the communication highway is getting broader and more crowded as people and cultures move more widely and rapidly. We are not developing into a global village but instead into a vast international mall, serviced by innumerable highways and a very large airport of ideas, with people perhaps eventually all speaking two or three languages, their own, maybe English — which, according to one authority, is now being spoken around the world in fifty-five varieties (Roger Antell, *Using English Around the World*, John Wiley, 1995) — and certainly the world-wide language of popular culture. It is vital that we academics understand that language of popular culture. It is imperative that we comprehend the details in the generalizations about other cultures, the stereotypes, in the international language of popular culture. Let me give you three examples of this need.

ITEM. On a large scale, tourism is mixing details of culture from one county to another and at the same time creating its own. Almost from the beginning of human kind's earliest travel it has been assumed that if people know more about one another, of their cultures and countries, human kind will get along better and be more peaceable. Marco Polo's early account in the 13th century to the court of Kublai Khan excited countless would-be travelers. Nineteenth-century American travelers by the score, like Nathaniel Hawthorne, Mark Twain and Henry James, lured Americans to Europe.

Currently, we are putting the value of tourism to the acid test and may soon reach a breaking point. Many American cities subsist on their tourism. Most of the residents accept or welcome the incursion. Most Europeans do too, but many are questioning whether all the tourism does not do more environmental damage than it is worth. For example, it is estimated that tourists abrade the height of the Alps four inches every year.

Almost all national parks in the U.S. and all game reservations are being swamped, even threatened by tourism worldwide. We have all seen footage of the leopard in the Serengeti resting in a tree and the camera sweeping down to show ten minivans of tourists, a hundred or so of the 70,000 who visit the park every year, standing around gawking. Ironically, it may be those gawking tourists who manage to save African wildlife. But how are we to save the Grand Canyon and the Yosemite and the giant brown bears on Kodiak Island from the destruction of the tourists? Before we close the book on the whole movement of tourism we need to know what good it does, what harm, and whether anything in particular should and could be done for it. In other words, we need more details.

ITEM. Fashion in women's looks. Increasingly around the world, women are becoming more conscious of how their bodies look. Japanese and South Korean women, and others, get cosmetic breast implants and facial surgery to make the eye rounder and the face more "Western." Are they falling prey to the feeling that, as Mary Douglas says, "the physical body is a microcosm of society, facing the center of power, contracting and expanding its claims in direct accordance with the increase and relaxation of social pressure (*Natural Symbols: Explorations in Cosmology*, p. 101) and are those pressures, then, changing the world? Fashion shows are popular in all first World countries and in many others. Is this more pressure? The choicest young women in the world might be those who pour out of the offices onto the streets of Tokyo during the lunch hour, where they spend all their earnings trying to look "Western." Half of the American women buy shoes that are at least a half a size too small. Do other women? Is this a throwback to the days when Chinese women's feet were bound to make them more beautiful and helpless? Is there a world-wide foot fetish?

American women show a great deal of skin, fashionable women and entertainers more than middle-class women. Australia has topless beaches; the U.S. has topless bars and bottomless restaurants. Everywhere amateur and professional shows have nude dancing girls. Several countries have nude beaches. The United States has bars where college girls are invited to undress and, according to the public invitation of one, "show what you have and see what your friends have." When, if ever, does female fashion tip over into pornography? The official Chinese Government policy is to keep out Western nudity as a sign of moral corruption. But theirs is a losing battle. According to *Newsweek* (Feb. 12, 1996, 41), there are lingerie billboards in Shanghai and Beijing (as well as throughout China) advertising the Wonderbra and thong panties. The author of the *Newsweek* piece feels that American popular culture "has transformed Asian women's idea of beauty" and how it should be displayed and enjoyed, where "Asia's growing class of affluent urban women is eager to flaunt their sexuality." "People want a good husband, and a push-up bra is part of the package," reads a large billboard in Canton, showing a Western woman reclining on a couch dressed only in scant bra and panties.

Are these ways of behavior pornographic? Is pornography a sign of decadence or the cutting edge of art and progress? Are women who assert these fashions exercising femininity or feminism? Will the changes in women's societies drive alterations that will be irreversible? And how are these moments being taken worldwide? Again, details are requisite.

ITEM. Bumper stickers. Since earliest times, people have decorated their caves and walls with pictures and scrawled statements. These graffiti have summarized people's feelings, observations, fears, hopes, dreams and realities. A generation ago such graffiti were considered vulgar displays. In the 1930s and 40s, there was a folk saying considered appropriate: "Fools' names and fools' faces always seen in public places." Now graffiti are widely affixed and sometimes accepted, at least by some groups. At times the use runs wild. Currently in Rio de Janeiro, for example, virtually every public building and all others accessible to the public, is defaced with gang graffiti, as are many buildings—and subway trains—in American cities.

Americans have long used the bumpers on their automobiles to make graffiti-like statements. Often these graffiti are vulgar invitations to violence, glaring examples of "in your face" confrontations, like the bristling of a male animal when it meets another of its kind and has to check out its intentions.

Vehicle owners in other countries are following the American example. On Brazilian highways, for example, these days one sees on trucks such bumper stickers as "So Jesus Christo Salva" (Only Jesus Christ is salvation), "Tudo e Forca" (Everything is force) and "Tudo por causa de teu olhar" (All for the sake of your glance). The person who collected these graffiti suggests that they fall into four categories: religion, love, work, and morality. They bear considerable difference from their American counterparts.

Carol Gardner, who must surely be one of America's authorities, in her latest book *Bumper Sticker Wisdom — America's Pulpit Above the Tailpipe* (Beyond Words Publishing, 1995), reports hundreds, many like, "So Many Pedestrians ... So Little Time," "Single Mormon Seeks Several Spouses," and "Happiness is Seeing Your Boss' Picture on the Back of a Milk Carton." Less grim ones read like, "If Reindeer Really Can fly ... Our Windshields Are in Big Trouble" and "Enjoy Life — This is Not a Rehearsal." Some bumper stickers are taken seriously. She reports that a construction worker lost his job on a university site because of anti–gay stickers, and a Kentucky pickup truck driver was killed because of a rebel flag sticker on his bumper.

In order to understand the differences between those stickers from different countries, one must dig into not only detail but also into context. Unfortunately, many popular culture scholars do not take their areas of research seriously enough to do all the background and sideground study necessary. The scholar who reported the Brazilian truck bumper stickers said that "some anthropologist should study these stickers" but failed to do so himself. If popular culture materials are worth studying, they are worth studying thoroughly, even if they are much more difficult to study and understand. Popular culture scholars need to be also anthropologists, sociologists, philosophers and everything else.

I could illustrate my point with other examples, but these should suffice. At this time, some of us will raise the question whether these kinds of culture are aesthetically worthy of being studied seriously. The answer is positively yes. Alan Gowans, a leading art historian, has said and demonstrated for many years that every cultural artifact, if understood thoroughly, is a microcosm of the culture in which it was created. And, as he says, art is not what it is but what it does. Art sells point of view, religion, automobiles, and deodorant. Of all purposes, perhaps the most important is telling a story since there are so many ramifications to storytelling. Sometimes the question of aesthetics— or effectiveness— might be relevant, for some stories are more interesting, more effective, than others. But scholars in Popular Culture Studies feel the question of aesthetics plays only a tangential and relatively unimportant role.

Academics tend to study only what they think is aesthetically valuable and to make whatever they study into something aesthetically rewarding. But such realizing is only imposing artificial qualities. And increasingly, scholars are recognizing that quality is largely in the eye of the beholder and we all want a bite from the aesthetic pie.

Further, and unfortunately, the aesthetics of artifacts are Western-value-laden. One such Western value is that fine art is genius-driven and crafts are everyday, utilitarian, and of little aesthetic value. The difference between the two is narrow or nonexistent and pushed by lack of knowledge and understanding. Present-day anthropologists are doing a great deal to demonstrate the artificiality and crippling negative results of judging the value of human creations by Western standards.

There is a much more profound answer to the question of aesthetic accomplishment. Newspaper columnist and TV commentator George Will believes that democracy is not an aesthetic experience. He is correct only in a superficial sense and absolutely wrong in the deepest sense. The true aesthetic experience is only superficially and by fiat nondemocratic. In its ultimate finality, the aesthetic experience, contrary to the elitist philosophy and practice, must be validated by the people or, unless protected by those in power, will go the way of all fads. Students trained into elitist points of view keep the canon alive. But for this artificial life machine, much of the canon alive today would be on an unending sabbatical or buried with a headstone to mark it.

This blind support of the canon may be most easily illustrated by the world of so-called "fine" art. It is estimated that half the fine art in the galleries and displayed in private collections are copies, reproductions. Yet so arbitrary is the art experience that owners of fine art will not admit it when they own a copy because, with such an admission, the financial and snobbish value would go down and its aesthetic value immediately become nil. Nobody has satisfactorily explained how a "masterpiece" which, in every detail is so exact that it fools the sharpest critic and is priceless, automatically becomes worthless when its authenticity is disproved. If the creative genius and the work skill of the original artist are so inspirational and valuable, why isn't an exact reproduction so skillfully done that it escapes detection just as valuable? Is it really the magical touch of genius that made the work so priceless or the artificial power usurped by the person or organization that owns a rare item and is determined to keep it not only rare but desired and priceless?

As a matter of fact, many art museums and private collectors tacitly prove the value of the copy and their own willingness to perpetuate their fraud by demonstrating the value and perfection of the copy. With the danger of theft and the high cost of insurance these days, it is estimated that many of the displayed items in museums and private collections are deliberately copied, fakes, placed there by the owners with the originals in secure keeping in safes. The reasoning is that the copy is good enough for the public since only the connoisseur can tell the difference. The question is, if only the connoisseur can tell the difference, is there really a difference? Who's doing what to whom in and about the art world?

The plot thickens. The anomaly of art appreciation has again been demonstrated. At the French Embassy complex in New York City, for ninety years a "classical" (Renaissance) statue of Cupid has gone unnoticed and unappreciated. As it stood around gathering dust and being derided by the cognoscenti passing by, it was assumed that the statue was just another piece of valueless statuary, surely with no vibes of greatness emanating from it. Francois Cusset of the French cultural staff reported that those who saw the statue thought it was "kitsch" and "laughed at the cute cheeks" (*Newsweek*, Feb. 5, 1996, 62). Then one dark evening, when Cupid was brightly lit up, one Dr. Kathleen Weil-Garris Brandt, of the New York Institute of Fine Arts, saw the statue really for the first time. Like a stroke from the heaven of art she realized that this cute little fellow was really the work of Michelangelo (1475–1564) and the only one in the United States. Now the United States and France are engaged in the Great Cupid War, the latter claiming the statue since it purchased the mansion in 1952, the U.S. wanting to borrow and display the statue on loan. Francois Cusset, quoted above, being a good Frenchman, says of Brandt's discovery, "It was a nice American example of personal ambition." So the War of the Cupid: from "kitsch" to treasure in a glance. Could it be that art is not in the eye of the beholder but in the pocketbook of the owner and the spiel of the seller?

But, as we used to say in the sixties, the times they are a-changin'. Economic necessity is driving toward democratization of art and will make the so-called fine arts a part of popular culture. The truth is that the art world for the past three hundred years has been the most priest-ridden of the arts. Calling artifacts "fine art" reveals the technique. The priests have maintained a small fraternity, admission to which has been more color of blood and stockings, and depth of pocket, than other credentials.

Those fraternity members' control has been so severe that they have exacted a heavy toll from all who wanted to enter. The world of "fine art" is the most flagrant of all arts in imposing a public mindset unconsciously accepted that is self-humiliating and self-debasing. "I like that but I don't know anything about art," is an admission that keeps outsiders in their place.

But we are discovering that those who claim to know about the fine arts are giving us a great wash of jargobabble that is losing its value as coin of the realm. The people, who speak it, like the Emperor who was wearing no clothes, are really without a significant language and standard of aesthetics. They are instead skilled at creating and maintaining a standard that does not exist in reality.

The popular arts are demonstrating that they—and the democratized so-called fine arts—can fulfill their original purposes and still be popular. Walt Disney may have been the greatest force in this shift. Comic strip artists were also powerful influences. Folk art has helped, as has children's art. Commercial art and computer art have made major strides. Perhaps we are seeing the beginning of a general revaluation of so-called fine art, which will make all worthwhile expressions in art, regardless of origin or proprietorship and original cost, available to us all. If somehow we can compensate the elitists for their loss. Or vote them out of power. Indeed, as we agreed at the beginning, the devil is in the details.

And he does change reality! Or at least he gives it a different spin!

These are some of the aspects of internationalizing Popular Culture Studies, which, it seems to me, we need to keep in mind. It is a large order but by no means too great. It's just that we need to reexamine our theses, our purposes and our means of trying to understand the very complicated and fast-moving world around us. We need a new renaissance in thinking, a break from the steel grip of the Germanic approach which has directed us for the past hundred and fifty years and dictated that we examine knowledge, and especially new knowledge from a core of established and accepted wisdom, a canon of approved readings. Such a canon can be mischievous because it implies, at least to the novice, that understanding of these approved works constitutes a sufficient knowledge and inquiry. But knowledge and learning are constantly expanding by new discoveries and new approaches to the new data. The canonic approach serves as an inhibitor, a restricting grip that changes if at all evolutionarily. We need a newer approach to reality, a new trip through Alice's Wonderland with a more recent explanation of why Father William behaves as he does.

Father Canon's Lament

> "They're fraud, Father Canon, the things that you teach,
> And your argument's become very static.
> Yet you persistently continue to preach
> When your attitude's undemocratic.
> Your logic is thin; your subjects are schmaltz,
> Though they sparkle so brilliant and sterling.
> They twirl us around in a dizzying waltz,
> And our heads are now put all a-whirling."
> "As academic," said the Canon, "I gave up my brain,
> And argued each case from my fear,
> So the deceptive strength I gained without strain
> Guaranteed a productive career.
> I've defended my bias, extolling my fluff,"
> Said the Father. "Just compromise personal cares.
> I have listened for ages to this kind of bluff.
> Be gone or we'll fall down the stairs."

Father Canon's recognition of the tenuousness of his representation is vital in Popular Culture Studies. We must take our subjects with disinterest, honesty and seriousness. And we must be well informed. In no other academic endeavor is there greater need for wide-ranging and deep study and understanding. The requirements are great, the task demanding, but the results will be more than rewarding for the individual and for knowledge in general.

11

The Vanishing Global Village

Playing off of Marshall McLuhan's famous probe that electronic communications were creating a global village, Browne posits that such a phenomenon may actually end up being further from reality due to electronic communication — perhaps using McLuhan's idea that such things eventually reverse into their opposite. Looking at how American popular culture fuses with other national popular cultures to create various multiplicities of "global culture," Browne suggests that economic realities, national and regional identities, and political forces pull away from the creation of a global village.

Written, unlike McLuhan's probe, after the rise of the Internet, Browne's survey of nationalistic TV, culturally appropriate McDonald's, politically scandalous Barbie Dolls and the popularity of Dolly Parton in Zimbabwe provides a fascinating litany of cultural blending and diversities. If the globe unifies at all, it seems it would have to be on American lines — specifically this line: E Pluribus Unum! Browne notes that mass electronic communication has changed the world, and the cultures in it, but that they retain their cultural integrity as they change.

McLuhan himself moved on to the term "Global Theater" and Browne notes that, if anything, we have created a "Global Mall." — The Editor

The rapid shrinkage of the cultural world and the intensified intercourse among peoples in political, commercial, and the resulting cultural activities make it imperative that all of us everywhere appreciate the power of the huge electronic media that are driving the inter-mixing of the peoples and cultures of the world — the drive toward world-wide democracy and its resulting popular cultures and powers. If we do not understand those popular cultures we leave the destiny of our cultures and those of other countries in the hands of the politicians, rabble rousers, merchants and media moguls who mayor may not be the most reliable and trustworthy creators and custodians of desirable cultures. If for one reason or another, we do not appreciate the great power unleashed in the democratization of the world, then perhaps the world deserves the turmoil and battling peoples and cultures that we will receive. As with the legal mandates, ignorance of the cultural laws is no excuse and no escape. We receive what we consciously or unconsciously create or have created around us.

But a misreading of the impact that the electronic media are exerting on the various cultures of the world can cause misleading, costly, and dangerous misassumptions in all societies, strong and weak, around the world. The slick spin to the story of the world for the last thirty years has been that the media — TV, movies, print, computers, etc.— are irre-sistibly and inevitably drawing the varied and extended communities around the world into a global village, presumably with citizens who are like-purposed, politically and cul-turally likeminded (at least to the degree that they can get along with one another) and happy. That's the clichéd reading of Marshall McLuhan's poetic vision of a global village, a concept that apparently promises peace and contentment to a world otherwise filled with wars, rumors of wars, obvious inequities, where in the words of another, very worried, poet, Matthew Arnold, "ignorant armies clash by night," and other people stand around like vultures encouraging the strife and gorging on the carnage. But poets are notorious for their visions, for foreseeing a future that never seems to come. Dreams and clichés spun by the spin-doctors, once established and cultivated through the constant reiteration of the media, are hard to erase. Hope and vision spring eternal, especially when so much is at stake in that hope and vision.

Elsewhere I have called the various geographical and cultural constituents pieces of a mosaic, all of which fit into a large pattern with the parts, moving slowly to adjust to shifting circumstances and developments. The operative words in this figure are slowly and evolutionarily. The notion, and hope, that the elements will move rapidly to form a peaceful global village pits the dynamics of electronic communication instant outreach to touch other peoples and elements of culture which may be very desirable — against human nature — nationalism, regionalism, parochialism, tribalism, cultism, religion, language and fear of change and of the unknown. The same electronic impulses which on the one hand pull us all closer together at the same time give us identity and significance in our separateness — in small groups — and in so doing make it unnecessary for us to join the larger community. When one has the mobility to move into and out of the global village, from and back to his or her "native" village, many opt for the smaller unit where life is looser, freer, and easier. It takes a lot of enlightened self-interest to overcome these inhibitions toward joining larger communities. Only Americans seem to have a natural proclivity to become part of a larger community. Human beings are capable of political and social revolutions on one scale or another. But cultural changes are more evolutionary than revolutionary, three steps forward and two backward.

Increasingly in our materialistic experiences, many people are looking around them to try to chart that global village but are finding instead a sheaf of forces working against construction of that village. They are grudgingly admitting that cobbling together a global village is a long and difficult task, given the many materials and working with the multifarious kinds of people throughout the world who must live in that village, if it is only a metaphor. Bringing people closer together electronically and through other means does not necessarily make them all happy villagers. So let us examine the interacting of the conflict between the communitarians and the nation-staters.

As I have said elsewhere there is nothing new in the intermixing of peoples around the world. According to Alison Brooks, of George Washington University, the history of intercultural trade is lost in the earliest traces of human societies. "Humans were using long-distance trading networks for the exchange of quality stone and other goods in Africa at least 100,000 years ago," she believes (55). In our more immediate past, since the 13th century when Marco Polo traveled the spice trail to Cathay to establish trading and cultural relations, it has been assumed that trade-intercourse is one activity through which people get to know and appreciate one another. It has been a given, also, that with travel has come mutually beneficial interchange of cultures. Messer Rusticiano, who recorded Marco Polo's adventures in *Travels with Marco Polo*, felt, "It would be a very great pity did he [Marco Polo] not cause to be put in writing all the great marvels that he had seen, or on sure information heard of, so that other people who had not these adventures might, by his Book, get some knowledge" (Prologue). Sixteenth-century English philosopher Francis Bacon correctly observed, "Travel ... is a part of education." He listed some two-dozen kinds of activities the traveler should observe, and the advice that such a visitor to a foreign land should "sequester himself from the company of his countrymen" in order to more fully learn from his travels (123).

The interchange of cultures, driven electronically, has never been as powerful it is now. There is no question that today the U.S. has the strongest, largest, and most diverse popular culture in the world and that it touches every land and people. According to German scholar Peter Frees, American popular culture "is the most successful export article of the United States ... [and] has effected an ever increasing 'Americanization' of daily life in Germany, as well as in many other countries around the world" (Carlson and Vichcales x). Joseph Arpad bears out Frees' observation in stating that Hungarian popular culture today is virtually all foreign. "To see some that is Hungarian popular culture, not American, nor Western European, nor even Eastern European, is ... difficult" (9). Media mergers, according to Joseph Tukrow drive "the globalization of mass media activities" (687). *Newsweek* commented on one aspect of this outreach: "Entertainment is not just one of America's largest exports, it's also our culture gone global" (2). During the summer of 1996 American TV through CNN and NBC penetrated more and more deeply and widely into Mexico, and American professional football and baseball filled Mexican stadiums while playing pre-season games in various Mexican cities.

But the flow of American culture toward reshaping the world in America's image is not all one way. In the *New York Times* John Rockwell in his article, "The New Colossus: American Culture as Power Export," reports that "American popular culture has never been more dominant internationally" (30). But he suggests that this predominance of American cultures "is not so much emblems of American superiority as the simple acceptance by a developing world of a simple international standard of discourse.... They may represent not the monopolistic invasion by one country of all the others but the focal point of an international mass culture forming before our eyes" (31).

This international mass culture, which bears no national imprint, is a mixing of both the local and foreign, familiarizing all but not tainting the bloodstream of any nation with foreign virus. As Dutch scholar Mel van Elteren says: "In the modern world a 'national culture' is never purely locally produced; it always contains the traces of previous cultural borrowings or influences which have been a part of a thorough assimilation process and have become 'naturalized'" (68). His unquestionable example is American popular music. "Jazz and American rock music have been assimilated in the European cultural repertoire to such an extent that they have become inalienable components of it," he believes. "'Globalization,' he adds, "is powerfully dislocating national cultural identities" in what he called "time-space compression" (69). Anthropologist Richard Fardon backs up van Elteren's generalizations in asserting that people in his field now feel the small community and the global are the same; "Global is also local and vice versa" (2).

But these various observers may have universalized from too few and atypical data. The interchange of cultures between the U.S. and Europe is relatively easy. We share a centuries old "Western Tradition" of culture. In the loosest sense possible ours are cultures with low border barriers.

But in these nations there are groups, which for one reason or another are trying to become smaller and more discreet entities of linguistic, political, cultural or some other kind of cohesion. The Basques want freedom from Spain more than the regional autonomy that they were granted in 1980. The Northern Irish do or do not want closer ties with Ireland

and looser ones with Britain. The Quebecois narrowly defeated a plebiscite to separate from Canada. Scotland after three centuries of being totally under political control from Whitehall has just been granted limited self-government by Parliament. Wales, with a population around two million, prints its road signs in both English and Welsh. On the border between the two countries the two designations are the same size. The farther you drive into Wales the smaller the English letters become. Welsh humor still keeps John Bull in his place.

The success of radio, TV, and the computer in making all people throughout the world into a culturally discreet unity has been at best qualified, as was that of newspapers and magazines before them. True, TV has furthered the movement that had been intensified by radio and travel in making people from various parts of the world aware of, imitative of, and culturally similar to those from other cultures.

Television by its very nature has been at least partially successful in separating people from their physical and cultural territory, a necessary action before they can be assimilated into new and larger configurations. "The relationship between group identity and group territory is tied to the traditional relationship between place and information access," said Joshua Meyrowitz. "By severing the traditional link between physical location and social situation," he continued, "electronic media may begin to blur previously distinct group identities by allowing people to 'escape' informationally from place-defined groups...." (57). At the same time media allow one to enter a new group informationally and through that new group become comfortable in a new physical place.

In America, where the television barrage has been most effective in breaking down barriers, regional dialectal differences have been largely eliminated, so that people from all parts of the country in effect speak general "standard" English. Other aspects of culture — dress, food, entertainments, transportation, and architecture — have been standardized and democratized.

But TV, at the same time it is breaking down barriers between elements of culture, is revealing strengths in the differences between those elements. It is exerting a counter-thrust against the blurring of cultures as one group discovers the perceived strengths of its unit and an unwillingness to give it up. This strength may have unexpected lasting endurance. People dwell in cultural communities— political, linguistic, and social. They must develop through these discreet "villages" of commonality from small to large, maybe eventually into an international or "global" village. But the many forces working against development of the larger communities have a profound and lasting tenacity.

One of the strongest is lateral cultural constancy. In the past when a person moved from one cultural community to another, he usually went in a small unit, himself and per-haps close family and associates. He took his unit of culture with him. In the new cultural community he was urged or forced to melt into the larger one around him. For example, when the immigrant came to America, he or she was thrown into the "melting pot" and prospered most easily if "Americanized." Though the immigrant might have lived in a ghetto or isolated cultural community, he or she was urged to learn English, dress American, live in an American-style house, and adopt the culture of the new community. It was not always easy to move from one culture to another and sometimes the shift was resisted.

Nowadays lateral cultural constancy is strengthened by the means of communication, which in the past was thought to be significant agents of intercultural mixing. Foodways are one of culture's strongest forces for continuity in tradition. Knowing that, and benefiting from at times costly experience, McDonald's fast food restaurants, though spreading rapidly around the world because they obviously fill a need, have modified their offerings under the golden arches to satisfy those customers who want fast food of their own country. In Amsterdam, for example, because the snack is a vital part of the Amsterdamer's life, McDonald's is known as "McSnack." In Bolivia, McDonald's offers concessions to the local cuisine by serving coca-leaf tea and Bolivian tomato sauce made with hot peppers. On the menu is a typical Andean dish of beef, potatoes, peas and hot peppers, all rolled in pastry. In Turkey no pork is served.

On another level, we all know Disney's gaffe in Euro-Disney until it recognized that the French are different from other people and started serving wine and otherwise Europeanizing its "world."

Television is found to be a strong stabilizer for those cultures, which do not want to change and disappear. This drive toward stabilization is a strong and explosive force, as Geoffrey Fox correctly says in *Hispanic Nation: Culture, Politics and the Constructing of Identity* and "is igniting nationalist movements around the world and ... the detonators include rapid economic changes [with the resulting power that comes with wealth] and new communications technology" (5) which drastically change a person's concept of him/herself and group, making them more powerful and satisfactory than they might have been before.

When television programs, especially such "domestic" ones as soap operas or musicals, for instance, are imported for broadcast they serve as a reminder of home and in so doing encourage people to continue to think of and act in the ways of the old country. In London, for example, every Saturday, tens of thousands of Indians rush to the television in order to see Indian soap opera. These programs serve to perpetuate the old order and the ways of home.

Television can also act as a promoter of minority, ethnic cultures in the midst of overwhelming saturation in television culture of the dominant society. Latino culture, for example, in various parts of the U.S., especially where Latin Americans are strong political and economic blocks, is now catered to with programs rebroadcast from the mother country. The Foto-novella, widely loved in Mexico and Latin America, is becoming increasingly popular in the U.S., especially the Southwest. Under these circumstances television acts as a linguistic and cultural cohesion, which reactivates and prolongs the Latin-American culture which many immigrants in the U.S. prefer not to abandon or forget.

Even more than television and movies, perhaps, American rock music, which contains the power of rebellion and individual achievement, has had a profound effect around the world. We all know how Europe sang Elvis and America sang the Beatles. But other cultures have reacted to American popular music in other ways. American country music in general and Dolly Parton in particular are loved by the people of Zimbabwe. Zimbabweans, especially women, render her success in America as a form of possible personal self-improvement, an American example of Zimbabwean possibilities. Making Dolly Parton a native of Zimbabwe is easily accomplished and powerful because of the Zimbabweans' knowledge vacuum about their own history and culture. When a people know little about their own culture, it is easy to fill their culture with that of outsiders. One Zimbabwean high school student made the point convincingly in stating, "Our own culture remains a mystery to us."

Such infiltration would be more difficult if the people knew and valued their own culture. Parton comes to Zimbabwe with force, glamour and sex appeal and is therefore attractive in the thinner folk culture. Unlike the cultures of the so-called First World countries, which are vibrant and broad enough to accept strains from other cultures without being displaced, Third World cultures such as that of Zimbabwe are likely to import the more glamorous from the outside. But the point must be made that though they import the foreign culture they make it their own. Parton takes on the cultural characteristics of the Zimbabweans rather than their taking on the Parton characteristics. She becomes more a citizen of their country than they of hers (Zilberg 114).

The development of Zimbabwean general culture, like that throughout Africa, is pulling against the controlling elite culture. As Karin Barber points out, "For the nationalist African elites, celebrating the 'traditional' was an affirmation of self-worth, an assertion that African civilization had long had their own artistic glories to compare with those of the colonizers" (1). But as she correctly perceives the cultures of the people have taken on the power of their numbers and of their creations. "They are not mere products of 'culture contact' either, speaking about — and to — the West that has 'corrupted' them. They are the work of local cultural producers [and users] speaking to local audiences about pressing concerns, experiences and struggles they all share." In so doing they strengthen the importance of African cultures to Africans.

An even firmer example of how people cope with needing and trying to establish their own identity can be found in the Mexican rock 'n' roll group called Cafe Tacuba, one of the three most successful groups working in Mexico City today. This group, according to Hope Dillon, is a microcosm of Mexico's search for a new identity, which in the words of the band's members, is a rediscovery of the past: "We try to create in accordance with our own roots, before it was thought that internationalism was gained by recording music in English, but the globalization of culture doesn't work that way, we have to take back our roots" (75).

Taking back or protecting cultures is being profoundly affected today by tourism, which is one of the strongest outreaches of first World cultures on destination countries. Increasingly it is being recognized by observant people that strong and self-respecting local cultures are needed to ward off being dramatically and rapidly changed. Local adjustments must be made to outside demands but in order to be viable tourist sites must retain their own integrity (Alarcon).

In accommodating tourism the vital problem is to encourage the visitors, with their monetary benefits but to maintain one's own culture. In doing so, a destination must accommodate the tourist culture by developing amenities that lure tourists yet at the same time it must maintain the integrity of the local customs to be attractive to those tourists once they are present. Though this accommodation may be driven by economics it is spiritualized and made more successful and peaceful if based on self-knowledge and pride in one's native culture. The present and future impact of tourism on another country, say Mexico, is staggering and may be overwhelming. Two examples, which could be duplicated a thousand times, will give some insight.

One kind of tourism is American retirees living in Mexico. This group is expected to reach half a million to a million and a quarter people by 2025 and pour into the local economies perhaps a billion dollars *a month*. In return for their money, these retirees will expect a dual world sufficiently Americanized to provide familiar comfort and amenities while at the same time retentive of its historical cultures and charms to make living there different, exotic and exciting.

Another apt case in point and an informative picture of the difficulty of change can be found in the small Mexican city of Cuetzalan, a 3–4-hour drive from Puebla, in south-central Mexico, with 19,000 inhabitants, mainly Nahua Indians. Forced by changes in the weather to turn from growing coffee, their traditional cash crop, to tourism, the locals have not found the change without its problems. Ideally consisting of all the qualities that make an environment attractive to tourists, the citizens of Cuetzalan must ease into changes where necessary and admit tourists where they can be accommodated. As the author of the study of the problems in Cuetzalan's adjustment observes, for people in such locations, "the importance of preserving their ethnicity, culture, architectural design, vegetation, and ultimately their tranquility is important to all. Here tourism would not exist if these things were lost," yet the mere existence of tourism threatens the stability demanded (Amador 936, 943).

Locals, of course, are caught in a bind. While desiring to lure the dollar into their economy, they do not want to do violence to their culture. The obvious tension and possible conflict can be eased and lessened if the local culture is strengthened by self-knowledge and self-respect. People who respect themselves can more comfortably deal with what appears to be attacks or slights by outsiders. With cultures as with individuals, if the people are comfortable and confident with themselves they are more likely to be secure and comfortable with others and can properly weigh their own societies against those that might be threatening to invade or substitute. Local cultures in these circumstances do not so quickly and easily fall to the outside power (Otero 914–21).

At times nations are caught in culture-development time warps. India, with its population of a billion people and thousands of differences in languages, attitudes, behaviors and other manifestations of culture, is an excellent case in point. India is a much more dense culture than some Third World cultures. On the 50th anniversary of its nationhood, it demonstrates how large nations, driving through Second World classification to first World, react to external cultural pressures, penetrations, and legacies. From the British, India adopted English as a lingua franca nationwide and a second first-language of commerce. It adopted also British bureaucracy and turned it into the slowest and most unworkable government practice imaginable. From America, India adapted the concept of democracy, capitalism, and democratic entertainment. Bombay, India's movie capital, produces over 300 films a year and is satirically known as Bollywood. Other forms of American business, as well as that from other countries, are slowly taking hold.

But these external forces so far have penetrated only skin deep. India has a large middle class, but more than half the population still lives in the most painful poverty. Fifty percent of the citizens are illiterate, 80 percent of the population still live in villages without any of the modem conveniences of life.

Yet India is not going the way of Britain, America, or any of the Asian nations culturally. Instead, according to best-selling novelist Salmon Rushdie, Indians are happy to be Indians, to maintain the many differences that make them Indians. They do not want to be melted down into one people or molded into a static mosaic. Instead they want the dynamics of a chaos of differences in which individuals, attitudes, successes, failures, loves, and hates are their very own. In this insular nationhood, India follows the pattern practiced by China for a thousand years in resisting all advances of outside cultures, and by Japan in its island superiority. Both China and Japan, however, are opening their cultural borders to the larger world; it is hard to resist the call of money. Time will tell how long India can maintain its national and cultural distinctness as it participates in, but also resists, activities of the world. The forces of cultism, tribalism, regionalism, and nationalism, perhaps because of the country's size and complexity, strengthen it for the time being.

There are many forces working against the concept of the global village whose only connection is electronic. We know that the "global village" is, in fact, an international mall, with clearly defined cultural separations and distinctions that prevent our melding into a cohesive group. In such a setting we would be a large mass but not a village mentality and culture. We fear that, in the words of poet Matthew Arnold, their only language might "be a cry." We dread the large concentration of people, as we have feared moving from the country into the city and in so doing losing our individual identity. We live in two worlds-the electronic and our "real" world. We leave the real world around us when we turn on the electronic media. But we come back when the screen goes black. When it lights, only a part of us is energized — perhaps the cognitive part, maybe the larger community spirit that longs to participate in the world community. But that spirit is not yet powerful enough to overcome the forces of greed, ego, cults, religion, language, and nationalism, which control us most of the time. Perhaps that should be known as the blank screen syndrome. It controls us and it will take a lot of electronic rewiring to free us from those demons of the past.

We also fear the power that comes with leadership of large concentrations of people. Power can be manipulated and it corrupts, not only the people who exercise it but also the people over whom it is exercised.

The forces for and against the actual development of the "global village" concept, as opposed to the rhetoric, which glorifies such a grouping of peoples of the world, are like currents of air acting independently and often flowing in opposite directions above us. They can be likened loosely to the world weather forecasts coming from a central spot, say New York or Atlanta. The forecaster consults his charts and tells us what weather science predicts for any spot on the globe. But whether we know is a local phenomenon. So we look out the window before venturing out.

In these times of developing democracy, the concept of the global village, instead of advancing, may in fact be receding as the American frontier did a hundred years ago. It may lessen or disappear as the physical frontier did. Human nature, with its many quirks, eccentricities, greed, and exercises in blind and unreasoning behavior, may, for better or worse, be a stronger force than electronic communication. With our love of labels and the magic that comes with them, we may in fact construct a bypass around the global village and center our attention on developing something else with the magic of a poetic metaphor.

The difficulty in achieving that poetic metaphor and, more important, the global village, can best be shown perhaps by Mattel Manufacturing and a Barbie doll. Mattel has recently added a new Puerto Rican Barbie to its "Dolls of the World" collection. For the physical attributes of the new Barbie the Institute of Puerto Rican Culture was consulted. She has a mulatto complexion, almond eyes, thick nose, plump lips, raven hair, and a local folkloric dress. To round off Barbie's appeal, the manufacturer printed on the doll what was thought would be an appealing nationalistic message: "Puerto Rico was granted permission to write our own constitution in 1952, and since then we have governed ourselves." But the Puerto Rican Barbie, instead of uniting the population, has split the four million living on the island and the 2.8 million living in the Continental U.S. into opposing war camps. Gina Rosario, a 46-year-old art director at an Alexandria, Virginia, school, who is of Puerto Rican descent, epitomizes the anti–Barbie forces: "She looks very, very Anglo, and what was written on the package was very condescending: 'the U.S. Government lets us govern ourselves.' If you're going to represent a culture, do it properly. Be politically honest," she urges. Meanwhile, a magazine editor in Puerto Rico who collects Barbies, says she was "honored" by the Puerto Rican Barbie, as outlined in an article by Mireya Navarro, "A New Barbie in Puerto Rico Divides Island and Mainland."

Such are the woof and warp of life swirling around a doll, and representative of cultures of the world today. If Barbie, whose main purpose is to sell widely and make people happy, becomes the center of a storm of controversy between like-cultured people, how can we possibly live in a village, no matter how widely separated physically? It takes a lot of compromise for us to minimize our differences and maximize our similarities. More, certainly, than a catch phrase and a dream in a poet's eyes.

Works Cited

Alarcon, Daniel Cooper. *The Aztec Palimpsest: Mexico in the Modern Imagination.* Tucson: University of Arizona Press, 1997.

Amador, Louisa M. Greathouse. "Ethnic, Cultural and Eco Tourism." *American Behavioral Scientist* 40.7 (June/July 1997): 936, 943.

Arpad, Joseph. "The Question of Hungarian Popular Culture." *Journal of Popular Culture* 29.2 (Fall 1995): 9–31.

Bacon, Francis. *Essays.* Oxford: Oxford University Press, 1930.

Barber, Karin. *Readings in African Popular Culture.* Bloomington: Indiana University Press, 1997: 1.

Brooks, Alison. "Trading Networks." *U.S. News* 20 May 1996: 55.

Carlson, Lewis H., and Kevin B. Vichcales, eds. *American Popular Culture at Home and Abroad.* Kalamazoo, MI: New Issues Press, 1996.

Dillon, Hope. "Cafe Tacuba: Forging a New Mexican Identity." *Journal of American Culture* 20.2 (Spring 1997): 75–83.

Fardon, Richard. *Counterworks: Managing the Diversity of Knowledge.* London: Routledge, 1996: 2.

Fox, Geoffrey E. *Hispanic Nation: Culture, Politics and the Constructing of Identity.* Tucson: University of Arizona Press, 1997: 5.

Meyrowitz, Joshua. *No Sense of Place: The Impact of Electronic Media on Social Behavior.* New York: Oxford UP, 1985: 57.

Navarro, Mireya. "A New Barbie in Puerto Rico Divides Island and Mainland." *New York Times* 27 Dec. 1997.

Newsweek 14 Aug. 1995: 2.

Otero, Lorena Melton Young. "U.S. Retired Persons in Mexico." *American Behavioral Scientist* 40.7 (June/July 1997): 914–21.

Rockwell, John. "The New Colossus: American Culture as Power Export." *New York Times* 30 Jan. 1994: 30–31.

Tukrow, Joseph. *Communication Research.* 1992.

van Elteren, Mel. "GATT and Beyond: World Trade, the Arts and American Popular Culture in Western Europe." *Journal of American Culture* 19.3 (Fall 1996): 59–73.

Zilberg, Jonathan. "Yes, It's True: Zimbabweans Love Dolly Parton." *Journal of Popular Culture* 29.1 (Summer 1995): 111–25.

Part Three

Topics and Examples

As previously discussed and demonstrated, Browne's scholarly interests were broad, deep, and wide-ranging. He once joked with me that had he not spent so much time fighting for the legitimacy of popular culture studies he "might have been able to create some lasting works of interest to at least a half-dozen or so like-minded intellectuals."

Joking aside, another volume could (and probably should) easily be compiled consisting of Browne's key and laudable works in folklore studies and literary criticism alone. Works on jump-rope rhymes, popular songbooks, taunts and teases, superstitions, folk medicine and more share the stage with numerous studies on the writings of Mark Twain, Herman Melville, William Shakespeare, Nathaniel Hawthorne and others. High quality aside, Browne gave new meaning to the term prodigious.

Add to those efforts his later works detailing examples of popular culture, not forgetting his other accomplishments, and the mind boggles at his discipline and fortitude. This section includes a mere smattering of such popular culture based examples, each chosen to illustrate how Browne was successfully able to tie his larger pedagogical issues to his more particular scholarship.

12

Whale Lore and Popular Print
in Mid-Nineteenth-Century America:
Sketches Toward a Profile

Browne's first scholarship on Melville was published in 1963, his landmark article "Billy Budd: Gospel of Democracy" in Nineteenth-Century Fiction. *Three other Melville pieces followed in the next few years. Then in 1971, versions of those articles became part of Browne's monumental book-length study* Melville's Drive to Humanism.

As he states in this article, Browne is out to use Melville to make a point. The vaunted and canonized great works of literature did not come to exist in a vacuum or spring into being whole and unique. They were part of larger cultural forces and concerns, part of the discourse of arts and letters of their time — including, of course, the workings of popular culture. The "great works" can better be understood when put in the broader context provided by popular culture studies.

To demonstrate this idea, Browne looks to the events and publications regarding whale lore around the time of the composing and publication of Moby Dick, with evidence of their probable influence on Melville's work, both directly and indirectly. Browne avoids a heavy hand as he deftly makes his case citing popular magazines, news accounts, ballads, minstrel shows, and joke-books.— The Editor

Newspapers and magazines—the popular print — of any time and place not only provide rich lodes from which profiles of what people read and talk about can be sketched; they also demonstrate how these media must be canvassed and appreciated if one would fully understand the culture, and literature, of the time.

In mid–nineteenth-century America, the sea was generally close to the consciousness of the people, especially on the East Coast, the major place of publication of most of these media. Naturally, then, the popular print of the eastern seaboard contained many items about the ocean. One of the most interesting aspects of this sea lore, because of its association with *Moby Dick*, had to do with whales. Articles on the subject were sometimes straightforward and informational, while many others were humorous. Some were illustrated with line drawings, but most were not. All, however, fill in the picture of what was the reading public's fare, and all demonstrate to us what Herman Melville, whose works were occasionally published anonymously in the magazines and whom I want to use to clinch a point, had to draw upon for his sources.

Whaling, a large and old business, made good copy. The straight informational pieces took several forms. One article, for example, "Seals and Whales," gave information about how numerous whaling ships had been forced to turn away from whaling as a business, going first to killing seals and subsequently to hauling timber.[1] Another account, "The Language of the Sea," nationalistically insisted that "the whole whaling diction is the contribution of America, or rather of Nantucket, New Bedford, and New London, aided by the islands of the Pacific and the mongreal Spanish ports of the South Seas."[2]

"How We Went Whaling Off the Cape of Good Hope," intended primarily to inform, at times sounds almost Melvilleian. At one point the whale is described with condescending jocularity: "our fat friend of the ocean is rolling himself about, as if such things as harpoons never existed; as if he were an infidel in javelins..."[3] An especially long article that appeared in *Harper's* contained a full and comprehensive account of all aspects of whaling, and in spots almost echoed *Moby Dick*.[4] It pointed out, for example, that the whale is subject to many infirmities, including dyspepsia (as Melville had reported), and the author advanced several theories about what causes ambergris (the concern of a chapter in *Moby Dick*). An anecdote was given about the sad fate of a harpooner named Tony, who, following sailors' practice, in the midst of a long voyage predicted that in the hunt that was to be undertaken for whales the next day, the whalers would "catch [their] last fish and [lose] a man." The other sailors derided Tony's prophecy, but the next day Tony's boat was gashed by the teeth of a vengeful whale, and Tony was destroyed. The account also included a tale — which sounds very much like Melville's flask talking — about a sailor who ate too much, fell asleep, and dreamed that he was a whale who was chased, harpooned, and finally brought alongside the ship and tried out. He reported that he woke up at the moment he was being tried out, and concluded his bizarre account with the moral: "It's no use to talk to me — whales has feelings; and I don't want to be one agin' as long as ile is in demand, and the supply is got by fryin' blubber."

Other aspects of whaling, or other areas for whaling, found in popular print were not so familiar. In 1854, *Harper's* carried an article entitled "Aboard a Sperm-whaler" which begins with a revealing statement: "We dare say the reader is sufficiently familiar with the many times-told story of the Greenland whale-fishery, but we may be permitted to doubt whether he knows much about the sperm-whale, and its capture in the far-off South Seas."[5] This article is straightforward, referring to the well-known story of the *Essex* being sunk by a sperm whale; the article, interestingly, suggests that people who want to know more about how whales attack ships should read Herman Melville. Furthermore, it cites and perpetuates other bits of whale lore, a practice not uncommon in the popular print. For example, the author asserts that when whaling boats are drawn underwater by diving whales, they are never floatworthy again because "such ... is the pressure of the water upon a boat when it descends to a certain depth, that on being drawn to the surface again, it will not float, owing to the fluid being forced into the pores of the planks, not only by the mere density of the ocean, but also by the rapid rate which the whale has dragged it."

The middle of the nineteenth century in the United States was the heyday of exaggeration, of so-called frontier humor, when the longbow was drawn in song and story by virtually everyone and when — as Melville wrote in both short story and novel — the confidence man was abroad in the land gulling the innocent and credulous in any and every possible way.

Though well known in some ways, the sea was to a great extent the mysterious deep, a place where the unusual and bizarre event occurred. The twin streams of the mysteriousness of the sea and the love of exaggeration and humor often coalesced in whale lore that sprayed into jibes and jests, in the conventional way of humorists. There were conundrums: "Why are some of the boats in New Bedford harbor probably like the head of Victoria's eldest son? Because they contain the prints of whales' teeth (the Prince of Wales teeth)."[6]

There were puns, both brief and extended. The following account is one that is developed at great length:

It is not often that we come across more natural punning than will be found in the following extract from a "Comical Report of a fish Convention." It is to be understood that all the marine monsters, big fish, and "small fry" of the great deep are assembled in conclave—the Whale "in the chair":

"He opened the Convention by stating that he did not wish to make a speech; he would take up as little room, and be no longer than possible.

"(Here the Shark whispered to the Sword-fish that it was not possible for the Whale to be much longer, as he was over eighty feet now. In his opinion, he only wanted a chance to spout: in fact, he considered him a regular old blower.)

"The Whale continued, and contended that he had been grossly insulted by man—he might say, lampooned; not that he would pun upon the use made of his fat, as he did not wish to make light of such a matter. He had been harpooned, at least. Men were sarcastic toward him, and their shafts were sharp and pointed. Some of his fellow-whales had been very much cut up, and exceedingly tried. He had lately learned that a substitute for oil had been invented, which might lessen the persecution of whales—but he feared it was all gas. The Whale alluded to a harpoon which had lately hit him; it had made a great impression on him, and, he feared, had affected him deeply.

"Here his feelings overpowered him, and he sat down (on the Shark) amidst a great blubber."[7]

There were also minstrel sermons delivered about him, as in this one called *De Whale* (which sounds very much like the cook's in *Moby Dick*), delivered by Mr. Julius Caesar Hannibal, in his lectures in "Black Diamonds":

I shall on dis great 'casion spoke to you 'bout de beasts and monsters ob de deep; and as I allers take de biggest end ob a joke fuss, I shall lecture dis ebenin' on de big cod-fish none 'mong de saylers as De Whale.

De Whale, my frens, am werry seldom found in enny odder place dan de Middleterrainin an' de Specific Oshuns. De whale am 'mong de fishes what de elemfant am 'mong de beastsesses-de biggest loafer ob dem all. A fisherman named Jona swallered one once; but it oberloaded he stomach to dat degree, dat in tree days he leff him up ag'in. It was too much for him.

De whale am de big fish; de cod-fish aristocracy ob de sea, de same as de big bugs am de cod-fish aristocracy ob de land; but de former hab got de 'wantage ob de latter, kaze notwithstanin' de whale dewours a good deal, he produces sumfin, but de lan' cod-fish aristocracy dewours ebery ting, and produces nuffin![8]

This is, to a large extent, the popular atmosphere in which Melville wrote *Moby Dick*, and it accounts for Melville's insistence that the events covered in the book could have happened, did in fact occur, and that all accounts of the seemingly incredible events transpiring on the whale hunt should be believed because whales and whalers were in actuality larger than nature. But Melville, it must be remembered, even in his straight-faced insistence, was following a well-established tradition and was also consciously telling tall tales and conning the public.

In this way, then, material about the sea was good copy. It was malleable. It could be given either straight or distorted, as the need required. I would like to use as an illustration an account of particular interest because of its relation to Melville's *Moby Dick*.

The good ship *Ann Alexander* (1805–51) of New Bedford, merchantman turned whaler, was attacked and sunk by a whale on August 20, 1851, at approximately 108o west longitude, 40 south latitude, and thus was catapulted into the popular print.

Under similar circumstances, the *Essex* had been sunk by a whale in 1845 and had become famous. Tales of that battered ship had filled newspapers and magazines and had become household lore. Melville, as he frequently did in his works, had drawn upon the event for use in *Moby Dick*. The fate of the *Ann Alexander*, coming so soon afterward, not only filled Melville with wonder and speculation, but also appealed to his feeling for the humorous. *Moby Dick* was at the printers when news of the *Ann Alexander*'s fate reached him. Evert Duyckinck sent him a letter (which Melville apparently received on November 6) telling the news. Although this letter seems to be lost, Melville outlined its contents in his reply:

> Your letter received last night had a sort of stunning effect on me. For some days past busily engaged in the woods with axe, wedge, and beetle, the Whale had almost completely slipped me for a time (and I was the merrier for it) when Crash! comes Moby Dick himself (as you justly say) and reminds me of what I have been about for part of the last year or two. It is really and truly a surprising coincidence — to say the least. I have no doubt it *is* Moby Dick himself, for there is no account of his capture after the sad fate of the *Pequod* about fourteen years ago. — Ye Gods! what a commentator is this *Ann Alexander* whale. What he has to say is short and pithy and very much to the point. I wonder if my evil art has raised this monster.[9]

Melville's tone here, as usual, reveals both sides of his character. He is serious, but he is also witty, ironic, and merry. In the comical pose, here as in many of his works, he is playing on his habit of feeding on the nation's bias for exaggeration in nearly all aspects of life and in nearly all kinds of stories, especially those concerning the sea.

The *Ann Alexander*'s fate filled newspapers and magazines with shock stories. Most accounts were serious treatments of the conditions under which the whale had first attacked the whaleboats, then the ship, and of the terrifying conditions resulting from a ship's being lost at sea. A long article in the March 1856 issue of *Harper's*, which included a line drawing, reported the event, citing it as a "recent example of the increasing intelligence of the whale," where the fight between the whale and the whalers was fairly conducted, and "where the pertinacity of human passions found a consistent antagonist in the monster fish." As a follow-up to the tragedy, the article reported:

> about four months after this catastrophe, the crew of the *Rebecca Sims*, of New Bedford, came up with, and captured a large whale, that permitted itself to be taken without any of the usual demonstrations of resistance. Two harpoons were found in its body, marked "*Ann Alexander*," its head was seriously injured, and from the huge wound projected pieces of a ship's timbers.[10]

Some newspaper and magazine accounts of the event, happy to feed on the frontier tradition of distortion and overkill, found the whole story of the destructive whale too large to swallow. These stories emphasized the absurdity of the entire escapade. An account in the *Utica* [New York] *Daily Gazette* of November 11, 1851, is a good example. Typically, it burlesques the affair, saying, "it gives a fearful idea of the courage of the whale that would give battle to a crew surpassing in their achievements Jack the Giant Killer or Saladin."

In ballad — which, with song, was especially popular at this time — the events surrounding the *Ann Alexander*'s fate were recounted at least once. In 1851, *Punch* printed a comical ballad called "The Wonderful Whalers" whose concluding line indicates that the account is mostly or altogether untrue and should not be taken seriously."[11] How extensively this song was reprinted, and how popular it became, is impossible to determine at this time. But the thousands of songsters and popular songbooks of the day contained hundreds of pieces just like it in spirit and execution, though not necessarily in subject matter. Professor Hennin Cohen, however, found a copy of the ballad in *The Harp of a Thousand*

Strings, an anthology of humor edited by S. P. Avery. Inclusion of the song in that volume might mean that the event was still in the minds of many readers—that the song was still popular. (But inclusion might just as well mean that it was considered a lively song, that it was available where copy was needed, and that Avery included it for his own reasons.)

The song reveals a good deal about this particular aspect of popular culture and popular print at the halfway mark of the nineteenth century in America. The ballad is lighthearted doggerel, which points out that such accounts of the activities of whales and the fate of whalers are figments of lively imaginations. It begins with the classical appeal to the Muses—in this instance, to Oratory—and to a more democratic teller of tall tales:

> Fathers of the Oratory,
> > Listen to my surprising tale,
> Hearken to a wonderous story
> > More than very like a whale;
> Each mesmeric marvel-monger,
> > Lend to me your ears likewise;
> If for miracles you hunger,
> > You shall ope both mouth and eyes.

> In the ship *Ann Alexander*,
> > Cruising in pursuit of whales,
> Bold John S. Deblois, Commander,
> > With a crew so gallant, sails.
> In the South Pacific Ocean,
> > Reaching to the Off Shore Ground,
> 'Mong the waves in wild commotion,
> > Several monstrous Whales they found.

> These two boats did follow after,
> > Larboard boat, and starboard too,
> And with shouts of glee and laughter,
> > The Leviathans pursue;
> When the larboard boat commanded
> > By the stout first Mate, did soon
> In a Whale, with force strong-handed,
> > Deeply plunge a shart harpoon.

> Off the mighty monster started;
> > Pain and anguish gave him cause;
> Suddenly he backwards darted,
> > Seized the boat between his jaws;
> Into smithereens he cracked it;
> > Or, as witnesses declare,
> Who beheld the thing transacted,
> > Bits no bigger than a chair!

In the starboard boat, the Captain
    Quickly to the rescue struck,
And, although the bark was snapt in
    Pieces, saved the crew-by luck.
Now the good *Ann Alexander*
    To their aid the waist-boat sent;
Half the band then having manned her,
    At the Whale again they went.

Soon the ocean-giant nearing,
    They prepared to give him fight,
Little thinking, never fearing,
    That the beast again would bite.
But without their host they reckon'd;
    At their boat he also flew;
Like the first he served the second.
    Snapped it into pieces too.

Sure his jaws, together clapping,
    Had the gallant seamen crushed;
But, when they perceived him snapping,
    Straight into the sea they rushed.
To afford the help they needed,
    Bold Deblois repaired again,
Once more, also, he succeeded,
    In the aim to save his men.

Tired, perhaps, of sports renewing,
    To the ship this time they hied,
When, behold, the Whale pursuing,
    With his jaws extended wide.
Gloating with revenge, he sought 'em;
    But with blubber pierced, and gored,
He was crippled, or had caught 'em;
    But they all got safe on board.

Risk the heroes little cared for;
    Speedily they set their sail.
In the ship herself-prepared for
    One more tussle with the Whale.
Now they reach'd him-plunged a lance in
    The infuriate monster's head;
Then-of course they had no chance in
    Close encounter-onward sped.

For the ship they saw him making,
    But the chase he soon gave o'er,

Which the animal forsaking,
    Down on him again they bore;
Fifty rods below the water
    There they saw the monster lie;
So, despairing him to slaughter,
    They resolved no more to try.

At this time, Deblois was standing
    Sternly on the larboard bow,
Ready, with harpoon in hand,
    To inflict a deadly blow:
Up he saw the monster rising,
    With velocity and power,
At the rate of speed surprising,
    Of full fifteen knots an hour!

In an instant-Heaven defend us!
    Low, the Whale had, near the keel
Struck, with such a force tremendous,
    That it made the vessel reel;
And her bottom knock'd a hole in,
    Into which the water pour'd;
And the sea so fierce did roll in,
    That the billows rush'd and roar'd.

Yet the ship was saved from sinking,
    Though so riddled by the Whale,
And Deblois and his unshrinking
    Crew survive to tell the tale,
Strong are all those daring fellows,
    Doubtless, the harpoon to throw:
And-to judge from what they tell us
    Stronger still to draw the bow![12]

The song's reversal of the well-known fact that the ship was indeed sunk is doubtless another broad indication that the account should not be taken seriously.

In *Moby Dick*, Melville says that a good laugh is a mighty good thing.

In this sense, as well as because of their common subject and their echoes of Shakespeare, "The Wonderful Whalers" and *Moby Dick* are related. The song is out-and-out spoof. On one level, of course, so is Melville's book. Both are examples of the popular culture of the time appearing in the popular media. And the similarity between the two demonstrates yet again how vital it is for anyone examining the literature of a period to consult contemporary newspapers and magazines.

Notes

1. *Harper's*, 3 (October, 1851), 766.

2. *Atlantic,* 2 (October, 1858), 578–84.

3. *Harper's,* 1 (November, 1850), 844–46.

4. *Harper's,* 12 (March, 1856), 466–82.

5. *Harper's,* 8 (April, 1854), 670–74.

6. *Harper's,* 10 (January, 1855), 276.

7. *Harper's,* 11 (September, 1855), 569.

8. *Harper's,* 10 (May, 1855), 853.

9. See Jay Leyda, *The Melville Log* (New York: Harcourt, 1951), I, 431–32.

10. 12 (March, 1856), 482.

11. *Punch,* 21 (1851), 242–43.

12. *The Harp of a Thousand Strings; Or Laughter fit for a Lifetime. Konceived, Comp., and Komically Konkokted, by Spavery ... Aided, Added, and Abetted by Over 200 Kurious Kuts, from Original Designs* (New York: Dick & fitzgerald, 1858), pp. 98–101.

I am grateful to Professor Hennin Cohen of the University of Pennsylvania for letting me use this song. I am also especially indebted to Mr. Richard Kugler of the Old Dartmouth Historical Society Whaling Museum in New Bedford, Mass., and to Mr. Charles R. Schultz, Librarian, the G.W. Blunt White Library, the Marine Historical Association, Mystic, Conn.

13

The Seat of Democracy:
The Privy Humor of "Chic" Sale

Vaudeville was an area of popular culture Browne considered infrequently, but with welcome results when he did. The strongest example may be his highly regarded and influential 1960 article "Shakespeare in American Vaudeville and Negro Minstrelsy," from American Quarterly, *in which he documents numerous popular parodies, satires, and burlesques of the bard and his works.*

In this article Browne turns his critical eye towards scatological humor, starting off with Freudian/medical references that make the reader wonder if Browne is totally serious himself, or perhaps engaging in some academic tricksterism.

Noting that folklore studies and historians have both regarded sexual behaviors and bodily eliminations as proper academic topics, Browne introduces readers to the now obscure performer "Chic" Sale and his (literally) out-house humor.

Browne lays out an interesting thesis to explain Sale's popularity between the two World Wars, and analyzes his importance as an unlikely (and probably unconscious) purveyor of democracy.

Though the argument is intriguing and well-handled, one still almost gets the idea that Browne may be mocking his own well-known penchant for uncovering the "long push to democracy" in unlikely places. Either way, the article is a strong example of Browne's contention that no subject or topic is without merit and potential useful insights, and warrants attention for that beyond its more obvious uses.— The Editor

Of all aspects of human life and activity, those dealing with the digestive and elimination processes of the human body have been the most tabooed and unspeakable. All parts of the body, especially the sexual ones, have been generally subject to discussion, particularly in regard to what you can do with and to them, but all kinds of people have been reluctant to deal openly and directly with the natural processes with which the human body must cope.

Norman O. Brown, in *Life Against Death*, feels that "the morbid attempt to get away from the body can only result in a morbid fascination [erotic cathexis] in the death of the body." He continues, "In more technical terms, sublimated anality presupposes the castration complex, the decisive death of the body which according to Freud desexualizes and paralyzes the penis. With the death of the penis the center of erotic attention is transferred to the dead body par excellence, the feces." Quoting Jonathan Swift and Coleridge, Brown agrees that what makes man a Yahoo is, "ironically, his disposition to negate the body and rise above it." "But the irony," again quoting Brown, "is that sublimation activates the morbid animality (anality), and the higher form of life, civilization, reveals that lower form of life, the Yahoo. To rise above the body is to equate the body with excrement."[1] Brown, in fact, places man's chauvinistic sexism and his fear of and feeling of superiority over women on the fact that woman's natural sexual eliminatory apertures are in close proximity to each other.

Even medical doctors, for reasons that must surely be nearly inexplicable, have only recently openly concerned themselves with such things. In a recent study a medical doctor and professor of gynecology and obstetrics published a group of sexual jokes under the title "Psychodynamics of Sexual Humor: 'Willing Women'" and explained their function and humor. For example:

> "The pretty young woman was about to go to bed with her blind date, when she suddenly sobbed 'I don't want you to get the wrong idea about me. I'm really not that kind of girl.'
> 'I believe you,' he comforted her.
> 'You're the first one,' she cried.
> 'The first one to make love to you?'
> 'No. You're the first one who believed me.'"

The impact of this joke, according to the gynecologist, is that it "structures a situation in which the reader believes that the female protagonist is adhering to and acting out the traditional good woman (sexual reluctance) pattern only to find at the end that her sexual posture has been a sham and the reader has been duped by the story teller. The excitement comes from each woman's admission of sexual interest."[2]

In yet another direction, in 1979 *McLean's Magazine* featured a story about a medical doctor who made news because he had been studying the causes and cures of a serious medical problem, gas on the stomach and in the bowels and its emission (13 times a day, by the way, is average). He was jeered at by the medical community and accused of "bringing status to flatus and class to gas." The folk have, of course, always recognized gas in its several manifestations and have all kinds of jokes about it, including numerous jokes and tall tales about its explosive potential (a scientific fact that in the current energy crisis, many scientists attest to). But they have been self conscious in talking about the whole activity. Gershon Legman's various serious studies in various kinds of bodily functions have generally had to be published against the hue and cry of fellow serious folklorists, and Vance Randolph's valuable collection of "pornographic" folklore had to lie hidden in the Library of Congress for years because nobody, including the Missouri Folklore Society which had published many of his other materials on Ozark folklife, dared bring it out. It was finally published under the title *Pissing in the Snow and Other Ozark Folktales* as an anticlimax.

In general elite culture has been above the subject, finding it indelicate, though there are numerous examples of its use, from the *Second Shepherd's Play*, Chaucer, Swift, Mark Twain, Herman Melville (who devotes a whole section to what happens when the giant whale Moby Dick has indigestion and has to pass air), to Ignatius Donnelly's two novels *Caesar's Column*, which has "excremental vision," and *The Golden Bottle*, and undoubtedly many others.

The importance of body gas, though it often goes undetected, as symbol is revealed by the practice of undertakers when they are preparing the corpse for viewing and burial inserting gaseous formaldehyde in the body cavities to "reanimate" it and make it look more lifelike. This "animate" look does not last long, as those of us who have observed the bloated bodies of dead animals very well have noted. Though most of us might feel reluctant to paraphrase Longfellow's *Psalm of Life* to read "Gas thou art, to gas returnest sure was spoken of the soul," most of us can recognize that perhaps Benjamin Franklin was unconsciously close to this feeling when he wrote in the 1776 edition of *Poor Richard's Almanac*: "He that lives on hope dies farting."[3]

One particular aspect of the bodily processes, which has been disguised in circumlocutions, has been the elimination of wastes. In Colonial America, William Byrd, in his *Secret Diary*, called it doing his "song and dance." Others have used circumlocutions and private language to avoid naming the parts and the functions.

Among the folk and the young, as everybody over forty knows, the outdoor privy, throughout rural America at least, has always been the source of a thousand jokes and a yearly ritual on Halloween of overturning it, that being apparently the funniest prank that could be pulled on anyone because it interrupted one of the most elemental and therefore most important aspects of bodily and thoughtful activity.

The importance of the privy, the stool, and the other names we have for the place and the process cannot be overstated. John Osborne in his play *Martin* has Martin Luther suffering from chronic constipation and quotes him: "I'm like a ripe stool in the world's straining anus, and at any moment we're about to let each other go."[4] Critic Simon Trussler declares, "Constipation, epilepsy and sweat distinguish Luther bodily." Norman O. Brown quotes sections of Luther, which strongly suggest that without his chronic constipation and other physical and consequent mental troubles, Luther might never have mounted the Reformation. For example:

> The words "just" and "justice of God" were a thunderbolt in my conscience. They soon struck terror in me who heard them. He is just, therefore He punishes. But once when in this tower I was meditating on those words, "the just lives by faith," "justice of God," I soon had the thought whether we ought to live justified by faith, and God's justice ought to be the salvation of every believer, and soon my soul was revived. Therefore it is God's justice which justifies us and saves us. And these words became a sweeter message for me. *This knowledge the Holy Spirit gave me on the privy in my tower* [my emphasis].

Throughout our history Americans have been extremely shy about talking sexual matters no matter how simple and detached. In the nineteenth century, for example, most Americans cursed the English sparrow, which had recently been introduced into this country, because it fornicated in public, as though unaware of the embarrassment of the situation! In current times, however, popular culture is freer in dealing with these kinds of things. For example, television, magazines, and all other media do not blush at advertising all types of cures for constipation, and hemorrhoids, and sanitary napkins and tampaxes. Alas, yesterday's hidden subjects are today's commonplaces— and humor.

Democratic humor can easily become condescension. And this kind of democratic humor easily and quickly becomes objects of ridicule, mainly because the popular mind is not quite comfortable with the words and concepts it uses. For example, in the early 1950s a candidate for the mayoralty in Los Angeles suggested that since the city desperately needed to save water each householder should put a brick in the water tank of his toilet, and thereby save the county millions of gallons of water a day. His opponent immediately dubbed him with all kinds of embarrassing names, and the candidate of course lost the election. In 1976 Wyoming Republican State Senator Malcolm Wallop defeated three-term democratic United States Senator Gale McGee, and part of his success hinged on ridicule. The federal government had advocated that restrooms should be provided in every workplace, no matter how small. Ridiculing this law, candidate Wallop tied this "absurd" legislation to Senator McGee, who of course represented the government, and had a TV ad show a cowboy dragging a privy jouncing and bouncing across the countryside. This is an association that one cannot counter and few can overcome.[5]

In the world of popular literature one writer, Charles "Chic" Sale, made the outdoor privy the subject of his major works. In these works he played upon the memories, prejudices, biases and pleasures of his former country life, and used the outdoor privy to express his profound attitudes and philosophy about the virtues of country life and to demonstrate the movement in America during the 1920s and 1930s away from the country to the city and the need for a cushion to soften the blow of the people who were wrenched from one and tossed into the other. It is not too much to say that Sale, consciously or unconsciously, in a way somewhat paralleling Martin Luther's preoccupation, realized that the privy was the most democratic of all institutions in America, and was using it as an icon to assert to a world where democracy was beginning to split into "elite" and common areas that the democracy of the earlier days should be recaptured and preserved.

Charles "Chic" Sale was born in Huron, S.D., in 1885. When he was a small lad his family moved to Urbana, Illinois, the country of Abraham Lincoln, who was to become and remain his idol throughout life. By the age of 15 Sale had a local reputation as a mimic. In 1908 he left Urbana for Chicago, where he tried out at the Majestic Theater, Chicago's leading vaudeville house, but was considered too green to succeed in the big-time. He drifted, determined to be an actor, until he wound up in Bellefontaine, Ohio, where he was successful. He thus began his career in what was called in those days "corn tassel and high-grass characters," which consisted of the sentimental rube speaking in a twangy nasal voice about country affairs. After one unsuccessful tryout in the Bronx in 1911 Sale succeeded in New York two years later. By 1923 he was a vaudeville headliner playing hayseed sketches and sentimental characters like that of the GAR veteran "wending his way down the dusty road to the poor house," which, according to the New York *Evening World*, "was always good for a tear." In 1930 Sale wrote the daily column for the *World*, called "Good Ev'nin'— Chic Sale" but it was not as popular as Will Rogers', whom Sale imitated. Sale was a GAR veteran in Shubert's *Gay Paree* in 1925, played in *So This Is Paris* in 1930, in *An Elephant Never Forgets* in 1934, appeared at the Winter Garden in several reviews, and made a dozen or so movies (such as *Stranger in Town, Star Witness, Comin' Round the Mountain, When a Feller Needs a Friend, The Expert* and *Lucky Dog*). He always prided himself on the fact that he looked a great deal like Lincoln, and his finest role, he felt, was an MGM sketch in which he read the *Gettysburg Address* to a rebel soldier; this movie was still being shown in public schools as late as the end of the 1930s. Sale died in Hollywood in 1936, aged 51. In the obituaries, generally, no mention was made of his activities in two fields. He made at least two phonograph records and wrote three books. The third book—*The Champion Cornhusker Crashes the Movies* (1933) was a series of letters written by a hick in Hollywood to a friend back home outlining how the sucker gets taken in the city. In this work, Sale had gotten too far away from his strong subject to be effective. In the two earlier books, however, he had been a smashing success.

The Specialist, his first book, published in St. Louis in 1929, was an instant sensation because it humorously bridged the gap between country and city life, eased the pain of those persons who were leaving the farm for the city, and because it brought back memories—fun and nostalgia—of life on the farm, by centering on the outdoor privy. Sale had made the transition from country to city and undoubtedly the people who purchased the book were city people not long from the farm who might well have been a little uncomfortable in their new role and liked the democratic implications of Sale's message, and people on the farm who were at least aware of what going to the city meant. As one John D. Wells in a poem printed in the Buffalo, N.Y. *Courier Express* put it, Sale was the perfect democrat:

> Gentle, too;
> Not like play-act fellers do-
> *Others of 'em*— who proclaim
> Something kin to mortal shame
> 'Cause a feller's country-bred
> *Ignorance*, I've always said!
> Chic, though, he jist ripples on,
> Smiles and swears a soft "Doggone!"
> Then he speckylates on who
> God made *first*, us fokes or you
> City fokes; and by an' by
> He'll declare the vote a tie —
> Says he thinks we *both* are good
> If we're only understood —

After a lengthy catalogue of country practices and habits, elements of folk culture, the poet concludes that Sale's appeal, though multifaceted, probably is his touching on nostalgia:

> Mebbe it's his brand O' jokes
> or his knack of ape-in folks,
> Or — like enuff — he brings to mind
> Things I've loved *an' left behind*!

Attention to this nostalgic appeal was highlighted in a Foreword to the book by W.S. McClevey, of St. Louis, who speculated that "Humor, when enjoyed to the full, is that which is based on events, experiences, or intimate knowledge of the subject described; or a mixture of all three. And if the subject is one which is not usually discussed, yet is of a character incident to the home life of each family, that also, adds to the zest with which one listens to the story told; or if printed, intensifies the interest of the reader."

The Specialist therefore "sought to portray generally-but-seldom mentioned incidents of every day life," and, as McClevey makes clear, the main element was the democratic subject of body functions.

McClevey's is a fair definition of much humor of the time, and undoubtedly says as much about the appeal of the presentation as of the subject.

In 1911 Sale had tried out his vaudeville act in the Bronx and failed because, as the *New York Times* said, the people knew nothing of the soil and cared little for "twangy lectures on rural architecture."

In this first book Sale put on paper the elements of "rural architecture" that the New Yorkers had not understood, and the "generally-known-but seldom-mentioned-incidents of every day life" (that is life around and in the outdoor privy). Writing as one Lem Putt, Sale describes the various kinds of privies he can build: one-holers to eight-holers, those anchored to the ground, and those just sitting on it, those constructed with two-by-fours or four-by-fours, the kinds of ventilation holes one can use, from quarter moons, to stars, the kinds of ground they should be built on for day and night visits and wet and dry times of the year, the proper geographical location; and he manifests a certain delicacy and regard for feelings by pointing out that the proper place to construct such a utilitarian building is on a direct line with the woodpile so that easily embarrassed women can camouflage their real purpose in heading in that direction by bringing back a load of wood on their return. Sale brings a smile to the lips of every reader by complaining at some length about the quality of the Sears-Roebuck catalogue always found there, and states that he is going to write his complaints to the manufacturer about the quality and ask that the catalogues be made thicker so that they will last from one printing to the next. He dwells some time on the country practice mentioned earlier, that of the pranksters who loved to overturn privies at Halloween. But Sale did not dwell exclusively on the utilitarian aspects of his work. He was an artist, and his privies were things of beauty. He ended *The Specialist* with this paean which was part satire, part parody, and part genuine feeling: discussing the beauty of his triumph in architecture and setting, Sale wrote:

> There sits that privy on that knoll near the woodpile, painted red and white, mornin' glories growin' up over her and Mr. Sun bathin' her in a burst of yeller color as he drops back of them hills. You can hear the dog barkin' in the distance, bringin' the cows up fer milkin', and the slow squeak of Elmer's windmill pumpin' away day after day the same as me.

On the last page of the book there is an illustration of this triumph of art over nature with the Biblical caption which immediately reminds us of Luther's fixation on the Bible, though the Bible was the most common book of the time in America: "The Cup Overfloweth."

This book was an immense success. Running to only 32 pages it sold for a dollar in boards, $3 in leather. These were steep prices even for 1929. According to *Publisher's Weekly*, this little book "without any advertising whatever except word of mouth, sold 200,000 copies within the space of three or four months and ran neck and neck with *All Quiet on the Western Front* on the best seller list during the summer of 1929." A year later Sale's publisher was claiming that *The Specialist* had sold more than a million copies and was still selling briskly. Apparently it was widely read. In 1980, everybody over the age of fifty, at least in the Midwest and South, remembered it.

In 1930 Sale tried to duplicate his success with another book on the same subject, *I'll Tell You Why*. The Introduction, written by a certain O. O. McIntyre, points out the recognizable characteristics of Sale's literary strength: "Chic Sale is one of the bright eyed robins of life who has preserved our vanishing emotional nexus with the turkey wing stove duster, the carpeted brick door-holder, wax doves under glass on the parlor mantle and other mid–Victorian what-nots." McIntyre lays the real thrust of Sale's intentions on the line: "He was an actor, and a good one, and did not know he could write until he seized upon a homely topic, usually mentioned in whispers, and gave it the whimsical charm of a Barrie play or a nursery tale by Milne."

The author of the Introduction claims that in this second volume Sale "has a greater subtlety, and its philosophy is deeper" than in the earlier book. Indeed, although it is on precisely the same topic as *The Specialist*, *I'll Tell You Why* is a somewhat different book. In the latter effort, with the success of the earlier book as reassurance, Sale tinctured his humor with more satire and social purpose than he had managed a year earlier; although he mentions his triumph as being a two-story privy, he doesn't describe how it works. The thrust of *I'll Tell You Why*, though still blunted and tipped with nostalgia, is somewhat more direct and less shielded by its humor.

The speaker is addressing the members of the Young Men's Business Breakfast Club, and has been asked to "talk on and point out such problems and pitfalls as confront the business man of today." He assures these young executives that if they will follow his advice they will succeed as he has:

> The same things— the very same things— that made me a big success in my specializin' will be a big help to you, too, if you practice what I'm going to tell you." He insists that if a businessman will be "honest, sincere, trustworthy and give service," success will generally take care of itself. He admits that sometimes the customer can be indecisive; in which case the executive should be "firm" and tell the customer what he wants. Sale insists that, "fair competition never hurt any-body. You can always meet it half way, an' it stimulates business." The speaker counsels that the successful businessman must have very little sentiment because, "gentlemen, sentiment in business won't work."

Sale pleads for the specialist, not the "common post–hole digger," but warns against the kind of fast-talking salesman who sold a dance pavilion an eight-holer, which had holes that were too small.

In a contradiction of his earlier statements in words that reveal his basic conservatism, Sale insists that he does not experiment and create unnecessarily. He always sticks to the standard type, "adding every year, such improvements as I've tried out and found fool-proof.... Experimentin' round is liable to prove costly — and it's the customer that pays fer it in the long run."

Although there are certainly echoes of Luther's experience in these words by Sale, in a much closer parallel to Luther's attack on the Catholic Church, Sale affirms that to him pride is dangerous, "Pride will nearly always make a feller over–estimate his ability!" He concludes this book, as he had the earlier one, on a Biblical homily that Pride goeth before a fall, and with his own philosophy, common in the thirties, especially among country people who had had to work hard to survive, "It ain't where you start that counts— it's where you finish."

In effect, what we have in the privy humor of Chic Sale is an amusing play on nostalgia and memory turned on a hush-hush subject, utilizing a vivid memory of life on the farm and in the small town, written by a conservative man, who though he has in fact conquered the world around him, is somewhat fidgety in it and although he could wear the clothes of the city slicker did not desire to get all the hayseed out of his hair or the twang out of his voice. He represents the Transitional — or Disrupted — man of the Thirties.

Such a message is not uncommon, and was especially widespread in the twenties and thirties when "an interest in farm fiction reached its peak among the urban population who had left their farms for city comforts but who looked back nostalgically to their simpler and seemingly purer rural past with its rural virtues,"[6] and the fruits of the business man, the specialist, lay in shambles all around him, thus making the virtues of the country life look more and more appealing — at least in memory. *The Grapes of Wrath* (1939) were grow-ing on *God's Little Acre* (1933), and people were fleeing. But if one poked back in the dirt before those vines had matured, they could find the pure soil that had produced the golden age in America.

These two books are especially useful in demonstrating how a person in transition — as millions of Americans were —from the farm to the city suffered pangs of regret and nostalgia, the kinds of humor that appealed to him/her, and how at least one individual bridged the move from Urbana to Hollywood. They are, in this light, valuable records of that history.

But on a deeper and more universal scale, Sale's choice of the privy as the metaphor of his world and of society undoubtedly runs on a level and a profundity that we might easily overlook. One does not have to agree totally with John Osborne or Norman O. Brown that the Reformation was a great bodily/psychological purgative for Martin Luther to understand that these basic aspects of life have deep-felt ramifications, nor that Sale was consciously or unconsciously paralleling Luther's preoccupation with anal philosophy, though it is obvious that both were concerned with the same objective, that of democratizing society.

As for Sale himself, what was his obvious ultimate success? As an actor his reputation suffered an eclipse. His books are no longer available, though there is some interest in having them made available again.* They were obviously widely read, especially in the rural sections of the U.S. Nearly everyone in these sections of the country over the age of 50 remembers the outdoor privy as a "Chic Sale." Sale did not achieve the immortality of George Crapper or that promised by the makers of the portable potty when they wanted to name it, "H-e-e-e-r-e's Johnny." But for fifty years the outdoor privy in a large section of the United States became the "Chic Sale"— and in the course of human events having one's name attached to such a democratic instrument of daily life for half a century is surely no mean accomplishment.

Notes

1. See Norman O. Brown, *Life Against Death: The Psychoanalytical Meaning of History* (Middletown, Conn.: Wesleyan University Press), especially Chapter XIII, "The Execremental Vision."
2. Malcolm G. Freeman, "Psychodynamics of Sexual Humor: 'Willing' Women," *Medical Aspects of Human Sexuality*, April 1980, pp. 130–136.
3. The best study of farting is by a sociologist, David Voigt, in, of all places, *Hustler*, July 1978, under the title "Fear of Farting." Voigt uses the Franklin quote.
4. Simon Trussler, *The Plays of John Osborne* (London: Gollancz, 1969).
5. Roy A. Jordan and Tim R. Miller, "The Politics of Cowboy Culture," in *Annals of Wyoming*, 52, No.1, Spring 1980.
6. Catherine McLay, "Crocus, Saskatchewan: A Country of the Mind," *Journal of Popular Culture*, 14:2 (Fall 1980).

*The first two volumes were eventually reprinted in facsimile editions.— The Editor

14

Sherlock Holmes as
Christian Detective:
The Case of the Invisible Thief

One of Browne's dominant interests throughout his career was detective fiction, and we have seen references to it in several of the pieces included herein. He edited at least three detective fiction anthologies and one collection of academic articles and wrote three books devoted to aspects of the topic. He also co-founded the journal Clues: A Journal of Detection.

Browne's interest was highest for the various guises and variations of the hard-boiled detective of popular crime fiction, ranging from the earliest adventures of Sam Spade, through the pulp fiction exploits of largely unknown characters and writers, to the popular authors of the post–World War II paperback explosion, and into contemporary examples from writers concentrating on Native American experiences and issues.

Browne's development of themes and issues in this area is notable and profound. This piece is in a lighter vein, but has its own validity and pleasures. For one, Browne rarely dealt with the most famous fictional detective of all, Sherlock Holmes, and he does so here.

At first glance the piece seems to be little more than a book review of a minor addition to Holmesiana. But more is going on here than meets that first glance. Browne begins by noting that Holmes remains ubiquitous in the popular media and details a few of the more interesting of the then-recent examples to support his case for the cultural adaptability and vibrancy of the character.

Browne then brings up the issue of conservative born-again Christian Fundamentalism and notes that Holmes has also been subsumed into that particular cultural wave. The essay then seems to proceed with a standard analysis of a particular book's development of fundamentalist Christian ideology by using the Holmes literary conventions as a template.

At heart, though, Browne is exemplifying his belief that even the most mundane and even "failed" elements of popular culture—he emphasizes the book's lack of success when so many things Holmesian are successful—can tell us something useful about ourselves and our culture. And the attentive scholar can accomplish this nearly simultaneously with the phenomena, not waiting for the hindsight of history.

Browne accomplishes these goals in a light, discursive manner. Those not familiar with Browne's larger pedagogic goals would likely miss out on the deeper aspect implied by the piece. But for those familiar with them, what may seem to be a slight effort takes on a most "singular" significance.

The original publication in Clues *jumbled the order of some paragraphs. When the article was republished, Browne simply omitted those sections. This reconstruction is the first proper and complete publication of this article.— The Editor*

In our society with its decided political and religious swing to the right there has been, curiously, a tilt (or rather a rush) also back to Sherlock Holmes, despite the fact that on the surface at least, Holmes, although obviously a political and cultural conservative, was hardly a practitioner of Fundamental born again Christianity. The two movements may be merely coincidental, but in at least one instance there is a direct connection.

In the swing back to Holmes there have been numerous reissues of all his works in new paperback editions. And there have been numerous (over three dozen) resuscitators and imitators. There have been, for example, such books as *Sherlock Holmes in New York*, based on the NBC adventure written by Alvin Sapinsley, adapted by D.R. Bensen (1976). *Murder by Decree* (1979) is an adaptation by Robert Weverka from the screenplay by John Hopkins; it centers on Jack the Ripper. Arthur Byron Cover projects a series of murders into the future in *An East Wind Coming* (1979). In this fantasy the murderer is the Wolfman, in a society peopled by newspaper people and godlike men and women.

An amusing and bizarre story in this line is *Sherlock Holmes vs. Dracula; or The Adventure of the Sanguinary Count* (1978), by Loren D. Estleman. In this updating of the Dracula legend, the bloodsucker comes again to England, on board a ship, with the captain strapped to the mast, lifeless and bloodless. Dracula escapes Holmes' best efforts, but Holmes feels that he is on top of the situation. That impossible story is aided and abetted by one yet more preposterous, Fred Saberhagen's *The Holmes-Dracula File* (1978). It ends with a conversation between Holmes and Watson about what an adventure between the great detective and a vampire should be called. Watson thinks: "I would say that any story involving Sherlock Holmes, the art of ratiocination, *and* vampires, cannot fail to appear more than a little preposterous." And Holmes agrees, but he adds, "So does life."

At least three books deal with extraordinary events and devices. *The Earthquake Machine (1976)* by Austin Mitchelson and Nicholas Utechin, features an "organized gang of criminals, which has as its goal war, riot and complete disorder"; this is a gang far worse than the one Holmes once broke up headed by Moriarty. Another book, *Hellbirds* (1976), by the same authors, covers the lethal activities of a flock of birds headed by the German evil master spy Van Bork. In yet a third treatment of pre–World War I intrigue, *The Infernal Device* (1978), by Michael Kurland, the evil is so great that Moriarty and Holmes must work together to put it down. After triumph, Moriarty opines that he and Holmes work so effectively together that perhaps they should continue their association, but Holmes, primly, says that their association is over. As he leaves, Mrs. H., the housekeeper, remarks to Professor Moriarty about Holmes: "An unforgiving lad."

The usual rivalry between Holmes and Professor Moriarty, in his former role as mastermind and evil genius, is furthered in two books by John Gardner, *The Return of Moriarty* and *The Revenge of Moriarty* (1976). In the latter, Moriarty has killed off all his enemies and become the head of all Europe's criminals, with unlimited wealth and power at his back. His aim is to cripple and destroy Holmes by cutting off his supply of cocaine.

Another interesting thrust in this general tradition of resuscitating Holmes is Michael Dibdin's *The Last Sherlock Holmes Story* (1978), one of numerous stories based upon the sensational and terrifying near-obsession of writers with a particular kind of violence and fear and hatred of women as seen in a reexamination of the Jack the Ripper story. In Dibdin's story the information for the study is drawn exclusively from *The Complete Jack the Ripper*, by W.H. Allen, 1975. Holmes, under the influence of Prof. Moriarty is shown to be Jack the Ripper, and dies falling from the Swiss mountain cliff into the Reichenbach chasm, in the same way he had fallen in Doyle's original story.

Realizing that there can be only so many hitherto lost manuscripts about the adventures of Sherlock Holmes, lucky authors have come across the hitherto unpublished accounts of Mycroft Holmes, Sherlock's shadowy and intellectually superior brother. *Enter the Lion* (1979), by Michael P. Hodel and Sean M. Wright, recounts an episode of Mycroft getting himself involved in a plot to overthrow the American government and reestablish British control through the Confederacy. In *The Adventures of Sherlock Holmes' Smarter Brother* (1975), by Gilbert Pearlman, based on a screenplay by Gene Wilder, a new brother, named Sigerson Holmes, is involved in what is in comparison with the original sedate adventures a wild and burlesque tale of sex and ridiculous adventures.

The idea of Sigerson Holmes apparently grew from a hint in the conclusion of the famous *Seven-Per-Cent Solution* (1974), by Nicholas Meyer, in which Holmes, who has been in Vienna working with and being the subject of work by Sigmund Freud, refuses to return to London; asked about his future, he remarks, "to keep track of my whereabouts, simply follow the concert career of a violinist named Sigerson." Now that the "discoverers" have found that Holmes had a secret life that Watson did not reveal they are building on it in various directions. In *The Adventures of Creighton Holmes* (1979), by Ned Hubbell, Creighton Holmes is the grandson of the great Sherlock. Dr. Watson had failed to mention that Sherlock in his youth married a beautiful girl who died almost immediately, leaving behind a son, whom Sherlock in his sorrow gave away to be raised. The son grew up to hate his biological father. Creighton, the grandson of the great sleuth, at first also hated his grandfather, but, having trained to become a lawyer, found more pleasure in "following his peculiar gift was, indeed, much like that of his illustrious forebear." Creighton's Watson is a reporter for the Manchester *Guardian*.

The appeal of Holmes and his world has proved most popular. There are perhaps a dozen volumes of detective works by Doyle's contemporaries, for example three volumes edited by Hugh Green, *The Rivals of Sherlock Holmes* (1970), *More Rivals of Sherlock Holmes* (1971) and *The Further Rivals of Sherlock Holmes* (1973), *The Rivals of Sherlock Holmes* (1978) edited by Alan K. Russell, *A Treasury of Victorian Detective Stories*, edited by Everett F. Bleiler (1979) and *Beyond Baker Street*, edited by Michael Harrison (1976). These and various others contain stories by Victorians who complemented if they did not rival Holmes and the detective story of the time.

The best evidence that a person has been taken completely into the culture is that demonstrated by humorous examples. If imitation is the highest form of flattery, then loving laughter is the highest form of affection. Two books in this tradition reveal the range and dimensions of this form of Holmesiana. *The World's Sherlock Holmes Quiz Book* (1976), by Dale Copps, provides "A guided tour through the wonders of Holmesiana" and the tour is both exciting and frustrating. Filled with all kinds of approaches to Holmesiana and his world, it covers such areas as "partners in crime," "pick a murder," "animal kingdom," "a relationship," and a good dozen more. At times the areas of research are not elementary. For example: "Who knocked out Holmes' left canine and where did it happen?"

Another marvelous feint in Holmesiana is Robert L. Fish's *Schlock Homes* (1959–1966); [fish is] also the author of *Memoirs of Schlock Homes*. In the Introduction Anthony Boucher correctly states that "gentle mockery is an assured sign of affection" and cites the first example of such mockery of Holmes in *Strand* in July 1891. In May 1892, again according to Boucher, the *Idler* published "Detective Stories Gone Wrong: The Adventures of Sherlaw Kombs," by Luke Short (Robert Barr). This collection of twelve adventures is top drawer burlesque.

Perhaps the most remarkable treatment of the new Doyle-Holmes factory is the dazzling study of the Holmes canon and person by Samuel Rosenberg (1974), *Naked is the Best Disguise: The Death and Resurrection of Sherlock Holmes*, which follows in the tradition of the earlier study, *The Private Life of Sherlock Holmes*, by Vincent Starrett (1933, 1960, 1975). Rosenberg, who has filled among many positions that of monitoring for the movies all outright, apparent and even faintly insinuated acts of plagiarism, demonstrates in his famous book that Sherlock Holmes was, among other persons, collectively and individually, Friedrich Nietzsche, Oscar Wilde, Dionysus, John Bunyan, Robert Browning, Boccaccio, Napoleon, Frankenstein and his Monster, Gustave Flaubert, George Sand, Plato and Socrates, Anthony and Cleopatra, Henry Ward Beecher and Sodom and Gomorrah. As Tennyson had Ulysses boast that he was a part of all that he had met, so Doyle, according to Rosenberg, was a part of all that he had read — or rather all that he had ever read was a part of him and evidenced itself in the thousand faces of his hero Sherlock Holmes.

One of those faces is the imitation Holmes story, *The Case of The Invisible Thief*, part of a series of *Baker Street Mysteries* by Thomas Brace Haughey (Bethany Fellowship Inc., Minneapolis, 1978). The novel is less flamboyant than some of the previously mentioned works, but entirely interesting. This is one of the few if not the only detective fiction series written by a confessed born-again Christian whose open and avowed purpose is to demonstrate the need for Christianity and power of prayer and at times does so in the most unexpected and dangerous places and times.

Haughey is, or was, the English Program Director of missionary radio station KVMV-FM in McAllen, Texas. According to the information in the front of his book, he holds a Th.M. from Capital Bible Seminary, a diploma from Rio Grande Bible Institute Language School, and has done evangelism and youth work in Mexico and has taught in a Bible School. He has also edited a Jesus Paper and done considerable writing.

Despite his zeal Haughey feels somewhat nervous and defensive about using detective fiction as an instrument for evangelizing. In the preface to *The Case of The Invisible Thief* he self-consciously defends the medium by pointing out that there is nothing wrong with escapism. Such great Americans as Abraham Lincoln and FDR used mysteries during war time, delighting in seeing a villain "get his comeuppance." Undoubtedly Lincoln and Roosevelt were not unaware of the similarity with their wartime goals, for as Haughey points out further in the Preface, "ever since Medieval times, morality plays have demonstrated that virtue pays. Sin destroys. That same theme lies at the heart of virtually every detective story worthy of the name. Crime is followed by doing time. The good get the goods on the hoods…. Deep down [the readers] know that situational ethics is baloney. And they welcome the simplicity of clear-cut right and wrong."

Not all readers like the stories for this clear-cut change, of course, and Haughey admits that not all detectives have been "pillars of virtue." But each fought "against an evil greater than his own." And undoubtedly Haughey, whose favorite detectives are Perry Mason* and Miss Marple feels that his fight against irreligion is a greater battle than against mere mortal evil. Haughey's detective, Geoffrey Weston, is "the only detective old enough to vote who— as Jimmy Carter would put it — has been born again. Weston battles evil with a passion."

Mason may be Haughey's favorite detective, but obviously his model is Sherlock Holmes. Haughey's parallel is close. The book begins with Geoffrey Weston, the detective, and his Watson (the narrator, named significantly John Taylor) having breakfast in their

---

*Mason, is of course, not a detective, per se. — The Editor

bachelor apartment at 31 Baker Street, a site chosen because Weston "took delight in recreating the rustic air that so characterized his grandfather Mycroft's celebrated brother," and selecting this Baker Street address which "Gave us a mystique that had attracted clients," for this enterprise of "Sleuths, Ltd., London's Consulting Detective firm" "God had been good" to them. Weston has all of Holmes' prescience and air of playing tricks. For example, at the very beginning of the book when Taylor unconsciously glances at the ledger, Weston surprises him with a whole paragraph about how one should work for pleasure and not worry about money. And in another bit of Holmesian stagecraft, Weston announces before the man arrives and knocks on the door that there is a stranger coming who needs their help.

The setting for the mystery of the story is about as closed as it could possibly be. From the Pinehurst Laboratory in England, which was absolutely security safe, some valuable papers have been taken directly from a safe in an office which has keys held only by reliable persons and is under 24 hour surveillance of cameras and guards. A real question is how somebody could have gotten in without the camera eye having seen him or her. That problem, however, is soon solved by a demonstration that since TV cameras have no depth perception it is relatively easy to provide a fake wall of the same color as the real wall behind which one can walk. Furthermore, the safe was opened while an invention was used in the camera to create the illusion that the machine was not there. The author's explanation was that "The invention used in the robbery created the same illusion from every angle. The thief was encapsulated, as it were. Memory circuits froze the picture while the safe was being opened."

Of far greater importance in the story is the question of what kind of secret work was going on in the laboratory. It eventually becomes clear that the work was ungodly and conducted by people who do not believe in Christian principles, in God himself, or even in Spirit. Therefore it is easy to believe that the secret work being conducted at the laboratory is genetic engineering, as eventually comes out.

Working from the assumption that cloning is the most ungodly of activities because it denies God, strips people of spirit and humanness, Haughey repeatedly hammers away at his concept of what constitutes a good Christian and the needs of a Christian society.

Weston discusses the existence of God and the needs of a Christian society with a learned scientist who is a moralistic materialist. Weston insists, "law only works with people who consider it to be grounded in an absolute — sometimes not even then." Without citizens that have convictions concerning right and wrong society would crumble." Weston insists that the scientist's "definition of law makes law (if you will allow the use of the term) evil."

Not believing in God is bad enough. Not performing Christian rituals is evil. But apparently not living a Christian life is even worse. One of the scientists in the book is a Hindu, for example, and that mere fact alone makes him suspect as a murderer. When the Hindu starts lamenting that there is no love, no good on earth and, under hypnosis, tries to commit suicide because of his desperation and loneliness, Weston grabs his gun and tries to wake him. He reassures the despondent man by telling him "There's god. There's truth,"— that is, of course, Christian truth. And Weston punctuates his reassurances with slaps on the man's face, apparently believing that at times any heathen deserves a little bit of muscular Christianity.

Although experiments in cloning are still being carried on at the laboratory, and there are large fish tanks containing little fetuses and operating as their "mother," according to Weston, apparently there are clones already abroad in the city. Or evil forces that conspire with the clones, because Weston penetrates a Satanic cult meeting of clones one night and saves himself only by invoking the name of Jesus Christ, just as John Taylor one night on a stakeout had saved himself from the crushing weight of evil only by invoking the name of Jesus Christ. Perhaps author Thomas Haughey is closer to the truth than we recognize. For Sam Rosenberg in his book postulates that Doyle had "Holmes equate himself with Jesus."

As the plot winds down, the robbery at the Laboratory is revealed to have been done by the young "man" named Peter Heath, who was not a human being but a clone. He did it; he killed his foster father, Arthur Heath, to prevent him from revealing his unnatural parentage and the kind of experiments taking place at the laboratory. Peter, although immune to most reasoning and pressure, has to reveal his identity and the truth about his act when, as in witchcraft exercises through the ages, he is commanded in the name of God: "IN THE NAME OF JESUS CHRIST, I COMMAND YOU TO ANSWER. WHO ARE YOU?" Weston commands. With a cackling giggle and saliva drooling from between bared teeth, the clone with "A halting, rasping, hollow hiss breathed an ancient message: 'I AM LEGION, FOR WE ARE ... MANY.'"

This twist on cloning had been tried a year earlier in the book *Exit Sherlock Holmes*, by Robert Lee Hall, with even a more bizarre twist, where genetic engineering had made Holmes and Moriarty from apparently part of the same genes, and as Holmes says "more than brothers." In that book the union is destructive.

But in *The Case of the Invisible Thief* Weston checkmates the evil done by the cloning and by the materialistic belief that there is no such thing as spirit and soul. He convinces the scientists that their ungodly materialism is destructive. Even the official on the police force, Inspector Twiggs, confesses that he would like to hear more about Jesus Christ, and John Taylor, the narrator, smilingly says that he has all night to talk about that subject.

Now if you think that this book sounds like an insufferable sermon about a bigoted and stupid detective who interrupts his detecting at crucial and dangerous moments to pray then you are not quite correct.

Haughey does interrupt the flow of the story to deliver philosophical-religious debates and homilies. For example, he once sermonizes: "You remind me of a man who once asked 'What is truth?' If you really want to see what a soul is, look at the souled. Then look at the soulless. Subtract the second from the first. What you have left is the essence of humanity." His tilt is openly foursquare and born-again Christianity. His points are made in uppercase emphasis.

But there is a general geniality and lightheartedness about this Holmes-Watson pair, which in some ways is as pleasant as the originals. These latter-day Holmes-Watsons have very jolly times in their bachelor quarters in the vicinity of their models. They enjoy their Holmes-Watson breakfasts and general actions. Weston eats Spanish peanuts instead of shooting cocaine, and listens to stereo records instead of playing the violin as Holmes always did. In general Haughey does not take himself too seriously. He is delighted with his punning, which can go on to embarrassing lengths, on the name of the Inspector, Twiggs. For example: "Ah, Twigg! You're just the sapling we've been looking for. We'd as leaf have Twigg as any tree in the forest." There is little violence, and it is conducted offstage where possible and there is none of the heavy-handed prose of such right wing writers as Mickey Spillane. All in all, the book is an amusing and pleasant experience.

It may be difficult, therefore, to see why the author was not successful with this detective pair. Apparently he wrote two other books in the series, but they are not readily available.

If, as Sam Rosenberg had insisted, Doyle had created Holmes at least in one of his many guises as Jesus Christ, the parallel is too subdued and covered to be effective in the present world. Maybe the detective mode is not the right vehicle to teach Christianity and love per se. Perhaps readers would like to say that the swing in America to the right is not as far and as complete as we have been told. Perhaps not. However, the truth apparently is that despite the obvious and far-reaching resuscitation and continued vitality of Holmes in nearly every other area of present day American life, the right wing, regardless of its size, is not reading detective fiction. Perhaps these people are not interested in stories of Jesus Christ as detective. Perhaps that is the only present-day area in which the ubiquitous Holmes does not work well.

Bibliography

The following is a reasonably though obviously not totally complete check list of Holmesiana written by authors other than the genuine A. Conan Doyle. Most examples are in the form of "recently found" or recently authorized for publication manuscripts. Readers can undoubtedly add to it from their own library or from bookstores. The study of this new area in Holmes scholarship is fascinating, and deserves a complete analysis.

Boyer, Richard L. *The Giant Rat of Sumatra.* New York: Warner, 1976.

Copps, Dale. *The World's Greatest Sherlock Holmes Quiz Book.* New York: Berkley, 1976.

Cover, Arthur Byron. *An East Wind Coming* New York: Berkley, 1979.

Estleman, Loren D. *Sherlock Holmes vs. Dracula; or Adventure of the Sanguinary Count.* New York: Penguin, 1978.

_____. *Dr. Jekyll and Mr. Holmes* New York: Penguin, 1980.

Fish, Robert L. *The Incredible Schlock Homes* (1959–1966). Gardner, John. *The Revenge of Moriarty* New York: Berkley, 1978.

Haughey, Thomas Brace. *The Case of the Invisible Thief* Minneapolis, MN: Bethany Fellowship, 1978.

Hodel, Michael P. and Sean M. Wright. *Enter the Lion* New York: Playboy Press, 1979.

Hubbell, Ned. *The Adventures of Creighton Holmes* New York: Popular Library, 1979.

Kurland, Michael. *The Infernal Device.* New York: Signet, 1978.

Lewis, Arthur H. *Copper Beeches* New York: Pocket Books, 1972. The Sons of the Copper Beeches is a society "to perpetuate the legend that Mr. Sherlock Holmes is not a legend."

Meyer, Nicholas. *The Seven-Per-Cent Solution* New York: Ballantine, 1974.

Mitchelson, Austin and Nicholas Utechin. *The Earthquake Machine* New York: Belmont Tower, 1976.

_____ and _____. *Hellbirds* New York: Belmont Tower, 1976.

Pearlman, Gilbert. *The Adventure of Sherlock Holmes' Smarter Brother* New York: Ballantine, 1975.

Queen, Ellery. *Ellery Queen vs. Jack the Ripper* (New York: Lancer, 1969).

Titus, Eve. *Basil of Baker Street* New York Archway Paperback, 1958. (Mice parallels to Holmes and Watson).

Symons, Julian. *A Three Pipe Problem* London: Penguin, 1977.

Wellman, Manly W. and Wade Wellman. *Sherlock Holmes' War of the Worlds* New York: Warner, 1975.

Weverka, Robert. *Murder by Decree* New York: Ballantine, 1979.

Part Four

Meanderings and Excursions

Browne composed many essays that capture him "thinking out loud" as it were. Longer ones take on a semi-autobiographical aspect at times, while the shorter ones can be opinion-editorials, sometimes becoming polemics. In many of the volumes he edited, Browne included not only his introductions, but also some of these more informal "ponderings and questionings" of topics and ideas. A handful of the more intriguing are presented here.

As mentioned in the general introduction, Browne wrote over a thousand scholarly reviews. They range in length from a brief descriptive paragraph to nearly article size critical analyses. Many of them exhibit Browne's mix of acerbic observation with whimsical humor and wordplay. Included here are a mere handful, selected for the notoriety of the book or subject reviewed, or for the manner and tone of Browne's commentary.

15

The Rape of the Vulnerable

A wonderful invective by Browne, tied to a loose analysis of capitalism and cultural malaise. Those who think of popular culture studies as overly celebratory should take note.

Critics may want the analysis of the issues of capitalism to be buttressed with greater significance, but it isn't that kind of a piece. Browne is not interested in clearly demonstrating some sort of quasi–Marxist or economic-determinist explanation for the abusive actions done in the name of religion. He is interested in the actions themselves and what they say about the people and culture in the broader spectrum. So, he tosses off a possible connection, leaving its follow-up or refutation to those so inclined.

Once again, Browne's humor when riled is terse and wry. Note that part of his anger is because of the betrayal of democracy. The religious robber barons achieved success not necessarily through their hard work, etc., but by exploiting the innocence of their fellow citizens when those citizens were downtrodden. We see, then, the justification for the intended and all too real venom in Browne's title.— The Editor

The Holy Wars that often break out among the American merchants of religion reveal much about the nature of these purveyors of religious fervor as well as the culture in which they grow and prosper — as well as over-extend and fail.

Religion and religious fervor and activities are not the sole product but they may be one of the domains of democracy.

Religious fervor is likely to follow the vagaries of capitalism, feeding on the same drives that fuel unbridled and unchecked capitalism — wealth, lust, greed and power — and frequently fall as capitalism gets out of control — as the Stock Market seemed to be in early 1987 just as key religious scandals erupted — and pays the price for its unbridled grab for the so-called fruits of capitalism.

The nature of the robber barons, as they once were called, by and large has been to grab for power and wealth among themselves, frequently leaving alone the small investor who does not represent enough wealth for the robber baron to bother with. But the nature of the religion merchants is to prey more on the poor than the rich, the vulnerable than the strong. In seeking small but steady contributors, the religion merchants, while getting much of their contributions from the steady middle-class which constitutes a steady source of wealth, has two fields open to them where the income, though perhaps not as large and steady, is sure. These two are the young and the old, both classes vulnerable to the honey-tongue blandishments, which work through idealism and fear, the former being particularly the province of the young, the latter particularly the dread of the old.

The young proved an especially fruitful field. Perhaps the reasons can easily be found. Conservative administrations' attempts through the years to put prayer back into the schools were efforts to breach the gap established by the U.S. Constitution to keep church and state separate. These proposals to put the church back into the state shows obvious contempt for the Constitution and demonstrated to school children — public school and college and university — that the gap between the two can and should be breached, and they are happy to try.

This attitude reveals, among other things, a weakness in American culture. Throughout history, a culture with goals, with purposes in life, with things to do is ordinarily a culture with people less interested in themselves than in the world around them. Call it materialism, pragmatism, call it interest in the world, but such an attitude tends to keep people's minds off the warts of their own lives and outside themselves. The people tend therefore to be mentally more stable and healthier.

On the contrary, the culture and society that seems to be without goals, without outside motivation and reasons for being tends to get worried over the fate of the individuals, to be more concerned with the spirit and heart of the individual than with society and history.

The causes of such malaise lie deep. Perhaps one of them is a natural consequence of history and national growth. Apparently after over two hundred years of generally unrestricted development and growth the United States has run out of frontier and open territory for development and has had to stop to take a breather, to regroup for further development, or to stagnate. Whatever the future movement, such a halt in development undoubtedly causes some concern among the young about their future. When they get scared, they turn to what people have always turned to in time of stress, religion and ritual of one kind or another. They thus become easy prey for the person in the business of peddling religion, whose product is ritual and promises security.

Another cause of malaise in American life is obviously education. In the past American education has been empirical or generally pragmatic with enough of the ideal to keep the head of individuals up and the eyes looking toward the sky. Now, the young and educable have found that the education of their fathers and mothers is not enough for them, not enough to prepare them psychologically or vocationally for the future. Disquieted, they are easy prey for the merchant of religion. So God has gone back to school, if not in the form of instructor then surely as companion to the thinking students who carry with them easy susceptibility in their intellectual baggage.

According to *Newsweek's On-Campus* (Nov. 1986), Velma Ferrell, adviser to the Baptist Student Union at Duke University, said, "There is a desire to have somebody telling you what to do, whether it be God or President Reagan." Apparently the magnitude of the fears of current life are too large for parents or professors to solve: so the young are going to the highest authority.

The natural herding instincts of students, when aroused, insist that they become a conservative and conserved member of a larger group, and religion provides the magnitude needed. *Newsweek's On-Campus*, again, quoted a representation of this herd-instinct in its excerpt from a recent Brown University prayer meeting: "We praise you for the fervency you've given us and ask you to increase it. Start a fire burning. There's nothing we desire more than for God to sweep across this campus." The same issue of the magazine pointed out another fruit of the religious fervor, an ethnic identity where people find their own roots and bush growth, a seeking, dangerously, which can lead to bigotry and blindness. *Newsweek's On-Campus*, again quoted Rabbi Marc Gopin, adviser to the Orthodox Jewish community at Brandeis University, as saying, "People are clinging an inordinate amount to ethnic identification and not enough to spiritual ideals." Students see and worship the tree but not the forest; the particular but not the general. According to Gopin, "Say anything about Israel and people start screaming; say anything about God and people shrug their shoulders." Any group that can see outside its own boundaries recognize that there is danger in such narrow ethnicity.

So students are vulnerable in putting vague mysticism, and good intentions ahead of common sense driven by observations and practicality. They drive with all the strength and potential damage at their command, wholly committed.

Older people are likewise vulnerable for almost the same reasons. They are weighed down by the problems of the world, many of which they could not correct in their active years and for which they may feel responsible. But mainly they seem to be lonely in their daily life and frightened by their short future. Preachers may talk excitedly about the glories of the life after death and about how much they yearn to get to heaven and start enjoying the physical and spiritual delights of the place, but generally they are not eager to change locations. Even Oral Roberts, whose position in the hierarchy of heaven was presumably well established, looked upon God's threat to call him "home" unless he raised $8 million to revitalize his medical college at Oral Roberts University as more of a punishment than a reward, and he was not happy to make the switch from earth's vale of tears to heaven's streets of gold. So the vulnerable elderly give money that they could more properly spend on themselves to support the wealthy churches that threaten them if they don't support the churches and promise them consolation if they do. Little wonder that the elderly give up the necessities of their lives for the promised certainties of the after-life.

Along with the cultural uncertainties that weaken the fabric and faith of our daily lives, there is another very real aspect of life that religion merchants have always railed against and occasionally dallied in — sex. It is easy to see why. Psychologists have demonstrated that the drives of sex and religion are not unrelated — both develop fervor, for example, and one might well develop along with the other. Both have a common drive in power. Power over evil and one's self and power over one of the great drives of humanity, sex, which is often called the power of Satan. Often people in the religion business get caught up in the Satan of sex. In America, the witchcraft of early Salem has often been ascribed to the puberty awakening of the girls of the village. Nathaniel Hawthorne depicted vividly the weakness of the flesh when in *The Scarlet Letter* he had the Reverend Arthur Dimmesdale fall prey to the physical attractions of Hester Prynne. Hester Prynne was forced to wear the scarlet "A" on her bosom for Adulteress, but Dimmesdale was destroyed by his own sense of guilt. At a much later time, Sinclair Lewis pointed out in his novel *Elmer Gantry* that one reason preachers liked their job so much was that it supplied them with the finer things of life: chicken to eat and ladies' knees to look at every Sunday. There are also other perks.

And it is the other perks that have dragged real-life ministers of God into trouble throughout America's history. The Rev. Henry Ward Beecher, called in the years before the Civil War, "the greatest preacher since Saint Paul," and a preacher who earned the unheard-of salary of $40,000 a year, was one of the early ministers who apparently dallied with female members of his congregation. Aimee Semple McPherson, flamboyant, attractive and somewhat erratic Los Angeles evangelical preacher, wore her low-cut flowing white gowns and charmed her audience, until she disappeared one afternoon in May, 1926, with one of her employees. Sex was the downfall of Billy James Hargis in 1976, when a magazine reported that Hargis was enjoying the pleasures of this world with both male and female students. It has been observed that preachers, especially young powerhouses on television, seem to be sex symbols; it is little wonder that sometimes they give in to their fatal flaw and stoop to folly.

Such was the great crescendo of noise that shook the televangelism business to the base of its golden feet in the mid and late 1980s. And the heaven-shaking event of the revelation of sexual irregularities among God's (self–) anointed brought into (at least temporary) question the whole business of selling God through the media and with powerful gusto.

The crisis was precipitated when it was revealed that Jim Bakker, husband of Tammy Faye Bakker, and head of the television show *PTL* ("Praise the Lord," or as some have said less respectfully, "Pass the Loot") had had a one-night tryst with a former church secretary named Jessica Hahn and had subsequently paid her blackmail. Many people (especially the large number of preachers who could take sides in this *cause célèbre*) felt that the devil in the drama was Jimmy Swaggart, an evangelist based in Louisiana, who was happy to exploit the discomfort of the Bakker family. Oral Roberts denounced Swaggart, as did Robert Schuller, from his $18 million Crystal Cathedral in California. Jerry Falwell, who took over *PTL* when Bakker resigned, and Pat Robertson, flexing his muscles to become a serious contender for the Presidency of the United States, both played the issue down the middle, seeing opportunity in the situation to clean house and improve the act.

Who, then, are today's televangelists and who their audience? In both cases the answers are fairly clear. The preachers are generally people with poor and impoverished backgrounds who had to overcome many privations to succeed in this land of opportunity. Frustrated in other directions, these people saw big bucks in peddling religion and, apparently with the sincerest beliefs in their product, turned their emotions into big business. And their business and profits are indeed large. Before their fall, the Bakkers had the *PTL* organization with a reported $129 million annual revenues; included in their empire was the 2,300-acre theme park *Heritage USA* in Ft. Mill, S.C. Jimmy Swaggart's weekly *Jimmy Swaggart Hour* played in more than 2 million households; his revenues reached $142 million in 1986. Robert Schuller reached a claimed 1.7 million weekly with his Reformed Church in America; his 12-story Crystal Cathedral cost $18 million. 547,000 weekly presumably watched Jerry Falwell's *Old Time Gospel Hour*; his income in 1986 was reportedly $73.5 million including that from the Liberty Broadcasting Network and Liberty University. Pat Robertson reputedly reached 468,000 with his daily *700 Club* broadcast; he apparently had an income from his Christian Broadcasting Network of $129 million in 1986. The Dean of them all, Oral Roberts, a Pentecostal minister, has outclassed all his competitors, perhaps. His weekly broadcasts were supposed to reach 1.1 million households.

His earthly assets included the City of Faith medical center, Oral Roberts University and religious enterprises in seven countries. There is no way to assess the personal wealth of these individuals, since they would not reveal what they claim are their modest salaries nor the numerous and wealthy perks that come as a part of their positions, including lavish homes, the finest in transportation, and perks for the immediate scions of these servants of God. But it has come to light that the Bakkers' annual salary before the Fall was $1.6 million.

Other than the young and the old, who are the people who support these ministers and their more recent ilk? Mainly, they are just like the ministers, with poor and stress-strewn backgrounds, who see in the ministers what they wish they themselves could accomplish. According to Jeffrey Hadden, University of Virginia sociologist and coauthor of the study of such ministers *Prime Time Preachers*, as reported in *Newsweek*, April 6, 1987, "The people who like and follow them see them as real human beings who are 'like me and have problems like me, but are more successful.'" In other words, the audience, who are perennial television watchers and who might be just too tired to get up and turn the TV dial, seem to be engaged in a kind of double-dupe. They are willing to support the duping of the American public because by doing that these people are getting back at a society that has not been as kind and beneficial to them as it should have been. They are willing to use God to get back at people and life.

Is the whole gang sincere? Are the televangelists sincere? And are the supporters sincere? The question and value of sincerity seems a charade. Tammy Faye Bakker was surely sincere because she has worried her problems through before accepting and feeling comfortable with them. For example, Tammy was quite free to tell how she first tried cosmetics, liked them but expected to be struck by lightning for using them. But God told her that it was perfectly all right for her to use cosmetics. Because of this Godly approval, Tammy then started manufacturing and selling cosmetics— undoubtedly dedicating the profits of the sales to the glorification of God, the Great Franchiser (apparently God is female, as novelist Dr. Andrew Greeley insists, and therefore understands the need of women to use and buy cosmetics). Tammy was also addicted to prescription drugs and tried to break the addiction. Was Jim Bakker sincere? He and Tammy Faye had always been open with the public. For example, their marital crisis in the early 1980s was a public affair, a soap opera that people enjoyed and forgave. When he was forced to admit the public into the affairs of his "sexual encounter," his admitted fling into infidelity, he suffered the agony of the sinner. But being the self-appointed spokesman for the Divine, Jim reported that God had forgiven him his transgression. According to *Newsweek*, April 6, 1987, psychologist and *PTL* family member Fred Gross revealed to Bakker's *PTL* club the circumstances by which young Jim received forgiveness: "He was sobbing. He was shaking so violently I had to hold him. In 10 minutes we were on the floor. His face was buried in the carpet. He was sobbing and kicking and screaming.... If there has ever been a release, that was a release." Some people might think that such actions were more befitting a child's temper tantrum than forgiveness by God, but apparently not. Like God, Bakker's vast following seemed also prepared to forgive him, as they would forgive themselves. But Jerry Falwell, with his eye on either the bounties of the ministry or on the Great Bookkeeper, was less quick to forgive. "The ministry of God is a great responsibility," he was reported in *Newsweek*, April 6, 1987, to have said: "You don't get two shots at it." But as sociologist Todd Gitlin (reported by Mike Duffy of Knight-Ridder Services) said. "If you can be born twice, why not a third time?" If God gives franchises to every poor soul who claims a second birth, why not renew the franchise if the franchisee will simply clean up his act? That makes good business sense.

If there were drama in the Jim and Tammy Faye affair, there was even more in the Oral Roberts Ordeal, which was running at the same time in a different theater across the country. The Bakker affair was indeed truly soap opera. And the actors may still have a future.* Mike Duffy, cited above, reported that sociologist Todd Gitlin said: "If they can't get back on the *PTL* show, maybe they can guest star on *Dynasty*." But Oral Roberts' drama was Faustian in every way. Roberts apparently had unconsciously mortgaged his soul to a greedy and lonely God who was going to take him "home" to Heaven if he did not start

---

*Jim Bakker's future included a prison stretch for financial misdeeds and divorce from Tammy. Tammy Faye got remarried to a well-known fundamentalist Christian architect noted for designing huge, elaborate and very expensive church-complexes. Jimmy Swaggart soon had his own sex scandal.— The Editor

immediately doing much more good in this lowly world, this time in the form of an $8 million enhancement of his hospital services. Thus there began a mortal tussle between the supernatural desires of God and the very material wishes of the materialistically wealthy citizens of America for the body and soul of God's servant. The stakes could hardly have been higher. The richest nation in the world vs. God!

Observant people might have noticed that this country is overrun with hospital beds that cannot be filled, that Oral's enhancement of God through the hospital was merely the fattening of his own ego. And wags might have well have said that God could not be so lonely that he wanted to enrich his life prematurely with the presence of Oral. But the contributions poured in, despite the fact that many media outlets, the public in general and even fellow evangelists, probably because of sheer envy at the magnitude of the gulling, decried Roberts' threat of being snatched from the earth unless his devout public dug even deeper into their pockets and found money to keep him among us. They might have observed that it would be far cheaper for them if Oral went on to Heaven where apparently the streets are already paved with gold. But Roberts finally raised his $8 million, the last $1.4 coming from a man who had raised his money on dog racing. But money raised through gambling interests can easily be laundered and made appropriate for God's work.

What are the futures of the televangelists after these major crises, and others? One could have hoped that they could not continue to prosper, to prey on the weak and vulnerable, that the Roberts-Bakker affairs shamed them, tainted this kind of huckstering in religion, and lowed the value of their stock on the Heavenly Stock Exchange. In a sense, the explosions were merely part of a Great Religious Franchise War, a battle not dissimilar from say that between fast food outlets or soft-drink corporations, and schemes devised that recovered the ground that may or may not have been lost by the shame of Oral Roberts' gulling the public about their buying his salvation from death or the naiveté of a young man who discovered that sexual desires have very little conscience or even religious probity. Apparently God is not indeed on 24-hour vigil.

But how long will the public be gulled? Probably as long as the public does not have some definite purpose in mind, some national and personal goal that will pull them out of themselves and give them something serious and worthwhile to occupy their time. God should be conceived of as big and generous, not as small and petty. There must be some question about whether God was really concerned over whether Tammy uses cosmetics or not. Perhaps that was within the purview of her beauty operator and dermatologist. God surely would not want to interfere with free enterprise.

The overriding question is what are the characteristics of the culture in which those people work. Kind and charitable, long-suffering and gullible — those are not necessarily undesirable traits of our democratic society. But there are perhaps grounds and room for some kind of different attitude toward those religious robber barons who may be seducing the innocent and vulnerable, and with the understanding and even the approval of the people who ought to know better. There is, after all, more to society than the ego gratification of those who are serving themselves when they call themselves the servants of God.

16

Class Reunion as a Folk Festival

In this rumination on his high-school reunion, Browne weaves little bits of general cultural analysis into his account of the proceedings. The reader feels as if they are inside Browne's mind as he thinks to himself what this event means to him on a personal, often emotional level, as he ties it to the conventional understandings of such rituals.

It makes for a richly unique essay, but this is not a formal study, or an investigation of serious rigor. Rather, it is a reverie with insights, a languid conversation with the self. In the personal, we find the common shared experience.— The Editor

The larger and more "sophisticated" the high school reunion the more it operates in the rituals of mass culture and less in those of a somewhat different strain — folk culture.

The mass culture reunion, though obviously based upon and exploiting the same basic human needs, develops in a society where contact and basic communication with other people, especially those with whom we have had no recent and therefore no "lasting" social or business intercourse, tends to be more casual, less "heartfelt" and less significant than it is with more "folkish" communities.

Class reunions from small classes in small towns tend to be more folkloristic, more based on what the participants feel are the "genuine" and heart-felt connections that geographic and historical chance created, and are therefore less inhibited and more "natural" in their manifestations. Though nostalgia, pride in accomplishment in life, disdain for those people whom we knew at a more tender and less sophisticated age, and a genuine curiosity to see how others who pretty much shared the opportunity we did to "get along in life" really "got along," the sharp edge of superiority, assumed or otherwise, that the more "sophisticated" graduates tend to gird themselves with for class reunions tends to be modified or blunted in the reunions of the smaller groups. This is especially true if the reunion is the first or second in many years. At the reunion of a class of oldsters in the "folk" community, there is of course the curiosity, and undoubtedly the delight at seeing how badly old rivals and enemies, old smart-alecs, have fared. But since many of the people have scattered literally to the four corners of this country, there is less feeling of competition among the members, more genuine delight in how well one's old classmates have fared and the genuine delight at seeing them again, though perhaps one re-seeing, one reunion, will be all that some people will attend or will want to attend.

Some interesting sidelights might be gained from a recent class reunion of my class of 1940. My hometown, Millport, Alabama, was and still is small. My class of 1940 had 18 people in it. We were bussed in from the surrounding country and small towns, and mixed with the local students, who consisted of people of all social and financial ranks within the town. Though some students came to school well housed, well fed and well dressed, some came from just exactly the opposite environments: ill-dressed, ill-fed and ill-housed. Yet all seemed to mix well in school, though there was some condescension from the town students, regardless of their financial and social conditions, toward those who were bussed in from surrounding towns and farms and a limited amount of awareness of difference in social and financial status among the in-town students.

Yet there did develop a sense of "family" in the class that would not have existed under other circumstances. One looked forward every morning to seeing his or her friends. Days in school were pleasant, with more love and friendship than envy and hate. One did not pal around with all the other students, to be sure; some were obnoxious, cruel, slovenly, dishonest, uneducable; some went to jail for various kinds of offenses while still in school; some were obviously mentally "slow." But in general the small group settled into its cliques, its habits of behavior and learning easily and all got along with very little friction.

The announcement of the first class reunion in 40 years therefore, in the instance I am talking about, was something of a momentous proclamation. Although I had visited Millport several times after graduating in 1940, I had pretty much lost contact with most of the families and individuals I had grown up with. Most faces and names had settled into a roseate hue that left them all reflecting clouds of glory that I knew never really existed except in my memory.

Having pretty much lived with the feeling that nostalgia is nonsense I wondered if the reunion was something to be appreciated or something to be apologized for. Through the years I had felt that people who look back are those who have lost their forward momentum. I had observed that reunions are only for those people who have nowhere else to go, and they go so that they can parade their accomplishments in life through lies or misrepresentations. Also I was thoroughly under the impression that everybody at the reunion would be old, fat and ugly — and pretentious; that forty years and millions of miles would have scarred those students of years ago who had managed to survive; that the "wake" for years gone by would be comforting for some but embarrassing for others.

I felt that perhaps the ones who would appreciate the reunion most would be the teachers who had suffered this batch of students years before, teachers who had taught for years (some as many as fifty years) and who still lived in the community, retired and respected. and who still remembered each and every one of their students among the hundreds they had spent so much time with in the past.

With these teachers, again, the difference between the small "folk" community and that of larger classes in larger communities is joyfully evident. I knew that our old teachers (many of whom had kept in touch through the years with the former students through letters, visits, and other ways) would be the honored guests at the reunion because they were more than teachers: they had been teachers, counselors, religious guides and genuine friends to us while we were in school and for many of the graduates continued to be afterwards. Through seeing us again, these teachers would be able to relive some of their past, see what "miracles" they had wrought through their teaching, and genuinely appreciate (the feeling of camaraderie and good cheer that our presence there would create. So I felt that if for no other reason, perhaps out of a feeling of gratitude and deep love we all had for our ex-teachers perhaps the reunion would be worthwhile.

The reunion went off with pretty much the usual superficial, though abbreviated, rituals. We all met in Millport, a town of 1,000 (virtually the same now as when I graduated there 40 years ago) in west central Alabama. After extensive planning by a self-appointed committee of three or four who had kept together through the years by virtue of the fact that they have all lived in and around Birmingham, and considerable correspondence, we met in Millport at the school Saturday afternoon. There was the usual activity at such functions. We had the nametags, the pictures, the usual milling around trying to see young faces through the wrinkles and youthful bodies in the fat and sagging torsos before us. Some of us had not seen one another literally for forty years, and it is not easy to see behind a beard or mustache a face that you used to go fishing with every day. But we did. We saw one another again, and remembered a time when life seemed to show very little but promise for all of us. We reminisced more than we talked of current things. There was a great deal of "remember whens" because we were tentative about talking of more serious things among people whose minds and biases when we knew them had been largely unshaped and whom we did not now want to offend by discussing politics, race relations, financial situations and other issues which when seen in light of the reason for our meeting were really relatively unimportant at least for the day. Naturally, there was no drinking of hard liquor. I assume that so deeply ingrained was the dryness of the area as it had existed forty years ago that no one would have thought about having a drink here no matter how much he might have drunk at home before he left or would consume once he got back.

After the general get-together, many of us took the obligatory tour of the school building, where we revisited the class rooms where we had spent so much time years ago, looked at the pictures of ourselves and our classmates now hanging from the walls, and tried to become young and innocent again, even if just for the night. This exercise was indeed a trip in nostalgia.

We left the general get-together and walked half a block to the site for dinner. The dinner was a ritual about as near folk culture as could be achieved nowadays. We milled around more, moving among more people than we had managed to talk with in the earlier, more general session, drinking soft drinks and making more personal inquiries than we had made earlier. Here we were joined by our former teachers who had spent their lives in Millport teaching at this school but had not come to the earlier event, and by several others who, after having taught for a short period of time in this town had got married, moved on to other assignments or quit teaching altogether. In effect, then, we had three generations mixing here for the moment: the senior teachers, the junior teachers (who were in effect very few years older than we — in fact one teacher present said that when she taught her first class at Millport, her students were older than she was), and ourselves, who were all approaching our late fifties and early sixties.

In general there was free mixing of people from all three groups, though by now some of the groups that had formed earlier and found that they had things to talk about tended to sit together and to talk among themselves. One of the most poignant moments of the evening came when a citizen of Millport, from a later class, came in to the group just for the moment because he had wanted especially to see some members of the older class whom he had not seen for forty years but remembered with great pleasure.

After the meeting there were the usual ritualistic activities needed to cement the occasion into something significant. There was the prize for the person who had traveled the farthest distance to get to the reunion. The distance was determined by each person announcing how far he or she had traveled; interestingly and typically, after the prize had been awarded, one of the ex-younger teachers confessed to those around her that she had traveled farther than the one who got the prize but she felt that it was appropriate that the prize go to one of the "students" rather than to an ex-teacher. Other prizes and mementoes were awarded. The Committee that had arranged this reunion were introduced, explained how much difficulty it had been to arrange it, and freely acknowledged that they would be glad to step down to allow others to arrange for the next. They were encouraged to keep their positions and to do as well with the next reunion as they had done with this one. When the question arose as to when the next reunion should be, there was a considerable debate. Some people suggested that since we were all so scattered perhaps we should not meet again for five years. Others said that since we were all getting along in years and no one could anticipate the future we should meet in two years.

At this time and with the truth of the observation quite obvious, there was present other evidence of the folk quality of this reunion.

Many people felt that there would be somewhat fewer people at the next reunion, death having reduced the number. Though this probability was treated lightheartedly, as a natural phenomenon, there was deep-felt sadness evident. These people, who throughout their lives have lived more closely to and more honestly with death, smiled at the thought that not all of us would be able to meet in two years, but their smiles were more stoical than amused.

Furthermore there was the realization that if you scratch the surface of these good people you find close to the surface of their persons and their lives the heated blood of religion that sustains them in life, and there was comfort in the realization that if we cannot all get together at the next earthly reunion there is a greater reunion that we might anticipate attending.

In addition to this one sadness there was another that permeated the gathering. Where were the people who were not there; and why had they not come? The answers are rather complex but deeply emotional and politically capitalistic.

Most of the people who were present had come considerable distances for the meeting. They had traveled from Montgomery, various cities in Mississippi, Birmingham, northern Alabama, and from great distances in other states. We had come back braced with the realization that to a certain extent we had "succeeded" or could pose as successes because not many people there would want to challenge the fact, or the unstated assumption that if in no other way we had succeeded by moving away from the mother nest. Some others, however, had not. For various reasons, often by choice, they still lived in town and on surrounding farms, not having "enjoyed" life away from Millport. Some not present surely had seen most of the people at the reunion lately; perhaps they saw them frequently. So perhaps they had sufficient reason for not spending the time and money to attend. But others had not come because they felt they would not be comfortable, would not be welcomed freely and looked upon as successful. They had not succeeded in life. So, some of the old feats and feelings of inferiority of youth still directed the attitudes and actions of these older people. I remember in particular one old friend that I asked about and was told that domestic unhappiness and general failure in life had made him confess that he would be uneasy at the reunion but that he hoped I particularly would look him up. These people perhaps felt that they could not dress appropriately, could not present themselves as successful, as the rest of us would consciously or unconsciously do. In another dimension in fact there was a great deal of apologizing for the lack of success in life on the part of those students who had shown early signs of predicted great success, those who had in the yearbook been voted "brightest," "most likely to succeed," and had served as valedictorian or salutatorian at the final exercises in school years ago. So there was a good deal of raking of old ashes and reexamining of potentials in life, generally with the best of cheer though with some obvious poignancy and I suspect, a good deal of human envy: of others' success, of others' better looks, slimmer figures, fancier automobile, etc. There is the assumption, furthermore, that some of the bon hommie and camaraderie that lasted through the afternoon and evening of the reunion might have worn thin through time. But that bon hommie and camaraderie is very real; it exists deep and has grown through time. Going back "home" to the reunion even for only a little while indicates how deeply the "locals" have brooded over the high-school experience through the years, partially because perhaps they never went any higher in education themselves and partly because of their deep affection for those people who did go on. Sometimes one discovers this brooding taking strange turns, indicating a life-long interest in old classmates. For example, one man whom I grew up with surprised me by saying, "Ray, you know I can prove that you and I are cousins." Since I had grown up with him and had never heard this mentioned before I was skeptical—amused and sympathetic, but skeptical. Imagine my surprise later when this man sent a document showing that our great-grandparents had in fact been siblings. In that area of the United States, where everyone knows that there have been through the years a great deal of South-wide extended-family relations, it might be surprising to discover just how many people not hitherto recognized as relatives are distantly blood-related.

Among a people who spend a lot of their time studying their families and relations, perhaps it is not surprising that the ritual of high-school class reunions means more than it would in other communities.

Thus the ritual, though perhaps no more frequently observed than among more sophisticated societies, is deeply appreciated. It simply means more to such people. The ritual is more appreciated, its meaning more profoundly felt, the mark made by the observance more deeply and lastingly etched. It is more anthropological, more earthy, more moving.

Reunions are not only celebrations of life but they are also memorials to death (to the death of the past) and vicarious anticipations of the rituals of coming death. On a larger scale the human being actually enjoys the ritual of vicariously experiencing death by seeing it in murder and funerals or reading about it in newspapers and books, or seeing it on television shows and in movies. As Stephen King, best-selling author of various kinds of gothic novels, points out in a parallel and similar kind of ritual: "The great appeal of horror fiction through the ages is that it serves as a rehearsal for our own deaths" (*Night Shift*, p. xvi). So too do the reunions: they link the dead past with the dying future. The strength of this feeling is achieved partially by the fact that the reunions build on the old belief, still demonstrated by elderly people, that death has a quota to be filled every day-week-month-year. The elderly will hear about the death of others their ages and will take obvious satisfaction in the fact that the quota has been filled for the period and nobody else need die, that they have outlived the other people. The feeling is apparently as old as consciousness of mortality and still strong.

Thus in the experience of going back and reliving the old death one gains a renewed strength to face the future.

But the going back also has been salubrious. Perhaps one cannot go home again—*permanently*—but one can visit and the visit often is life sustaining, providing to the visitor an ore for present and future worth far more than gold.

So reunions are anthropological rituals deeply imbedded in the lifeblood of the human race. Though through the years they change as superficial lifestyles change, the rituals still have a deeply needed and beneficial effect. Trying to go home again, though perhaps futile and perhaps not even desired, is worth the effort.

17

The ASA and Its Friends

In this intriguing piece Browne uses a self-evaluative theme issue of American Quarterly *to gently chide the American Studies Association for failing to live up to its potential. The article is of historical interest for the strong implication that if the ASA had been less rigid and "elitist"— Browne's term — the popular culture studies movement might have been contained within the field of American Studies as one of its specializations.*

Browne's remonstrations take on added significance when it is noted that he had successfully formed the American Culture Association and its flagship publication the Journal of American Culture *the year prior to this work's appearance. Browne was apparently not alone in his evaluations of the ASA's shortcomings.*

In addressing the question of what academia would have been like today if there had never been any American Studies movement, any American Studies Association or any *American Quarterly,* some profound and sometimes disquieting questions arise:

1. In the age of continuing specialization can an interdisciplinary or multidisciplinary approach to the humanities and cultural studies thrive in America?
2. Was the timing of the American Studies movement premature, and did it therefore suffer from being the first pioneer on the frontier?
3 Has the American Studies movement been too narrow, too fixed in the conventional disciplines (literature, history, philosophy), with only token interest in other related disciplines and therefore unable to become more widely based?
4 Has the whole movement been a real success? Probably the answers lie in a qualified yes and no to all questions.

Obviously many worthwhile accomplishments in academia have resulted from the concept. If there had never been the impulses which motivated the people to institute the movement in the first place, academia would have been more endarkened and less flexible than it is now because it would have centered too closely on conventional modes of approach although it would have allowed or encouraged new disciplines, and this hidebound approach would have inhibited new synthesis and associations. But like all human impulses the sensible dreams of the founders of the ASA have not come to fruition despite the hard work of second and third generation American Studies people.

I first came to take the American Studies movement seriously in 1950 when I went to UCLA as a graduate student. I was interested in folklore, American history and American literature, as well as allied fields, and felt, naturally, that American Studies contained the approach for me. UCLA did not offer any work in American Studies, but with the direct intervention and direction of Leon Howard, in English, and Wayland Hand, in folklore, I hammered out a program that reasonably suited my tastes. Working with Howard I helped put together one or two programs in folk music that he was going to deliver at the national meeting of the ASA.

But I pretty quickly saw that the ASA was somehow falling short of its potential. One person (obviously a friend of the movement) lamented that the ASA was like a train: the goal was first-rate but most of the passengers were on second-class tickets. Although I could not believe the accusation, I felt that if there were any grounds for the feeling, effort should be made to get first-class ticket-holders aboard the train.

Toward that end (to keep up the metaphor), in an attempt to get the train to touch more points in its long run and to pick up more first-rate passengers, I tried through my early years to get people in other disciplines interested in the ASA and the ASA interested in more and different people and organizations, in other words to get a different and larger mix. I especially tried to get the ASA and the American Folklore Society to hold joint meetings. After all, Richard Dorson — one of the leading folklorists in the country — had been the recipient of the second American Studies Ph.D. at Harvard, and the AFS though relatively small was an old and vital organization. I was perturbed when I was told by the ASA that there could be no worthwhile purpose in getting mixed up with the AFS and by the AFS that they could see no reason for meeting with a group of people who would only condescend to them. Sad but true, we had here two groups of people whose purposes paralleled but who would not work together because one felt itself elite and the other inferior, and the "inferior" one naturally resented not being recognized for its true worth.

In an effort to break down this feeling and to demonstrate how these groups could benefit by working together, while at Purdue University, in 1965 I organized a Mid-American Conference on Literature, History, Popular Culture and Folklore. Participants included the late Leo Stoller and Louis J. Budd (literature), Edwin Cady and Russel B. Nye (American Studies), Tristram P. Coffin and Americo Paredes (folklore) and Bruno Nettl (ethnomusicology), as well as others.

In the introduction to the volume of papers published from the Conference I made a plea that, "The time has come when serious scholars in these various disciplines— American Studies, folklore, and others should realize the nature of one another's work and the potential value and need each field has for the others. To be comprehensive, American Studies, that is, the examination of American life and culture, must include subculture —folk and popular cultures— as well ... the folk aesthetic as well as the more sophisticated one." The Conference, I concluded, "spoke emphatically and conclusively to the point that in the various fields and levels of American Studies and folklore, a broader and more liberal approach would be a more proper study."[1]

A second Mid-American Conference in 1966 made the conclusion even more obvious. The fields represented were wider than they had been in the earlier conference. Participants included such persons as E. McClung Fleming (Winterthur Museum); Herbert M. Schueller, C. Hugh Holman and Frederick J. Hoffman (literature); William H. Gass (Philosophy); Leslie A. Fiedler (literature and popular culture); Richard M. Dorson (folklore); and a half dozen others.[2]

For both conferences Robert F. Lucid, executive secretary of the ASA, cooperated fully.

Both conferences confirmed in my mind more solidly that the ASA ought to be more inclusive, less elitist, in its attitude and approach; it should be seeking outside the conventional and "respectable" fields for new materials, new ways of looking at the humanities, at scholarship, at new inter–and multi-disciplinary approaches to American culture and civilization. Yet I felt that no matter how hard the leaders in the ASA tried to revamp their thinking, in effect their first loyalties — psychologically at least — lay in their first disciplines, their conventional or narrowly broadened methodologies — that they were settlers in new lands rather than explorers.

The political, social and academic turmoil of the sixties and seventies set in motion, as I see it, two forces working on the ASA — one to broaden and make contemporary the interests of the organization; and the other, in a counter movement, to make the ASA more "respectable" because it was under considerable fire and suspicion. Unfortunately, the second impulse — purposely or inadvertently — often got equated with the ambiguous and loaded term *standards* — with some unfortunate consequences. The two drives were not incompatible and could, of course, have been interwoven into a strong cord, as many people undoubtedly wanted. But in the minds of some people, broadening meant *lowering* of standards; thus maintaining standards became being less experimental, less searching, living less "dangerously" — being safer.

Broadening the approach would have meant bringing in new sometimes untried and perhaps even second-rate scholars and subjects whose importance was open to question or whose value had not been demonstrated. The leadership of the ASA and editor of the *AQ* believed, apparently, that the purpose of the ASA and the *AQ* was to use eminent authorities to point the way lesser scholars should go, and to maintain the "highest" standards. Thus the ASA continued to be nailed to the cross of the futile debate over methodologies, never really being able to agree with Henry Nash Smith and others who insisted that a single methodology in the American Studies approach would be counterproductive.

These ideas have, of course, to a certain extent been modified in the last five years or so, but not enough. The ASA needs to be younger in attitude, more daring, less self-conscious, less concerned with what the rest of the academic establishment will think of it. It is time that the ASA quit being defensive about its value; anybody who is still fighting against such a program will never be convinced of its value; therefore he or she may as well be ignored.

As we say in another context, some of my best friends belong to the ASA, and I have been friendly with the officers of the organization and the editors of *AQ* all along. I wish it nothing but a bright future. But I am afraid that the society needs a strong shot in the arm, rap on the head or kick in the seat of the pants to propel it forward with real momentum. In academia these are desperate times, as we fight against financial and curriculum retrenchment. Although the ASA is not the white knight to ride up and save the whole system, it surely has enough potential to be a leading warrior in the battle.

It can provide new ideas in education and cultural studies — for academics as well as for non-academics — if it will shake itself fully awake and become more consciously aware of and responsive to the study of the world around us. The ASA's future impact depends on whether it will go much further than it has gone in its latest reorganization and honestly take stock, weighing its strengths and recognizing its weaknesses. The ASA cannot — should not — remain essentially Establishment. It owes the debt to itself and to America to branch out and become more inclusive geographically and more democratic and comprehensive in subject matter. It needs to seek out with complete democracy new areas of study and new ways of studying them. Each area should be given examination without prejudice and then awarded the justified time and place in the large scheme of culture.

Recent trends in both directions are proper, but they need to be expanded and made more obvious.

Notes

1. Ray B. Browne, Donald M. Winkelman, Allen Hayman, eds., *New Voices in American Studies* (Purdue University Studies, 1966).

2. Ray B. Browne, Richard H. Crowder, Virgil L. Lokke, William T. Stafford, eds., *Frontiers of American Culture* (Purdue University Studies, 1968).

18

Folklore to Populore

In this brief essay Browne summarizes and restates his long-held ideas about the connections between the fields of folklore and popular culture. Here though, he goes another step further, proposing that the studies now be termed "populore."

Browne is certainly serious in his comments about the connections between the two fields as his decades of work demonstrate. But how serious is he with his neologism? It is hard to tell, but more likely than not it is a pleasant rhetorical strategy that makes his point in an endearing fashion.

Writing a brief chapter on the role popular culture studies should play in a folklore program is in most ways stating the obvious. It is a three-way sermon — preaching to the choir; haranguing the audience in the front row; and pleading with the scoffers who came to doubt and sneer.

Folklore studies are well established in the public mind and in academia. The Library of Congress has a magnificent collection, recognized worldwide, and each year holds a festival attended by tens of thousands. Government money, procured largely through the tireless energies of folklorist Archie Green, provide funding for various activities. Society at large approves the study, and academics, especially those with proven track records, teach various thrusts in numerous kinds of folklore. Yet courses are being phased out and students in the field constantly ask questions about their future. To a certain extent historically, folklorists have been too narrow in their approaches and have vociferously engaged in what might be called discipline defense; that is, raising the walls of self-assurance of their purpose too high and being too exclusive. Perhaps the walls should now be lowered or at least penetrated.

To a large extent the task before us is to make definitions clear. Historically, folklore has been thought to be the life culture of the mass that made up the majority of any population's present or past. Folklore is the manifestation of some element of historical development, generally presented in an artistic form. It is nostalgia to some degree, a desire to revisit the time and place in which the culture occurred. People in any culture other than their own, wish for the imagined good old days, places, and societies. Folklore is a yearning to return to yesteryear, yesterplace, and yesterculture. People may or may not feel a stirring in their blood for the beauty and magic of some element of folklore but they feel they can hold onto the past through the reenactment of its lore. It is especially appealing when the society one finds oneself in is a polyglot of hundreds or thousands of bits of cultures congregated from all over the world.

One may not be able or even desire to leave the lore of one's environment, and the physical trip is not necessary. We can use the magic wings of folklore to travel from the present, and go to a more desired location of our real world. In the new land we still feel the throb of the home country blood, and can return at will. In the United States, we maintain nominal linkage with the pasts through linking ourselves to the points of origin of our ancestors. We are German Americans, English Americans, Latin Americans, Japanese Americans, Native Americans, and African Americans. We enrich our emotional lives through reenactment of the human, daily practices and arts of the country and people of the "old" country.

As time has compressed the boundaries of mixed countries and cultures, folklorists have increasingly looked upon folklore as the magic heritage of a people, which defined them, and was to be used by scholars as a cultural pantry from which old ways of life could be extracted. This trip down memory lane has been a kind of cultural security blanket from which old ways of life, which we have raised to the level of ideal, have become the practice of dealing in antiques, a practice which actually bled the life from the lore and left skeletons from which DNA had to be extracted to provide paleo-anthropological evidence of the locale and tribe of the past.

This attitude involved tunnel vision and putting blinders on us that directed scholars and the populace at large to make false readings. Looking toward the past has given us a false sense of reality. We don't have folk anymore in this country; they probably disappeared in Europe in the 15th century and never were alive in the United States. Instead of folk we have a general population. The members of the population at large or of groups do have, to be sure, traditions and memories of earlier days and societal groups. To a certain extent these traditions and memories influence our attitudes and patterns of behavior and are the groupings of an earlier national and cultural identity.

But the past is past though not dead, and cultures have been modified or changed. That means folklore is surviving in and being influenced by different dynamics—the mass media, new cultural concepts, different ways of life. This changed world forces a modified folklore. Culture is broader and deeper, civilizations march to different drums; the "lore" of culture, whatever that is, has changed. American society is now the result of, and ruled by, its popular culture. Popular culture consists of the aspects of attitudes, behavior, beliefs, customs, and tastes that define the people of any society. Popular culture is, in the historic use of the term, *the culture of the people.*

Popular culture and folklore are twin bodies joined at the heart and head, popular culture looking to the present and past, folklore viewing reality from the past to the present. Folklorists are beginning to recognize the attachment. Linda Degh (1996), called by Alan Dundes "our most distinguished folklorist," had led the way in the new thinking on folkloristics, especially vis-a-vis the mass media:

> The mass media liberate folklore from its earlier confinement to the so-called lower layers of society and from the prejudice—both pro and con—that stigmatized it. Folklore belongs to everyone, not only to the underprivileged, uneducated masses. It is a common cultural property characterizing our ways of thinking, believing, and dreaming, and our modes of defining our identity. The observer of emergent folklore may be able to decipher the interpretations through the accessibility of modern media. We are eyewitnesses to a new era in which folklore gains power and prestige as an authoritative dream, and hope; the voice of all humanity alienated and fractured by electronic efficiency. The task of folklorists is to read these meanings of folklore, and this task makes folkloristics an important interdisciplinary science, now more than ever before [2].

Numerous other folklorists are advocating the use of a wider umbrella to cover the subject. Alan Dundes, one of the more learned and amusing folklorists working today, has the Freudian approach to humor and folklore, especially published in several books on the folklore of present-day duplicating machines. Roger D. Abrahams broadens the study in *Singing the Master: The Emergence of African American Culture in the Plantation South* (1992) in a whole geographical region's culture. Archie Green (1993), one of the fiercest exponents of folklore studies, recognized the influence of everyday culture on folklore and was willing to subdivide the term into "folk, popular, plebeian" (*Wobblies, Pile Butts, and Other Heroes*, 238).

Other scholars have turned to value what are considered the most threatening media of all — TV and movies. Bruce Jackson wanted to clutch the movies to his bosom:

> Film is the dominant narrative mode of our time. Film and television provide much of the sense of community in a mobile and electronic world; the verbal and imaginative referents we utilize in ordinary face-to-face encounters are as likely to come from our separate — but shared media experience as anywhere else. Film and television are far too important to be left to the media studies and literature scholars [*JAF* 102, 388–389].

The suggestion is carried into somewhat greater detail by Mikel J. Koven:

> Folklore studies have examined or at least recognized the importance of examining, popular cinema from a number of perspectives. At one level folklorists are able to observe and trace the process of homogenizing cultural expressions through the mass media. On the other hand, a great deal of folklore scholarship has explored those traditional narrative types and motifs when they appear in popular film and television, Yet, still other folklorists have noted further areas for fruitful exploration of popular culture texts, such as how popular culture texts reflect contemporary belief traditions, ethnographies of fan culture, the rituals involved with popular cultural consumption, narratives about technology and technological industries, and the existence of multiple versions of seemingly fixed texts [*JAF* 116, 176–195].

Shakespeare's question, "What's in a name?" should be answered, "Quite a lot," especially when the name is the flag that a whole academic and public community has been serving under for a hundred years. The word directs and limits a group's direction and vision. Notice how closely Degh's new definition of folklore, quoted above, parallels my definition of popular culture.* She and I have carried on our thinking independently but have arrived at the same conclusions.

If therefore folklore and popular culture are but two tracks for the same train to run on, why shouldn't the name be modernized and brought up to date? I believe the word *folklore* should be changed to *populore*, since it is no longer the lore of the past but the living, vibrant culture around us, past and present, that we are concerned with. If I were naming a folklore program today I would call it *populore*. Blending popular culture and folklore courses can only be logical and beneficial, no matter what the name might be. Nothing would be lost and a great deal gained by both the instructors and the students. The latter will flock to the classes and the faculty will have to grow with more staff. The education the students get will be richer and broader and more useful. Not bad for a program that has much to offer a campus-wide curriculum.

*See, for example, this volume's "Prologue."— The Editor

Bibliography

Abrahams, Roger D. *Singing the Master: The Emergence of African American Culture in the Plantation South*. New York: Pantheon Books, 1992.

Degh, Linda. *American Folklore and the Mass Media*. Bloomington: Indiana University Press, 1994.

Green, Archie. *Wobblies, Pile Butts, and Other Heroes*. Urbana: University of Illinois Press, 1993.

19

Replying to a Rejoinder

Browne gives himself the last word in a friendly little give-and-take between himself and scholar Richard Gid Powers. Powers had gently chided Browne for what Powers saw as Browne's refusal to accede to even a generalist theory for Popular Culture Studies, or the approximation of broad standards of evaluation in popular culture products and artifacts. Of course, Powers' concerns and points have been (and are) shared by many.

So, Browne mounts a defense, serious, though light in tone. It ends up being one of his more approachable and succinct explanations of his point of view. His discussion of the origin of Marxist thought is hilarious, and tellingly leads to a statement explaining why he took popular culture studies so seriously: "In human society the name of the game is power, and forcing its release through access to knowledge and understanding is ultimately the goal of Popular Culture Studies." That statement bears several re-readings.—The Editor

Dick Powers and I, though with our eyes on the same star, seem to be separated by a common academic curse. I failed to make my position clear (or he refuses to see it!) and he teases my argument by pulling on a string of particulars that does not lead to the core of my position (or I think he does!). So we smile at each other over my chasm of insufficient development while he wanders around through his swamp of a different agenda.

In my essay I tried to heed Lincoln's observation that if we know where we are and where we are going we might get to our goal more quickly. So I described our present launching pad to our Society of Heart's Desire and suggested that if we keep our determination up and our minds open we can move toward our goal. I suggested that (my point three) after all our stepping from rock to rock on our trip through the swamp of human existence perhaps our realization that empathy among all peoples is a large platform on which we might catch some breathing time before slogging on to peace and happiness. I tried to be no more precise because I did not want to rest on smaller particular stones that will soon sink in the mire of changed theories or will be quarantined because they will be covered with deadly academic gases.

It is the academic gases that I know and fear, not the intellectual or seeming nonintellectual inquiring mind, and I want more inquiry by all kinds of minds. Contrary to the monster Dick thinks I see in all "leftist" political bias, I pride myself on being of such persuasion. But I do have trouble with Marxist doctrinaire thinkers who ride on Marx's coattails without at all thinking about his thinking. One does not need years in the British Museum to realize that capitalism, organized religion and academia—but less so than all forms of totalitarian governments and the hierarchies in other animal societies—exploit the poor and weak by withholding the power of equal knowledge, equal rights and equal opportunity. In human society the name of the game is power, and forcing its release through access to knowledge and understanding is ultimately the goal of Popular Culture Studies. But that goal can hardly be achieved as long as intellectuals have their feet caught in the underwater netting of doctrinaire ideologies. Experience in scholarship teaches us that nearly all theories are mere milestones leading down the highway around which are piled numerous skeletons of abandoned theories. All too frequently these mounds become shrines for scholars who cannot or will not abandon them.

Democracy is the dynamic of movement on that highway of scholarly development; as Dick correctly puts it, "Democracy in popular culture is evolutionary." I believe society is always becoming, is gradually moving, and never is finished. That is the democratic process. The immediately present dynamic in the democratic movement — with the explosive surges of tribalism, ethno-piety, regionalism, nationalism and individual definitions of personal rights— is a powder keg that takes us to a new mixture of folk and popular cultures, where the drive for immediate development from the former to a sophisticated version of the latter may create unbearable tensions and actions that test whether the center or the edges of human existence can hold. Surely the dynamic in its convulsions of development is going to remake the body of world society.

These convulsions will demonstrate that society is far more than aesthetics, the union of perfection in God. In fact it can demonstrably be charged that aesthetics is another artificial standard imposed by those in power. Beauty is largely in the eye of the possessor. I would not want to be caught in bed with Romantic nonsense that a medium of artistic expression — like, say, a slab of marble — has its aesthetic statement enfolded in its nature and the aesthetician's role is merely to allow the marble to speak. Nor would I subscribe to countless other ways of describing quality, perfection or privilege. In the world of collectible art I would agree with the perceptive de-canonizing remarks of art historian Jon Huer, "Never has there been a greater mixture of comedy and insanity in an institution than that displayed in the Art Establishment" (2), in which at least half of the so-called masterpieces are hoaxes and apparently just as effective as the genuine until proven to be inauthentic. Then they become worthless, having been stripped of the cachet of being by one of the masters. There must be more to life than so-called beauty, at least as defended by those who claim to have a special appreciation of it. How about justice, or self or societal development? It may be that after equity, equality and justice have been achieved, then beauty — genuine beauty, not that declared by the elitists— becomes life's object. So far, however, such theory is largely a mote in the aesthetician's eye that he is trying to use to blur the public's vision.

So, not to get impaled on Dick's paradox of God's sense of beauty, I would think that if God is not interested in more than beauty then we don't want to waste our time on Him or on the question of whether She exists. The urge is to try to allow human society to survive and develop. I believe that it can — perhaps only — if human existence grows more democratic and I think that Popular Culture Studies properly driven are a great academic agent for that development, if those studies are considered to be the humanities.

Academia is hardly in the driver's seat in the world today. "Things are in the saddle / And ride mankind," observed Emerson over a hundred years ago. These things are generally electronic or their spin-offs. But academia can still play a role in society's development in the humanities if academicians can keep up with the real world rather than the ones they create or perpetuate in their own heads. Popular culture studies are a major link to that real world.

Work Cited

Huer, Jon. *The Great Art Hoax: Essays in the Comedy and Insanity of Collectible Art*. Bowling Green, OH: Bowling Green State University Popular Press, 1990.

20

American Studies and Humanity's Dream

When Browne edited a special anniversary issue of the Journal of American Culture he wrote this brief essay as part of the introductory remarks. This short but passionate piece is a call for American Studies to become even more of a field of cross-cultural understanding and to be wary of misplaced, insular, patriotic nationalism.— The Editor

Today's American political-military-financial-driven muscle overpowers the world. With this power goes cultural saturation unequaled since the nineteenth century. Just as the western world aped Rome during the imperial days and bowed to Great Britain when the sun never set on its political, commercial, and cultural influence, the feeling today throughout the world seems to be that if something is American, it must be imitated or held in contempt.

As America's cultural influence expands, it is imperative that scholars and laypeople in the United States and around the world understand it. American society has great depth and swirling mixtures. The many cultures that have been transferred alive to the United States have brought with them deep histories and cultural imperatives. These histories, mixed with those that existed among the Indians who were here when this old world became the "New World," have continued to be a mixing cauldron that gets more and more complex as each constituent continues to grow and to recognize and demand what it considers its rights. Americans' understanding of the complexity and power of America's many elements can help spread the concept of democracy and its possible accomplishments worldwide by modifying the tenor of the vocabulary about America and by removing from American concepts and vocabulary the exclusionary, self-congratulatory labels such as "American Way of Life" and "American Dream." We are fortunate to live in the United States of America and to enjoy the "American Way of Life" and the "American Dream," but this does not automatically exclude cultures and peoples from partaking of the dreams of their cultures. The "American Dream," after all, is not an end in itself but a step in the climb to make life better for all of humanity. We should therefore make it clear to the peoples of the world that they should be driving toward "Humanity's Dream," which may not always carry on it the label "Made in America." The key is to wash away the lines between various hopes for the best life with the astringent of clear and careful communication.

Not to do so in the present world is to toy with determined people who are driven with the fierce determination to develop their own fates, sometimes with the fantasy of the destruction of America and the way of life that they have not yet achieved. The drive feeds on one of humanity's most devilish characteristics: "If you can't have it, then destroy it."

Since the early 1950s, American scholars, through the American Studies programs in many schools in the United States and abroad, have tried to expand and enrich examination of American culture. Driven by the realization that knowledge and life are not two parallel lines of needed understanding, these scholars have interwoven several disciplines in the humanities, and in so doing have opened the thick book on the development of American studies and their influence at home and abroad to page one or two. But the book needs to have more pages turned, to include such areas as archaeology, anthropology, art history, communication studies at all times, folklore, toys and play, work and play, politics, iconography, and all of the other forces in life that make up a powerful and complex swirl of cultures. Expanding will enrich, and enriching will result from expansion.

The degree to which scholars in American culture studies have succeeded in their efforts to broaden and enrich may be open to interpretation. But every effort, no matter how strong or weak, can be looked upon as advancement.

21

Russel B. Nye:
The Richness of His Life

This is a simple and poignant memorial to a comrade who had been "in the trenches" with Browne since the beginning. Or, in some ways, even before. It is also of note for the brief comment on the development of the field.— The Editor

Russ Nye was one of the great experiences of my life. How, then, do I experience his death? In two ways: with great sadness that American academia no longer benefits from his presence and with joy that I knew him while he lived. And he did live, and brought new vigor and vitality to whatever life and whatever people he touched.

I first met Russ in about 1962 when I was at Purdue University, and he came down to talk about children's literature. After that, almost everything I proposed for investigation Russ responded to with the positive statement, "Why Not?" Why not, indeed. Everything deserved consideration and the chance to succeed, He pushed the parameters of investigation on all subjects, and he encouraged his students— and everybody else's students— to investigate, think and try. Students never had a better friend than Russ. Academics in general never had a better friend and colleague than Russ.

I experience Russ' death from two constituencies, myself and the Popular Culture Association and the American Culture Association. I stand on his shoulders, receiving vitality from the upward flow of his mind and personality. The thousands of members of these two associations which he helped me found and cultivate speak their gratitude through me. They too stand on his shoulders and feel the upward flowing current of vitality.

Russ was a man of the West, the New Nation. Westerners have a compliment they pay their heroes: those people stand from the ground. Russ stood from the ground and for the spirit. No finer monument need be sought than this realization.

22

Reviews

The Unembarrassed Muse

Browne's enthusiasm for his colleague-in-arms' book is palpable and arguably carries him away at the end of the review as he veers into "founding father" hyperbole.

Small matter. The book, an academic descendant of Gilbert Seldes' The Seven Lively Arts, did indeed turn out to be a benchmark effort, still held in highest regard. Browne can't resist a little analysis of his own, tying the book to the nostalgia wave of the late 1960s and early 1970s that was more or less concurrent with (and perhaps a reaction to) the then ongoing social upheavals.

He then uses his review to springboard into proclaiming the book's arrival signals the end of elitism in higher education and to proselytize for the gospel of popular culture studies. Points he would later develop more fully can be glimpsed here in passing embryonic form.

This volume's Prologue contains Browne's later minor self-chastisement at his and Nye's emphasis on the popular arts and how that misstep had far-reaching repercussions for the field.— The Editor

This book is both a storm maker and a haven of explanation for many anxious souls.

It will create storms because it will attack the tenets held by many conventional minds, those elitists who persist in seeing large gaps between elite art, popular art and folk art, the first and last as splendid and uplifting, the middle as meretricious, downgrading and the cause of most of the world's problems. Prof. Nye has demonstrated, however, that the gaps are only in the eye of the beholder, for when an observer honestly and dispassionately compares the three types of art he sees that one blends into the others, that none is perfect, none without blemish. Prof. Nye also demonstrates that the scale of esthetic achievement is not vertical, as elitists like to assert, with elite on top and mass art on bottom, but instead it is horizontal, something like an eye or flattened ellipsis: elite on one end, folk art on the other, with the largest portion of the center taken up by popular art, which includes mass art.

Prof. Nye corrects the long-held near-religious belief that popular art appeals to the lowest common denominator. Instead it is merely, as he says, the "largest common denominator," and the difference is significant. All kinds of art do and must exist concurrently, especially in a society like America's. In such a society the esthetic accomplishment is always being reassessed and changed. Everybody knows that esthetic evaluation depends to a large extent on faddism, on feelings and attitudes of critics, often on nothing more than age and approaching hardening of the critical arteries. And the real accomplishment of the art itself constantly changes. As Prof. Nye observes: "Sometimes, with skill and talent alone, a popular artist may transmute mediocre material into something much better than it is, something even good; the gradual improvement over the years of standards of performance in the popular arts provides sufficient proof of this."

Prof. Nye provides us with a three dimensional sweep of American popular arts from the Massachusetts days to the present, through fiction and poetry, the theater, newsstand arts, cowboys and spacemen, music and the media. It is a profile in depth of most of the dimensions of and the growth of the American mind and character.

The survey is rich, detailed, and perceptive. It reveals tellingly how our ancestors spent their time and how most of us spend it now.

A minor use the book serves is to ride the crest of the current wave of nostalgia that is sweeping across the oceans of our anxiety and frustration. This function is inadvertent but interesting. Although we may think there is something defensive, weak and frustrated almost to the point of sickness in our tendency nowadays to dreams of times past, this book, without condoning or condemning, will at least make the trend more understandable.

The power of the book, however, comes from the air of iconoclasm, which rises from virtually every page to influence the reader consciously or unconsciously. It is one of the true books recently published in the history of American development — true in the sense of not meaning to mislead, but to uplift, not to varnish over reality. For this book shows life like it is and has been. There is really nothing new about demonstrating that the popular arts have always been a vital part of American culture. The best cultural and literary historians have always recognized this. But the import of these messages has usually been blunted or ignored by lesser scholars and critics who have been unaware of the popular culture around them or have chosen to ignore it.

But to refuse to recognize reality is nonsensical as well as dangerous. The noted British critic Raymond Williams insists that every crisis in human life is a crisis of understanding, and if we can only understand we can confront and overcome the crisis. The crisis in popular arts is one of admission. The popular arts are with us, and to stay. It is time we quit trying to deny their existence. There are more than sixteen thousand theaters in this country, attended weekly by some sixty million Americans. At the rate people are glued to their TV sets, by the time a child is graduated from high school he will have spent eighteen thousand hours before the Tube and only 15,000 in classrooms. These are the facts of life — curse, some people would say. But Aristotle felt that it is better to enjoy art — good or bad — than not to have access to any. Undoubtedly it is better to learn to read on comic books than not to learn at all. But the Maginot Line of some people's minds still lies manned.

There are still some among us who insist that they would not allow the Tube in their homes. But these are undoubtedly the same kind of intellectuals who long ago insisted that the invention of the printing press was an abomination sure to produce books inferior to the old manuscript, to effect a "popularization" and therefore vulgarization of literature and art.

But many such elitists are less than candid with themselves and their constituents. Often the material they condemn in the professional hours they indulge in on the sly. In many ways the crisis is one of lack of candor. Many elitists have a bootleg psychology, consuming "illegal" goods they are ashamed to admit they traffic in. What we need is a Twenty-first amendment in culture.

Marshall McLuhan is correct in seeing the shrinking of the world through the mass media. The Technological Revolution is reversing the separation of the arts into "elite and popular" which was brought about by the Industrial Revolution. Susan Sontag is correct in saying that there is no difference between art now and that of earlier days—it is merely serving a different and more general purpose. Leon Edel calls Prof. Nye's book "a great documentary and guide to the fairy-tale mind of America," and Orson Welles once observed that, "The cinema is a ribbon of dreams." Both comments are off base in their assertions of the unreality of these popular arts. In many ways the popular arts are the reality, whether we like it or not, movies especially.

Undoubtedly the popular arts have been abused in the past. But there are encouraging signs that some "improvement" is coming. TV, for example, is slowly enriching at least some of its programs. With the underwriting of IBM, Xerox, Ford, Rockefeller, etc., NET, especially in *Sesame Street*, is just beginning to discover its potential. This potential is far more than TV's critics, especially the narrow academic critics, can visualize. In this age of growing disrespect for the so-called specialist, there is increasing respect for such a comment as that of Robert Sarnoff, Chairman of NBC, in observing, "If we listened to the eggheads, we'd be out of business in six months." If "eggheads" equals "academics," Sarnoff surely had a point. Academics often spend their lives trying to protect their positions, and in remaining inflexible. They are not so much interested in the development of ideas as in the protection of old notions. What they have they don't want to change. Someone has observed that if the Edsel had been introduced into the curriculum, it would still be taught. The only trouble with that observation is one of progress: in fact the motion to introduce the course would still be before the curriculum committee.

But a warming trend in the glacier of academia, and elitism, is evident. Condescension to the popular arts and to the study of them is decreasing. Courses are springing up on college and university campuses all over the country, in, for example, Introduction to Popular Culture, Popular Arts and Entertainments, Popular Literature, The Western, The Film, Science Fiction, Detective Fiction, etc.

Prof. Nye's book has provided a pair of ten-league boots for people to leap the culture gap in American academia. The book is an Academic *Declaration of Independence*, saying that people in the college and university (and public school) communities are tired of studying the old "truths," and want new materials and ideas, want to think for themselves. The book is also, at the same time, a Constitution for the federation of Popular Arts scholars. It will stand as such. But because the world of Popular Arts, in and out of academia, is in ferment, the outlines of the subject and the guidelines fluid—and may they ever remain so—students will insist on their *Bill of Rights* and other Amendments. These amendments will enlarge the area to include all of Popular Culture, as Prof. Nye would undoubtedly have done had the format of the series in which this book appeared permitted. Prof. Nye is the first President of the Popular Culture Association, and one of the powerful forces in making the study of Popular Culture "legitimate and respectable." His book will stand as a monument by one of the Founding Fathers.

The Study of Folklore

In this review (one of two he did on the book) of the recognized instant classic in the field of folklore, Browne relies on his knowledge of literature to find at least one particular weak spot in the volume. Overall, Browne is worried that folklore as a field will devolve into unconnected specialties, a fear he later had for popular culture studies, and congratulates the author for not falling into that particular trap.

Browne counters some known criticisms of the book, but ends up somewhat damning it with faint praise.— The Editor

Increasingly as folklorists become more and more insistent on their own professionalism, each in his own particular area, they are becoming more fragmented, and often more intolerant of and antagonistic to others. The schism is especially marked between the literature-folklorists and the anthropology-folklorists. In this age of specialization such a schism was perhaps inevitable, probably even desirable. But a real question arises as to whether it now has gone too far or has progressed to the point that it need go no further. Are people in our profession now arrived at that stage in their discipline-development that in becoming narrow they are losing some of the breadth and depth that make folklore rich and useful? I am not arguing for the minister dilettantism of the nineteenth century or for the gentlemanly casualness of the early twentieth.

Instead I am wondering whether folklore is not by definition interdisciplinary and therefore quite properly defiant of fragmentation into various sub-fields.

Professor Dundes recognizes the danger of this compartmentalization. Although he insists that folklore is a field of its own and should not be mistakenly subordinated to other disciplines, in this book he in fact tries to open an umbrella sufficiently wide to cover the whole field. He is trying to teach the student of literature more about anthropology-folklore, and the student of anthropology more about literature-folklore. Such a purpose is commendable.

The book is a collection of thirty-four essays, covering in greater or lesser depth practically every aspect of folklore. The names of the six groups into which the essays are divided are significant: "What is Folklore?" "The Search for Origins," "Form in Folklore," "The Transmission of Folklore," "The Functions of Folklore," and "Selected Studies of Folklore." The text was designed, as Dundes says, "to show the beginning folklore student something about what folklore is, how it might have originated, what some of its patterns are, how it is transmitted, how it functions and finally, how folklorists study it."

Dundes keenly and properly feels that the "teaching of folklore is definitely impeded by the extreme diversity of both the materials ... and the methods of studying these materials."

In trying to teach all specialists the materials of the others— especially the literature-anthropology extremes— he may have stretched himself too thin, and underdeveloped most areas. Perhaps folklore has now become so diversified that nothing short of an encyclopedia can in a single volume comprehend it all. Perhaps also Dundes over-compliments each specialist in his own field, assuming that he can seize a hint and blow it into a balloon.

I am most concerned with what I consider the shortcomings of the book on folklore and literature. The only essay Dundes includes on this major topic is Archer Taylor's "Folklore and the Student of Literature." This essay, admirable though it is, can hardly be focused to throw all the light needed into the nooks and crannies of a subject so large and profound. Dundes includes in a headnote, as he does for all sections, a bibliographical reference to other material, especially "Folklore in Literature: A Symposium," which appeared in the *Journal Of American Folklore*, LXX (1957). This reference is insufficient, if not worse.

At least two of the articles in that symposium should be at the fingertips of all instructors regardless of their bent or bias. Richard Dorson's "The Identification of Folklore in American Literature," for example, is indispensable. Perhaps even more vital to the beginning student is Daniel Hoffman's "Folklore in Literature: Notes Toward a Theory of Interpretation." The conclusion of this first-rate critic-scholar should be widely known: "The critic investigating literary uses of folk materials will be concerned not only with their function in their cultural contexts but also with the qualities they contribute to the literary works in which he finds them."

An excellent case in point of Hoffman's theory is Herman Melville. Not to know how fully and richly he used folklore in *Moby Dick* is to miss a large part of its message and potential power. Numerous sections of the book depend heavily on folklore for development. Some sections — the chapter entitled "Queen Mab," for instance — are understandable only in their folkloristic context. So too in the rest of Melville. Three passages in *Typee, Redburn,* and *Moby Dick,* all the same, turn on an obscene gesture, which is a kind of anal Shanghai Gesture. Such material must be known if Melville is to be understood fully.

One criticism of Dundes' book heard in the corridors of hotels and classroom buildings is that the material is better designed for graduate students than undergraduates. Such a criticism is, as Dundes has responded, without validity. A subject of this importance must not be watered down for babes. In *Moby Dick* in the magnificent chapter entitled "The Grand Armada," Melville recounts how whale's milk is "very sweet and rich; it has been tasted by man; it might do well with strawberries"— perhaps if it were diluted. But it should be taken full-strength by young and growing leviathans. Folklore also should be taken full-strength.

After all the real or presumed shortcomings of Dundes' book are cataloged most of us will agree — though sadly — that it is the best single text available.

The Benjamin Lee Whorf Legacy

Browne comes clean on his long-time friendship with the author but his positive review seems merited as he details some of the materials included in the study of and collection of materials by anthropological-linguist Benjamin Lee Whorf. Worf's ideas on language, communication, and culture had extensive influence, including on the field of popular culture studies, a fact of which Browne is clearly aware.— The Editor

The Benjamin Lee Whorf Legacy adds a new dimension to our understanding of the businessman/linguist associated with "the Sapir-Whorf Hypothesis." This electronic archive supplies primary and secondary materials to amplify Whorf's arguments about how languages shape perceptions; it also throws light on the 1920s controversy between science and religion.

The collection is edited by Peter C. Rollins, whose first conference paper on Whorf was delivered at an early meeting of the Popular Culture Association and later published in a special issue of *JPC* devoted to The Occult (Ed. Robert Galbreath). Later, the association endorsed a book-length study of Whorf (included on this CD-ROM). It was my great pleasure to be standing next to Marshall Fishwick at the Kellogg Center on the Michigan State University campus when the first paper on Whorf was given, and I have followed Rollins' study of Whorf as it evolved over the decades.

Previously unpublished articles by Whorf discuss the history of linguistic theory. Also in the collection of "new" articles are discussions of what Whorf derides as "scientific unanimity." Moving to the world of physics, this graduate of MIT (chemical engineering) proposed a "flux-outlet" theory of matter, which incorporated what at that time was called the "new physics." The supposed conflict between science and religion is considered in an imaginative essay entitled "The Newtonian Room and the Christian Rosebush." For scholars interested in the steps of Whorf's exposure to new ideas, there is an entry for "Library Books Read: 1924–1928," a list which evidences a concurrent interest in linguistics, psychology, and relativity — all synthesized in the famous linguistic relativity hypothesis associated with Whorf and his mentor, Edward Sapir.

During the trial of John T. Scopes, Whorf set out to answer H. L. Mencken, whom Whorf scorned for his lack of understanding of both religion (for which Mencken had contempt) and science (in which Mencken had no training). In 1925, Whorf sat down after work (at the Hartford Insurance Company) and, in fewer than six months, completed a novel titled *The Ruler of the Universe*. This idiosyncratic work of polemical fiction attempted to demonstrate by both argument and narrative that the sciences — especially the physics of Max Planck and the relativity theory of Albert Einstein — were not in conflict with an imaginative reading of Genesis. The novel predicts — by way of a dream — a future war in which airplane technology facilitates attacks on large cities; in the armaments race, scientists develop a weapon, which taps the basic energy of the universe. How prescient were such "fantasies" in 1925!

This collection includes three journal articles on Whorf, a book on Whorf, and even the hefty dissertation submitted to Harvard University's American studies program. An introduction to the collection takes a cultural studies approach to Whorf, and the dissertation will be of interest to scholars of the post–World War I decade because it places the discussions of religion, science, and language within a historical context. (After the "war to end all wars," Alexander Korzybski devised his famous "structural differential" and launched the General Semantics movement while Ludwig Zamenhof and others devised and popularized the artificial language of Esperanto — both efforts by Polish intellectuals to promote international understanding and peace.)

The "Sapir-Whorf Hypothesis" is discussed every day on the Internet, often with a "shock of recognition," to use Edmund Wilson's expression (borrowed from Melville). *The Legacy of Benjamin Lee Whorf* should provide a jump-start for new scholarly investigations into American popular perceptions.

There are some software needs connected with this scholarly tool, but the required items are already on most computers and, if not, are included on the CD-ROM for downloading. Many of the documents are word-searchable, an important aid for scholars who might be more interested in the issues of the 1920s and 1930s than with specifics about Whorf. I would urge every major university teaching linguistics, ESL, and anthropology to acquire this important scholar resource.

The Devil Gets His Due: The Uncollected Essays of Leslie Fiedler

This review is more Browne's quick ironically-satirical obituary for Leslie Fielder than a review of the actual book, and that, in essence, is its charm — The Editor

Since Fiedler's death in 2003, just before his eighty-sixth birthday, criticism of literature and indeed culture has regrettably lost a vital spark. Fiedler was the Serpent in the Garden who not only tempted but also urged. He had opinions on all subjects and expressed them rapidly and cogently no matter how foolish or wrong-headed — even uninformed — they might turn out to be. But Fiedler was always Fiedler, and was worthy to be heard. This collection is not the complete Fiedler but it will suffice until a fuller collection comes along. Serpents in the Garden change skins, and each deserves study.

A Theme Issue of the *Journal of Folklore Research*

Again, Browne finds a way to warn against the dangers of "grand theory" and it is clear that his message is not only intended for the Journal of Folklore Research. — *The Editor*

Indiana University and Indiana University Press have always been leaders in the study of folklore, the necessary but often overlooked and despised area of academic study. But *JFR* has persevered. Now it is bringing out a special issue dedicated to the question of why there is no "grand theory" in the study of folklore. The answer, of course, is that folklorists don't want to work in sweeping theories, preferring "to focus on the actuality of vernacular practice" (1). But to folklorists the total is contained in the miniscule, the big in the little. As long as folklorists continue to seek the general in the particular they will continue to add to human, and academic, knowledge.

Postmodernism and Popular Culture: A Cultural History

Browne uses this hilarious book review to rake excessive theory-heads over the coals. Pungent and punchy, it shows that Browne has had more than enough of such goings on. Agree with him or not, the reader has to laugh and delight in Browne's nimbleness. — The Editor

There is a great deal to be learned from this book, which really should have been named *The Education of John Docker*, or *The Ultimate Education of Every Person*. For that is precisely where we have recounted here. The development of the student — especially that graduate student — from the stage when he or she is impressed by the instructor into awe about a theory on which can be hung all knowledge (say, Modernism, Postmodernism, Marxism/Leninism, the Frankfurt School, etc.) and final development that such theories, as most unbiased observers finally determine are mere wasting skeletons on the side of the highway of intellectual development. Many theorists, of course, fondle the skeleton long after it has putrefied and been reduced to broken bones. But most scholarship is a trip down the road of life while looking backward, stumbling and rolling through new experiences and situations.

Docker, as he points out, made all the conventional decisions, and outlines here the appeal of the theories. He scraped at the feet of F.R. Leavis and his wife Q.D. Leavis until he was relieved of their blinding and self-serving elitism. He copes with Marxism/Leninism, with Theodor Adorno and Max Horkheimer and the Frankfurt School and its twist with Walter Benjamin, then he slept with Richard Hoggart's British cultural studies and its latest spin in Stuart Hall. Then he watched the flickering of the 1970s Screen Theory and the London journals *Screen* and *Screen Education*. He got singed by Frederic Jameson's flashing pan of latterday Marxism, from Structuralism and Post-structuralism, and others. Finally he arrived at what seems obvious to most of us on the downhill side of the road, that the great theorists were working out schemata and lines of theorizing that were useful to them, were obviously transitory, and that education — perhaps even an iota of wisdom — consists in working through those morasses and arriving at one's own little island in the swamp.

In this very revealing and useful book Docker works through his journey, outlines the attractions of theories to the unthinking mind and finally arrives at the freedom that comes with realization that all theories are just that and should be treated as such. We see in his *mea culpa* a lot of ourselves, and the book is therefore embarrassing. But from embarrassment can come wisdom, and the sooner the better. This volume should therefore be required reading for the child in the cradle. If that is a little too early, then grade school, middle school, high school, or undergraduate college. If not those times, then surely and definitely in graduate school, when the mind is most susceptible to fraud and smoke and mirrors. This book blows away the smoke and holds the mirror steady. For that reason it should be awarded the Self-Awareness and Knowledge Prize.

Re-Reading Popular Culture

Browne gives a generally positive review to a book that espouses the internationalization of popular culture studies, but takes the occasion to note that the conflation of the popular arts with popular culture continues and should be studiously avoided.— The Editor

This informative volume sets out to analyze the internationalizing qualities of popular entertainment. The author, who is a Lecturer in the Department of Media and Culture at the University of Amsterdam, outlines the purposes of her book to describe the merits and abilities of popular entertainment. First "popular culture makes us welcome and offers belonging. Its economic and celebratory logic (depending on its corporate-capitalist origins, or its users or reader provenance), after all, make it imperative that ever more buyers or like-minded fans are found." Second, is "the fascination" we have about statements in popular culture. Third, "popular culture links the domains of the public and the private and blurs their borderline more than any other institution or practice." Discussing and comparing American and Continental popular entertainments Hermes accomplishes her purposes clearly and convincingly. But her book raises a caveat and a problem that is becoming increasingly misleading. The title of her book is "Popular Culture," but all she discusses is popular entertainment, as though popular entertainment is the entirety of popular culture when it is only one portion. Popular culture includes far more than entertainment, just as elite culture (whatever that is) includes more than such entertainments of that culture than, say, opera and art galleries. The confusion of popular entertainment as all of popular culture continues and nurtures academics' continued examination of a supposed problem that was settled years ago, and in teaching this misinterpretation to students is only continuing misinformation that should not be used to confuse present-day students. Such misunderstanding and publication of what constitutes culture (popular and otherwise) has long since been settled, and readers for publishers should be chosen more carefully so that outdated concepts and theories should not be rehashed again and again.

Instructors in popular culture studies should also, of course, begin their studies with more current theses. Those objections having been said, this reviewer recommends this book, with a new title such as *Re-Reading Popular Entertainments*, as a useful study of the value of viewing the power of popular entertainment in spreading and mixing American with those of other nations.

Inventing Popular Culture

If Browne ever needed proof that the popular culture studies movement he had championed had won legitimacy and that his messages of its democratic impetus had been understood, this book and others like it surely must have done the trick. Knowing Browne, and reading his description of the book's point of view, the reader knows it will meet with significant favor.—The Editor

This is a sensible and usable handbook addition to the rushing tide of popular culture studies. [John] Storey recognizes that the term "popular culture" was an eighteenth-century invention used by the privileged to name and devalue the role of the underprivileged in society. The term grew from folk culture and meant the same thing. Through the years, however, folk and everyday culture have exercised their power and worked their way from the kitchen and barnyard into the living room and front parlor. Muscle and the vote (especially the heavy purse) have, of course, brought the disenfranchised more and more power. In our day, as Storey points out, popular culture has little or nothing to do with intrinsic value but with attitude and way of viewing. A so-called work of art may or may not have superior intrinsic value but is categorized as "high" or "low" by the owner and others who benefit from some categorization.

Storey also discusses the growing and irresistible power of popular culture. As the political power of people grows, their everyday culture becomes more a part of the worldwide level of global culture. What was at one time an American projection of global culture as American culture lived and practiced worldwide has now become a realization that global culture is going to be precisely that: a stew of roiling (often conflicting) local cultures by people who hang on to their own native cultures as their "everyday" ways of life. Such a development is inevitable and perhaps even desirable if people, especially in the First World countries, recognize and accept these concepts.

One of the strong aspects of this study of popular culture is its simple presentation and lack of academic pretentiousness. It traces the development of ideas from their origins and points out their class structure and blind development. But Storey's presentation is understandable and pleasurable.

Perhaps his conclusion carries the full burden of his book and needs to be emphasized. We do not need "a denial of difference but an insistence on seeing difference within the context of a shared humanity: in effect, to live in both the local and the global and share a "glocalized" culture. This would be a truly popular culture." Perhaps everyday culture has enough power to move the world. We can only hope to help it along. This fine book helps us see the way.

Society's Impact on Television: How the Viewing Public Shapes Television Programming

A short commentary on the expansion of television and a handful of pithy asides mark this as a good example of Browne's short book critiques. — The Editor

Behind every television screen there is a rainforest, which includes a jungle, inhabited by human beings. The rainforest grows in abundance animals with and without talent, it feeds those animals with the fruits of ego-gratification and money, and it develops the rain that falls on us all — sometimes to our pleasure and satisfaction, sometimes to our decay and rot. Into that forest often venture pith-heads who want to influence and change the climate — and always to comment on what is going on, sometimes with knowledge and often in complete bias and ignorance.

Gary Selnow, Professor at San Francisco State University and author of much on communication policy research, and Richard Gilbert, senior partner in the Daniels Group until 1989, Director of Policy Resources for NBC, try to bring information — and a point of view — to the jungle so that we inhabitants can better understand the world of television.

They succeed quite well, methodically, detailed and clearly. Through interviews with such people as Norman Lear, Gary David Goldberg, David Milch, and Steven Bochco they get the points of view of the writer-producer and the conflict between the attitudes of the two coasts — New York and Hollywood. The authors discuss the impact of government regulations, the impact of "pressure groups" (which should be called "interest groups"), of advertisers and of technology. They point out that in the rain forest each group is fighting for its own territory and growth, and is not necessarily a devil. Television never fully satisfies any of these groups because they are self-interest expert groups, narrow and self-serving. In a way all these groups are merely mouth-pieces for the public, who want TV to be both educational and entertaining. Perhaps, after all, it is, in the same way that life is. But if you think there are high spots and low spots now, just wait until we get 500 channels operating 24 hours a day, 365 days a year — it is enough to frighten the most brazen person. Most people admit that the ultimate critic of television is the person at home who has the power to influence both coasts — by tuning in another channel or turning the set off. If the bosses on the coasts are worried about "interest groups" now, just wait until each individual is a "group," and there are 10 billion such groups in the world. That will make programming rather difficult!

Meanwhile, people should read this book. It is an anatomy of the world of television broadcasting, and as such clears up many of the misconceptions about the industry, which, like the rain forest, provides broadcasting which rains on the just and the unjust, the alert and the indifferent, the informed and the uninformed — all of whom in one way support the business. We all should know our rainforests better.

The McDonaldization of Society: Revised Edition

In this breezily amusing but dismissive review Browne's mistrust of elitist perspectives causes him to look askance at the revised edition of a book that uses the global expansion of McDonald's fast-food chain as a metaphor for certain cultural developments in the USA.

Fairly or not, Browne can't help but see parallels between the disparagement of McDonald's with the disparagement of popular culture in general.— The Editor

Without McDonald's to chew on, George Ritzer could not have a happy life. He must spend his entire life eating at one of the thousands of available outlets, observing the customers, and trying to figure out ways to save America (and now the world) from the evil of fast food emporiums. So far he has failed, but sociologists throughout the United States tell him how valuable his study is and how they pray for his success. Now, Ritzer is dividing populations into two classes: the elite (that is, the rational who would rather starve than eat at McDonald's), and the unwashed and tasteless.

It takes us back to the old arguments of thirty years ago, when a few gifted and select members of society realized that the popular culture (and its denizens) of today was to be avoided, while a select few were to be appreciated as taste and style setters. Now, however, Ritzer has dwelled on the subject for so long that he has become tired of his fight and is only amused by it, realizing that, regardless of what he preaches, his choir has long since adjourned to the nearest McDonald's restaurant. He has reduced himself to name-calling — everything evil is a "Mc-something."

In his list of ways to avoid the evil, he generally has his tongue in cheek, such as when he suggests that to avoid McDonaldization, one should always stay out of domed stadiums or those with artificial grass, or avoid going to movies with Roman numerals after their names. Whatever else it is, this book is a charmer for adults, especially academics and others who want to save the world. As we say, one good laugh deserves a new revised edition.

Cowtown Wichita and The Wild, Wicked West

This piece is included as an example of the hundreds of short summary-reviews Browne has done.— The Editor

Those of us interested in the settling and development of the so-called Wild West must look at this book [by Stan Hoig]. Wichita grew from a settlement of Wichita Indians into a town in the plains where such notables as Billy the Kid, Wyatt Earp, Bat Masterson, and many less notorious characters such as Jesse Chisholm (for whom the Trail was named), Rowdy Joe and Rowdy Kate, Marshal Mike Meager, and Indian trader James Mead all of whom followed the founding of the city, Dutch Bill Greiffenstein. Like all settlements that grew in the West, Wichita continued to benefit from its position on the trail. It also benefits from this very readable account of the city's growth from nowhere to the leading city in the state. This book is readable and informative history and should not require the pointed gun to force one to read it.

Epilogue

Education: Forward
to Democratic Fluency

This piece has been edited by fusing two smaller essays of Browne's 1992 book The
Many Tongues of Literacy. *Somewhat against his will, Browne officially retired from teaching that year (though he did teach the occasional class after retirement) and the book had
a certain ironic feel as a result, in light of partial contents such as this that make a plea for
the value of education, and others that address the role of educators, formal and otherwise,
in a mass-media environment. As stated previously, Browne's core concern throughout all
of his academic work involves education as key to maintaining and developing democracy.
In that light, it seems fitting that this selection close the volume.*

*Browne urges his readers to keep open to all kinds of information and experiences, and
to not allow themselves to be stifled in their quest for understanding and life-enrichment.
As in the rest of the book that the piece is taken from, Browne extols the necessity for a new
literacy unbound by the previous narrow and limiting concept of the term. The book greatly
expands the ideas expressed in the article "Popular Culture: Medicine for Illiteracy and
Associated Educational Ills" included elsewhere in this collection. Only through unbounded
literacy, he contends, can the individual and societies thrive.*

*Near the end, Browne references Marshall McLuhan's noted metaphor of humanity
vainly trying to see the future through rear-view mirrors. Here, Browne agrees with
McLuhan's assessment but calls for us to get rid of the rear-view mirror through a free-ranging unbounded education, the education necessary to maintain and improve not only ourselves but also our democracy.*

*For Browne, the democratic ideal is achievable only when life, liberty, and the pursuit
of happiness can be, and are, freely engaged.— The Editor.*

Democracy and capitalism though seeming symbiotic partners that work well together
contain antagonistic stress in regard to power and powerlessness and, especially, in regard
to education. Democracy insists that politically and humanistically everyone is equal to the
rights of education. Capitalism, on the other hand, since it thrives on some people being
more equal than others, demands only that education be widespread and sufficiently
advanced to drive the machine of its own making. In many ways a well-informed people
is a threat to capitalism.

The result of the two competitive tracks is great stress on education, one that the people
in the education business have not been able to harmonize successfully. Throughout the
eighteenth and nineteenth centuries, the conflict was muted because of two constants in
the development of both thrusts into human associations and behavior. Those constants
were educating and education, each appealing to the "good," honest, up-lifting and ideal
in life. But, both bastions have been breaking down through the years.

Religion has long been suspect as the business of the quack, charlatan and crook, who exploited one of the most vulnerable aspects of the human being. Lately the suspicion has been made flesh in the spectacular examples of such people as televangelists Jim Bakker, Jerry Falwell and Jimmy Swaggart and scores of others whose venality has shown itself in their unprincipled exploitation of the public.

The crumbling of the house of religion left the citadel of education.

Now, however, with the disclosures that various colleges and universities have been robbing the government and administrators have been siphoning off vast funds from the educational budget — at the expense of the taxpayer and the student — the final citadel has crumbled. It has become clear that education — which has always been packaged as a treasure — has become merchandise, something to be sold for the benefit of educators' personal gain. The highest levels of administration manipulate moneys for their own personal and professional gains. Teachers insist that their personal fortunes be foremost in the business of education, no matter how much the children suffer.

Education has become the glitzy product that everybody trades in.

Talk is inexpensive. Politicians and educators realize that there is much to be gained by paying lip service to developing the minds of our students-and older citizens. But students are not the primary concern of those people in power, no matter how they protest that they are. Power and control — the acquiring and protecting of perks — are. It is almost as though the American Dream and the implementing of it have shifted. Being mortal we recognize that we must eventually pass on power and control. But being unwilling to admit mortality we withhold power as long as possible. The American Dream almost promises eternal power.

We care so little for children that we make them pawns in our tug of war for power. Literacy — our professed goal for everyone — is a battle of turf. Professors do not want to teach; they want released time for earning to teach what presumably they already know. Foundations and research groups subsidize non–teaching while educators teach themselves how to not-teach. Administrators give up teaching because administrating has become more important and beneficial. Government fights over who is to control education — the White House, Congress, Department of Education, National Endowment for the Humanities, governors, state legislators, teachers unions. All power blocks seem more interested in controlling education, in dictating its directions, than in guaranteeing its development and success.

Education is always the first casualty in a financial setback. Children cease being loved citizens of tomorrow and become instead small adults whose future must be sacrificed for the immediate benefit of the ruling adults. All such "frills" as music and sports programs must be eliminated, even while after working hours we devote our time assiduously to sports and music programs. Parents often entrust education to baby-sitters whose impact is going to be far below what one would expect parents to demand. Educators abuse their classes, often arguing — correctly or incorrectly that it is far more important to have happy teachers who teach small classes than to work hard themselves and demand dedicated application on the part of the students.

The failure of education has derived in part from the fact that the education we must advance has become so complex that people are unable to grasp it for the teaching. Thus people are driven into specialization, even while experience has convinced us that over-specialization frustrates and blunts the aims of education.

All education depends on fluency of communication, on people understanding the message no matter what language it is spoken in. Fluency levels the playing field and more nearly equalizes the game because it allows all people to understand the rules and techniques. To paraphrase Thomas Jefferson on education, a democratic people that is not fluent in the media of communication cannot create a society that will stand. Fluency means communication in a thousand media, the total media of existence. All such media speak various languages that contribute either to a cacophony of sounds or a thousand intelligible languages. We must examine them all and see how they can contribute to the needed education that is requisite to modern life.

To succeed in this examination we must first of all examine our own mind-set. If it is firmly set, intractable, closed — it needs to be opened. It needs to be effectible by new ideas, new concepts, and new approaches to the phenomena of life.

Education and democracy thrive only on newness and growth.

Wrestling with modernity's problems with the attitudes of the past guarantees inadequacy and failure. An open mind is the classroom of progress. Politicians, administrators, educators and students need to keep the mind open. Foremost, however, parents and adults must keep the mind receptive to new ideas and new ways of doing things. Ultimately, of course, it is from them that all educative power flows. In the final commitment the fate of education rests in their hands.

This commitment is both a sacred and very real trust. Adults cannot afford to waste or abuse it. Ultimately the fate of America, and indeed of the world, rests in our hands.

We ask ourselves, finally, what are the potentials of human development, and what are the most effective ways of edging toward our goals?

Without being starry-eyed perfectionists we can assume that although the development has been slow, erratic and halting, humanity has made some positive development in the last 100,000 years. We seem a little less eager to bare our fangs than we used to be, or we do it in a somewhat different way.

We are more likely to be aware of our problems and have learned at least tenuously to address them. There is no doubt that technologically we have made some giant steps— though whether forward, backward or circularly may be an open question. In the process we have learned a great deal about ourselves— our strengths and weaknesses— and about the world around us. We may have learned that, to paraphrase Socrates, the enquiring life is the only one worth living, though at times it seems that we have concluded that the only life worth living is greedy and self-indulgent.

Anyway, even the most sluggish minds among us are likely to be stimulated — we would call it making the adrenaline flow — by observing how much we can learn when assisted by all the devices around us, how much fun we can have when we utilize the fun-producing opportunities in our lives. Giant telescopes, searching microscopes, radiocarbon testing, and machines to keep the human body alive — all are interesting. They open up new avenues, new areas and new worlds to investigate.

The brave new worlds are there before us, waiting for our visit.

Our great task is to develop the mentality capable of handling the machines we will use. To do so we need a new orientation and calibration. We need to realize that our line of sight must be through the windshield of our hurtling machine looking forward rather than through the rearview mirror, gazing backward. Looking backward only tells us where we have been. The view might bathe us in nostalgia and recreate a pleasant though unreal experience, but it hardly prepares us for new experiences, which are inevitable.

Looking forward, on the contrary, we can become fluent in all the media of communication of the future, in the possibilities open to us. If we concentrate on the past we remain bound to the past; if we are lucky we are fluent in that past. But only sharp perception can allow us to change the fluency in the past for fluency in the future; they are not coins traded at equal value on the market of human experience. The past sells for less on the living market than the future does. The past is a commodity that can only fade and shrink; the future can develop and grow.

It is a promising personal and real world to those who prepare for it by becoming fluent in its media of communication. It is well worth the cost. The future, an education, and life — all are too important to abuse or waste. The United Negro College Fund uses as its motto, "A mind is a terrible thing to waste." Indeed it is. Similarly, opportunity is a terrible thing to abuse or waste. The investment is great, the potential unlimited. It is imperative that we realize the possible outcome.

Annotated Bibliography

"American Studies and Humanity's Dream," originally published as "Introduction." *Journal of American Culture* (2004) 27:2, p. 130–132.

In this brief piece Browne calls for American Studies to internationalize itself without becoming jingoistic.

"The ASA and Its Friends." *American Quarterly* (1979) 31:3, p. 354–358.

Browne challenges the American Studies Association to broaden its scope both in subjects and methodologies and uses the opportunity to explain that part of the justification for the birth of the popular culture studies field was the ASA's intransigence.

"Class Reunions as a Folk Festival." *Journal of Popular Culture* (Summer 1985) 19:1 p. 107–113.

Finding larger issues in personal responses, Browne's introspection about his own class reunion leads to a wistful (but not sentimental) analysis of the high school reunion as social marker.

"Education: Forward to Democratic Fluency," edited from "Preface" (p. i-iii) and "Windshield No Rear-View Mirror" (p. 194–195) in *The Many Tongues of Literacy*. Bowling Green, OH: BGSU Popular Press, 1992.

Browne earnestly notes that the only way to prepare for an uncertain future is to keep open to the possibilities for enlightenment and that a free-ranging education is therefore essential for the individuals as well as societies to thrive. He calls for education to teach fluency in all manner of mediated communications for this to be an achievable goal.

"The Face of the Hero in Democracy," edited from "The Concept of The Hero Against Democracy." *Profiles of Popular Culture: A Reader*. Edited by Ray B. Browne. Madison: University of Wisconsin Popular Press, 2005, p. 47–53; and "Hero with 2000 Faces." *The Hero in Transition*. Edited by Ray B. Browne and Marshall W. Fishwick. Bowling Green, OH: BGSU Popular Press, 1983. p. 91–106.

Browne surveys the forms and functions of the hero in fiction and reality, demonstrating how it alters according to cultural developments and needs. He then posits that a mature democratic culture may not need the hero, as traditionally defined.

"Folklore to Populore" *Popular Culture Studies Across the Curriculum*. Edited by Ray Browne. Jefferson, NC: McFarland, 2005, p. 24–27.

Browne justifies his call for popular culture studies to be recognized as another aspect of folklore studies and (jokingly?) suggests that the joint field of inquiry be termed "Populore."

"The Humanities as Redefined Through Popular Culture," edited from "Popular Culture as the New Humanities." *Journal of Popular Culture* (Spring 1984) 17:4, p. 1–8; and "Redefining the Humanities." *Pennsylvania English* 13 (Spring/Summer 1989), p. 16–28.

Browne explicates the thesis that a broader definition of the humanities as a field is needed and that misguided critics of the popular arts are failing to see them in their proper light as the "new humanities." As such, those critics do a major disservice to the distribution and expression of democratic impulses.

"Internationalizing Popular Culture Studies." *Journal of Popular Culture* (Summer 1996) 30:1, p. 21–37.

In this piece Browne argues against the dominating influence of the Westernized cultural canon, noting that electronic mass communication has accelerated cultural contact and increased cultural permeability. As a result, he contends that the study of culture from the bottom up and not the top down is the only practical panacea open to researchers of things cultural.

"The Many Faces of American Culture: The Long Push to Democracy." Speech given on November 2, 1977. Printed by Bowling Green State University, not officially published.

Browne contends that the plurality of American culture is a key component of its democracy. He chides those who deride and dismiss aspects of popular culture as being essentially anti-democratic and failing to see that popular culture is both a function of democracy and tool for its dissemination.

"On Redefining Cultural Studies." Unpublished essay fragment, 2005.

Browne posits that any study of culture(s) cannot be legitimate without serious consideration and inclusion of popular culture studies. He also recalls the early reaction to the birth of the popular culture studies movement.

"Popular Culture: Medicine for Illiteracy and Associated Educational Ills." *Journal of Popular Culture* (Winter 1987) 21:3, p. 1–15.

A redefinition of literacy is needed, Browne states, and with it a more inclusive study of communication and media. As a result of these steps, Browne contends that literacy and education will be improved and with them, democracy will be strengthened.

"Popular Culture: New Notes Toward a Definition." Edited by Jack Nachbar and Christopher Geist. *The Popular Culture Reader,* 3rd ed. Bowling Green, OH: BGSU Popular Press, 1983, p. 13–20.

A second attempt to set a broad definitional groundwork for the field is more successful than the first, though of course less radical as the field gained acceptance. Browne corrects and clarifies a few key points, but the piece is not really a reworking of the earlier article despite the implications of the title.

"Popular Culture: Notes Toward a Definition." *Popular Culture and Curricula.* Bowling Green, OH: BGSU Popular Press 1972, p. 3–11; and *The Popular Culture Explosion.* Edited by Ray Browne and David Madden. Dubuque, IA: Wm. C. Brown Co., 1972, p. 205–207. Originally printed in pamphlet form in 1970 by the Popular Culture Association.

In this significant article Browne attempts to define and explain the differences among such terms as mass culture, folk culture, and elite culture in order to arrive at a working definition of popular culture. He notes the tentativeness of his conclusions and did, in fact, later reconsider some key points.

"The Rape of the Vulnerable." *The God Pumpers: Religion in the Electronic Age.* Ray Browne and Marshall Fishwick, eds. BGSU Popular Press, 1987, p. 183–190.

An indignant Browne catalogs the then-recent scandals among evangelical leaders and proposes an analysis of why the evangelical movement is so popular and why the scandals have broken out at that particular time. Browne counsels

eternal vigilance against those who abuse the upward mobility drive of democratic-capitalistic culture.

"Replying to a Rejoinder." *Preview 2001+: Popular Culture Studies in the Future.* Edited by Ray Browne and Marshall Fishwick. Bowling Green, OH: BGSU Popular Press, 1995, p. 35–37.

Browne responds to a friendly critique of his generalist stance with a remarkably succinct statement of the driving principles he sees behind the popular culture studies movement.

"The Repressive Nature of TV Esthetics Criticism." *Journal of American Culture* (Fall 1983) 6:3, p. 117–122.

Television is used as an example of a mass media form of communication (and more) that hegemonic cultural forces attempt to control because of its potential to bolster democracy. Browne calls for TV to be studied as TV, and not as, or with tools appropriate for, some other form.

"Russel B. Nye: The Richness of His Life." *Journal of American Culture* 16:1, p. 1.

Browne provides a moving memorial to his colleague, friend, and "co-conspirator" in founding the Popular Culture Studies movement.

"The Seat of Democracy: The Privy Humor of 'Chic' Sale." *Journal of American Culture* (Fall 1980) 3:3 p. 409–416.

In this look at the humor of a now-obscure vaudevillian, Browne demonstrates his contention that no topic or subject is without merit if approached seriously. Browne ties Sale's humor to the growing urbanization of the US between World Wars and finds a strong democratic impulse in the proceedings.

"Sherlock Holmes as Christian Detective: *The Case of the Invisible Thief.*" *Clues: A Journal of Detection* (Spring/Summer 1983) 4:1, p. 79–91.

Browne uses a failed popular fiction work to discuss the figure of Sherlock Holmes and the rise of Christian fundamentalism, while demonstrating that an attentive scholar can find valid and useful cultural clues in even the most obscure popular culture elements.

"The Theory-Methodology Complex: The Critics' Jabberwock." *Journal of Popular Culture* (Fall 1995) 29:2, p. 143–156.

Browne surveys the formative strengths of the popular culture studies movement and its accompanying organization and journal, admonishing scholars not to be seduced into singular theoretical approaches or narrowing methodologies. He calls for a continuation of the eclectic and pragmatic approaches that have made the movement unique, and as he contends, necessary.

"Up from Elitism: The Aesthetics of Popular Fiction." *Studies In American Fiction*, 1981, 9, p. 217–231.

Browne attacks the defenders of elite culture by explicating the virtues of popular literature. The inherent inadequacies of elite aesthetics to deal with the full range of cultural productions are seen not just as misguided but as also serving to marginalize the democratizing forces of popular literatures.

"The Vanishing Global Village." *The Global Village: Dead or Alive?* Edited by Ray Browne and Marshall Fishwick. Bowling Green, OH: BGSU Popular Press, 1999, p. 24–35.

Rather than bring us together, as most theorize, Browne posits that the Global Village may be distancing peoples as cultural forms remix and blend. The shared global culture may be little more than a shallow veneer.

"Whale Lore and Popular Print in Mid-Nineteenth-Century America: Sketches Toward a Profile." *Prospects* 1 (1975), p. 29–40.

This article demonstrates the value in Browne's assertion that canonized classics can be better understood when placed in a broader context by applying popular culture studies. Melville's *Moby Dick* is seen through commonly known and appreciated whale lore at the time of its composition and creation.

Index